DISCOURSES *and* IDENTITIES *in* CONTEXTS *of* EDUCATIONAL CHANGE

COUNTERPOINTS

Studies in the Postmodern Theory of Education

Shirley R. Steinberg
General Editor

Vol. 387

The Counterpoints series is part of the Peter Lang Education list.
Every volume is peer reviewed and meets
the highest quality standards for content and production.

PETER LANG
New York • Washington, D.C./Baltimore • Bern
Frankfurt • Berlin • Brussels • Vienna • Oxford

DISCOURSES *and* IDENTITIES *in* CONTEXTS *of* EDUCATIONAL CHANGE

Contributions from the United States and Mexico

EDITED BY *Guadalupe López-Bonilla*
AND *Karen Englander*

PETER LANG
New York • Washington, D.C./Baltimore • Bern
Frankfurt • Berlin • Brussels • Vienna • Oxford

Library of Congress Cataloging-in-Publication Data

Discourses and identities in contexts of educational change:
contributions from the United States and Mexico /
edited by Guadalupe López-Bonilla, Karen Englander.
p. cm. — (Counterpoints, studies in the postmodern theory of education: 387)
Includes bibliographical references and index.
1. Postmodernism and education. I. López-Bonilla, Guadalupe.
II. Englander, Karen. III. Title.
LB14.7.L675 370.1—dc22 2009046842
ISBN 978-1-4331-0929-4 (hardcover)
ISBN 978-1-4331-0928-7 (paperback)
ISSN 1058-1634

Bibliographic information published by **Die Deutsche Nationalbibliothek**.
Die Deutsche Nationalbibliothek lists this publication in the "Deutsche Nationalbibliografie"; detailed bibliographic data is available on the Internet at http://dnb.d-nb.de/.

The paper in this book meets the guidelines for permanence and durability of the Committee on Production Guidelines for Book Longevity of the Council of Library Resources.

29 Broadway, 18th floor, New York, NY 10006
www.peterlang.com

Printed in the United States of America

Contents

Contributors

Alma Carrasco is a psychologist with graduate degrees in linguistics and education. Her main interest is reading and reading promotion. She is full professor of educational management at the graduate school of the Faculty of Administration of the Autonomous University of Puebla, Mexico. She was the founding president of Consejo Puebla de Lectura (Puebla Reading Council), a non-governmental organization devoted to promoting reading. She belongs to the Mexican Association of Educational Researchers (COMIE) and the International Reading Association.

Karen Englander is a professor in the Faculty of Languages at the Universidad Autónoma de Baja California in Ensenada, Mexico. She brings 25 years of teaching experience in English as a second/foreign language in Canada, California and Mexico, to her research in academic literacy. She is author (with David I. Hanauer) of the forthcoming *Scientific Writing in a Second Language*. Email: kenglander@uabc.mx

James Paul Gee is the Mary Lou Fulton Presidential Professor of Literacy Studies at Arizona State University. He has published in the areas of literacy studies, discourse analysis, learning theory, and digital media and learning. His books include *Social Linguistics and Literacies* (3rd Edition, 2007); *An Introduction to Discourse Analysis* (2nd Edition 2005); and *Situated Language and Learning* (2005). Email: james.gee@asu.edu.

Judith Green (Professor of Education, UCSB) engages in research on discourse and the social construction of disciplinary knowledge in linguistically and culturally diverse classrooms from preschool through higher education. She also writes on issues of epistemology related to collecting, archiving, searching and analyzing video records within ethnographic archives. She served as editor of the Handbook of Complementary Methods in Education in Education Research (Green, Camilli & Elmore, 2006) and is editor of the Review of Research in Education (2006, 2008, 2010). She is a Fellow of the American Anthropology Association and the

National Conference for Research in Language and Literacy.

Ana Inés Heras is a National Researcher in the National Career Track for the Council of Science and Technology (CONICET, Argentina). She is also a founding member of the Instituto para la Inclusión Social y el Desarrollo Humano [Institute for Social Inclusion and Human Development]. She has published in the areas of interactional sociolinguistics and ethnography as they apply to the study of human learning and social development. Her books include *Desarrollo Local* [*Local Development*] and *Trabajo, Desarrollo, Diversidad* [*Work, Development, Diversity*] both co-edited with David Burin. She has also published multimedia works (*Comunicación para la Inclusión [Communication for Inclusion]* and *Introducción al Uso del Video en Ciencias Sociales [Introduction to the Use of Video in the Social Sciences]*), using a combination of audiovisual and written language. She is currently the principal researcher on "Learning Processes in Autonomous Projects". Email: aninesheras@fibertel.com.ar

Rollin Kent is a sociologist with degrees in history and educational sociology and policy. He is full professor of educational management and public policy at the graduate school of the Faculty of Administration of the Autonomous University of Puebla, Mexico. He has been a visiting professor at the Harvard Graduate School of Education and the University of Oslo. He has done research in higher education policy, management and organization. Currently he investigates institutional change in Mexican science and technology organizations.

Nadia Khalil graduated with Honors in Human Development from UC San Diego in 2005. She has been teaching in elementary school and is now the Curriculum Specialist at Celerity Dyad Charter School in South Los Angeles.

Colin Lankshear is an Adjunct Professor of Education at McGill and Mount St. Vincent universities in Canada, and researches aspects of literacy and new technologies. He is author (with Michele Knobel) of *New Literacies: Everyday Practices and Classroom Learning.*

Guadalupe López-Bonilla is a Professor of Literacy Studies and Discourse Analysis at the Universidad Autónoma of Baja California. Her research interests include high school students' literacy practices, inequality in education, and youth's identities. She is coauthor (with Alma Carrasco and Alicia Peredo) of *La lectura desde el currículo de educación básica y media supe-*

rior en México (2008) [*Reading in language arts in the Mexican national K-12 curriculum*]. Email: lopezbonilla@gmail.com

Hugh Mehan is Professor of Sociology and Director of the Center for Research on Educational Equity, Access, and Teaching Excellence (CREATE) at UC San Diego, positions that link his commitments to unite theory with practice for the improvement of education for underserved youth. His recent book (written with Lea Hubbard and Mary Kay Stein), *Reform as Learning* documented the organizational culture and local politics surrounding the contentious educational reform recently implemented in San Diego.

Elizabeth Birr Moje is Arthur F. Thurnau Professor of Literacy, Language, and Culture in Educational Studies at the University of Michigan, Ann Arbor, and a Faculty Associate in the Institute for Social Research and in Latino/a Studies. Her research focuses on academic and youth literacy skills, practices, cultures, and texts. She is a co-editor, with Cynthia Lewis and Patricia Enciso, of *Reframing Sociocultural Research on Literacy: Identity, Agency, and Power.*

J. César Morales completed his BA in Spanish at California State University San Marcos in 1998, and his MA in Latin American Studies at UC San Diego in 2005. Since then, he has been a classroom teacher and is currently serving his second year as Principal in the Carlsbad Unified School District.

Carmen Pérez-Fragoso is a Professor of Distance Education at the Instituto de Investigación y Desarrollo Educativo, Universidad Autónoma de Baja California, Mexico. Her work has dealt mainly with Online education in Mexico, and she has co-authored two books on the subject. Currently, her research interests are on youth's use of ICTs inside and outside the classroom.

Guadalupe Tinajero-Villavicencio is a Professor at the Instituto de Investigación y Desarrollo Educativo, Universidad Autónoma de Baja California, Mexico. As a teacher in different undergraduate and graduate programs of the university, she has specialized in subjects related to public policies in education, and reform and change in baccalaureate and indigenous education.

Preface

Discourses and Identities in Contexts of Educational Change presents the work of scholars from the United States and Mexico. This book evolved out of discussions during a colloquium in Ensenada, Mexico, in 2008 and a symposium at the American Educational Research Association conference in 2009. Nine of the authors had gathered to share research based on a common interest in using discourse and identities as lenses for viewing and analyzing the educational contexts we saw around us. Five were based in Mexico, four in the United States, but we found that we shared a commitment to exploring inequity, intolerance and social paradigms of power and powerlessness. The fact that we were working in different countries with different languages and different communities enriched the dialogue. We found that the educational issues we raised crossed all these boundaries, while some are deeply situated. As a consequence of those discussions, we agreed to bring them to a wider audience. The outcome is this book, and a Spanish edition *Discursos e identitades en contextos de cambio educativo*, published by Plaza y Valdés-BUAP.

The authors explore current and changing educational contexts through the relationship between discourses and identities. These are contexts in which the participants must negotiate multiple, and sometimes conflicting, positions. The empirical studies reported here are grounded in contemporary theories of sociolinguistics and literacy practices, social relations conceptualized in dynamics of power, and identity representations.

The identities of the different agents of formal and informal educational process –students, teachers, scholar– are analized through the different opportunities for participation that members have within the context of the discourse communities they each belong to and through the mechanisms which enable these opportunties or the lack thereof.

Scholars and students with an interest in current educational issues will find in these pages rich discussions of pedagogical paradigms, institutional change and constraints, knowledge construction, language access, bilingualism, bicultural policy, technological innovation and learning outside the classroom. This volume uniquely contributes to the challenges facing different educational communities in specific contexts by using discourse and identity as the conceptual tools to analyze the problematic and often unclear relationship among diverse educational actors immersed in contexts of change at the local, national and global levels.

We greatly appreciate the commitment and enthusiasm of all the authors who participated in making this book a reality. We also deeply thank Dr. Lilia I. Bartolomé of the University of Massachusetts for her careful reading of the first draft of this manuscript.

Guadalupe López-Bonilla and Karen Englander
Ensenada, Mexico
December 2009

CHAPTER ONE

Introduction: Educational Progress and Social Order

COLIN LANKSHEAR

This book brings together a diverse group of collaborating authors from Mexico and the United States, predominantly from the neighboring states of California (United States) and Baja California. This creates very interesting possibilities for addressing the theme of discourses and identities within contexts of educational change within the current conjuncture, in view of such considerations as language and population demographics north of the border, immigration policies and dynamics, economic and wider cultural trends associated with the North American Free Trade Agreement (NAFTA), histories of academic collaboration (not to mention history itself), and the comparatively high levels of penetration of new (and not so new) technologies and their extension into everyday popular culture on both sides of the fence. These possibilities are amplified by the book's organization around three expansive themes that tap strongly into its focus on educational change: educational practices and identities; literacy, youth cultures and virtual spaces; and educational policies and professional identities. Each theme is addressed by North American and Mexican participants, infusing multiple perspectives into the discussion. The outcome is a nicely integrated discussion of wide-ranging aspects of discourse and identity in relation to engagement in formal education and non-formal learning under contemporary conditions.

Within the chapters that follow, we encounter first-hand accounts of the experiences of Mexican adolescents engaging in "team work" at high school and using new technologies under conditions of economic scarcity; of high academic achieving students of color from low socioeconomic status backgrounds negotiate challenges posed by the cultural and geographic distance between home and school; of indigenous educators taking up an official discourse of intercultural bilingual education within community settings in Baja California that are far removed and different from their own cultural roots and those of the indigenous groups they have been recruited to serve. We trace the steps of a Mexican academic developing a new discoursal identity—and the implications for his autobiographical identity—as the price for being accepted into membership of an elite discourse community publishing in "high impact" English language scientific journals; explore the impact of changes in California's policies on medium of instruction on opportunities for learning and potential identity construction within one teacher's fifth grade classrooms during 1993–2000; and get a perspective on the relationship between teachers' identities as members of the national teachers' union in Mexico and their identities and performances as pedagogical practitioners. And, we are presented with two complementary perspectives on relationships between discourses, identities and learning, focusing respectively on the role that knowledge-in-action plays within development of "disciplinary identities and disciplinary literacy and discourse skills," and on the potential of "game-like learning" for developing ways of reading, writing, speaking and thinking associated with deep learning.

This book could be read in many ways. My way reads it as a text that moves between forms of social research that speaks about questions of meaning, action and social order, on the one hand, and forms of educational inquiry undertaken with a view to contributing towards promoting better quality learning and more equitable academic achievement, on the other. In the final analysis, the book prompts difficult questions about the relationship between how formal learning is socially ordered and the ideal of enhancing learning on an equitable basis.

Meaning, Action and Social Order

In an interesting and useful paper concerned with developing an integrated theory of social practices, Andreas Reckwitz (2002) distinguishes within modern social theory three broad (idealized) approaches to understanding action and social order. He refers to these as purpose-oriented, norm-oriented and cultural theories, respectively.

Purpose-oriented theories explain action in terms of individual interests, purposes and intentions, and understand social order as the collective outcome of "single interests" (Reckwitz, 2002, p. 245). Norm-oriented social theories identify collective norms and values—shared rules [that] express a social "ought"—as the means for explaining human action, and *social* order is grounded in normative consensus. By contrast, cultural theories of action and social order—of which theories of social practices are a variant—understand and explain *social* phenomena by reference to shared symbolic structures of knowledge and meaning.

Cultural theories explain and understand (social) actions "by reconstructing...symbolic structures of knowledge [that] enable and constrain [human] agents to interpret the world according to certain forms and to behave in corresponding ways" (Reckwitz, 2002, pp. 245–246). Similarly, social order is seen as embedded in a "shared knowledge"—that is, "collective cognitive and symbolic structures"—that affords a socially shared way of making sense, or ascribing meaning, to the world and doing life on this basis.

Reckwitz distinguishes social practice theory from three other lines of cultural theories, which he refers to as "culturalist mentalism," "culturalist textualism" and "culturalist intersubjectivism," respectively. Cultural mentalism is based on the idea that "mind is a substance, place, or realm that houses a particular range of activities and attributes," or symbolic mental structures (Schatzki, 1996, p. 22). Human actions are "effects" of these structures, which are *shared* cognitive possessions and, for that reason, underpin social order. Reckwitz distinguishes an "objectivist" current of mentalism, exemplified by the early structuralism of de Saussure and the later anthropological tradition derived from Lévi-Strauss, from a "subjectivist" line in social phenomenonolgy following Alfred Schütz.

Culturalist textualism locates the social, and the order(liness) of social life in the external, "public" and material realm of texts: "in chains of signs, in symbols, discourse, communication...." (Reckwitz, 2002, p. 248). Reckwitz identifies three main fronts along which cultural textualism has mainly developed during recent decades: poststructuralism and semiotics, radical hermeneutics and constructivist theory of social action (following Niklas Luhmann). In varying ways, these theoretical lines construe mental attributes as "conceptual ascriptions in discourse", and locate knowledge and the social "beyond bodily acts" (p. 249). It is paradigmatically texts to which we turn in order to source, investigate, understand and explain action—recognizable human behavior—and social order.

Taking Habermas' theory of communicative action as the classic formulation, Reckwitz argues that culturalist intersubjectivism locates the social and its orderliness within symbolic communicative interactions, where "agents endowed with minds" interact with each other. Speech acts internalize objective rules, somewhat in the manner of a linguistic twist on norm-oriented sociological theories.

In contrast to these culturalist theories of action and social order, practice theory locates shared symbolic structures of knowledge and meaning in everyday social practices and identifies practices as the smallest units of social theory. Reckwitz (2002, pp. 249–250) describes a practice as

> a routinized type of behavior [that] consists of several elements, interconnected to one another: forms of bodily activities, forms of mental activities, 'things' and their use, a background knowledge in the form of understanding, know how, states of emotion and motivational knowledge. A practice...[forms] a 'block' whose existence necessarily depends on the existence and specific interconnectedness of these elements, and which cannot be reduced to any one of these single elements...[In short, a practice is] a routinized way in which bodies are moved, objects are handled, subjects are treated, things are described and the world is understood...Social practices are routines: routines of moving the body, of understanding and wanting, of using things, interconnected in a practice.

Humans are bearers or carriers of practices, through which they do and be, understand and make sense or meaning of their worlds. As carriers of practices, through participation in practices, individuals *perform* their bodies and their minds, their desires and ends, their emotions and values, and interact with things, in particular ways—thereby accomplishing identity and membership, roles and relationships, understandings and accountabilities. Practice theory, in other words, gives a particular "spin" to bodily performance, mental activities, using things (tools, technologies, artefacts), knowledge and language (oral, written, generic, discursive): a "spin" that resonates strongly with James Gee's (1997, 2001, 2007) conception of Discourses as "coordinations" as we will return to, numerous times, in the pages and chapters that follow.

Practices involve "the regular, skilful 'performance' of (human) bodies," and when we learn practices we learn to be bodies in particular ways—not just to *use* our bodies in certain ways. As the "site of the social," routinized bodily performance "give[s] the world of humans its visible orderliness" (Reckwitz, 2002, p. 251). Social practices are simultaneously patterned mental activities: "routinized ways of understanding the world, of desiring something, of knowing how to do something;" of interpreting, intending and aiming at, mobilizing emotions and desires and so on. These desires, emotions, intentions, forms of understanding and the like are not individual personal subjective states but, rather, are non-subjective, "collective" patterns integral to the practice, and that individuals take up, bear, carry and enact in recognizable ways. The "knowledge" of practice, then, is much more than propositional knowledge, including also ways of understanding, of knowing how, of wanting and feeling that are integrally connected to each other. The "things" that are taken up in practices, while "always-already interpreted" to a degree, are "things to be handled"—to be used—and "constitutive elements" of ways of doing and being: not merely things that are produced textually or in talk as meaningful—known and interpreted—entities.

For present purposes, three further points made by Reckwitz are especially germane. The first is that within practice theory language loses the predominance it assumes within textualism and intersubjectivism, while nonetheless remaining crucially important. Discursive practices, which construct the world meaningfully in language and other sign systems, are recognized as just one among various kinds of practice. At the same time, however, discursive practices are structurally of a piece with social practices at large: comprising "bodily patterns, routinized mental activities—forms of understanding, know-how (including...grammar and pragmatic rules of use), and motivation—and objects (from sounds to computers) that are linked to each other" (Reckwitz, 2002, p. 255).

Second, practice theory takes a distinctive line on the question of human agency and "individuality." Reckwitz does not address "identity" per se, having a larger and wider interest in social theory. Practice theory situates human agency in the performance of practices: agency is exercised and expressed in and through "carrying a practice," and in doing so in ways that are recognizable but to some degree distinctive. Individuality, by contrast, consists in the unique trajectories of persons through the multitude of practices in which they engage, and their manner of engagement. This, of course, is not quite "*identity*" in the sense that has become an increasingly visible preoccupation within pockets of social, psychological and educational research in recent decades. It does, however, locate the general "space" of identity concerns within practice theory.

Finally, in practice theory, social structure and social *order*—reproduction of social structure to establish a substantive order (and orderliness) within everyday social life—are seen to consist in the repetition of routinized social practices over the sequence of time (Reckwitz (2002, p. 255). This, however, does not imply stasis. In a point that becomes especially significant in the context of contemporary educational change and policy directions. According to Reckwitz (2002, p. 255), from the standpoint of practice theory,

> the "breaking" and "shifting" of structures [takes] place in everyday crises of routines, in constellations of interpretative indeterminacy and of the inadequacy of knowledge with which the agent, carrying out a practice, is confronted in the face of a "situation."

Such "crises" might be as seemingly simple as using a tool in a different way in order to try and do something, to cashing in on "indeterminacy" within the interpretation of educational policies to develop expansive ways of assessing and reporting learning outcomes.

One further point, not discussed by Reckwitz, although crucial to the ways discussion of discourses and identities are often taken up within educational inquiry and, specifically, in this book, concerns the "two layered" meaning of "social order," namely, "orderliness" and "hierarchy." In a formulation integral to the broad theoretical frame informing this book, as we will see in greater detail below, Gee (1996, p. 132) claims that Discourses

> are intimately related to the distribution of social power and hierarchical structure in society, which is why they are always and everywhere ideological. Control over certain Discourses can lead to the acquisition of social goods (money, power, status) in a society. These Discourses empower those groups who have the least conflicts with their other Discourses...Let us call Discourses that lead to social goods in a society *dominant Discourses*, and let us refer to those groups that have the fewest conflicts... *dominant groups*.

Discourses and Identities

It is time now to focus in from this brief account of "practice theory" to the conceptual terrain of Discourses and Identities as they frame discussion in this book. While occasional references are made to norm-oriented theory of action and social order (e.g., institutionalist sociology in Chapter 7), and to culturalist textualism (e.g., Foucault in Chapter 3), the book's theoretical and methodological core lies in tenets of practice theory.

Specifically, the book draws centrally on James Gee's well-known and influential theory of D/discourse and his account of identity as an analytic lens for educational research (e.g., Gee, 1996/2007, 1997, 2001, 2004, 2008). In various places, Gee notes that his concept of Discourse (with an upper case "D") is concerned with "important aspects" of what others refer to via such other constructs as "communities of practice" (e.g., Wenger, 1998), "actor-actant networks" (e.g., Latour, 1987), "activity systems" (e.g., Engestrom,1990), "practices" (e.g., Bourdieu, 1998) and "forms of life" (Wittgenstein, 1953). These terms are not synonymous (Gee, 2004, p. 110) but rather foreground different aspects of human beings doing certain things in certain ways in order to achieve certain purposes: in the process of which they use things and symbols in certain ways and, in the doing of all this, be(come) certain kinds of persons—recognizable to others, and "interactable" with these others—within particular contexts, thereby collectively accomplishing meaningful, recognizable, enduring and orderly forms of social-cultural life.

In "Reading as Situated Practice: A Sociocognitive Perspective" (Gee, 2001, p. 721), Gee presents a set of conceptual-theoretical "tools" for understanding language and literacy in sociocultural terms: "Discourses" (and "discourses"), "social languages," "genres" and "cultural models" as follows:

> **Discourses:** [These are] ways of combining and coordinating words, deeds, thoughts, values, bodies, objects, tools, and technologies, and other people (at appropriate times and places) so as to enact and recognize specific socially situated identities and activities.
>
> **Social languages:** [These are] ways with words (oral and written) within Discourses that relate form and meaning so as to express specific socially situated identities and activities.

> **Genres:** [These are] combinations of ways with words (oral and written) and actions that have become more or less routine within a Discourse in order to enact and recognize specific socially situated identities and activities in relatively stable and uniform ways (and, in doing so, we humans reproduce our Discourses and institutions through history).

> **Cultural models:** [These are] often tacit and taken for granted schemata, storylines, theories, images, or representations (partially represented inside people's heads and partially represented within their materials and practices) that tell a group of people within a Discourse what is typical or normal from the point of view of that Discourse.

In "Reading as Situated Practice," Gee applies these tools in a highly focused manner to an instance of a distinctive kind of interaction between a child, a parent and a book. He shows how they collectively enact a "moment" of situated social practice that can be seen as "co-constructing the child as a reader (and, indeed, a person) of a particular type" (Gee, 2001, p. 723). The particular type of reader that this interaction–event–situation contributes to "shaping up"—in conjunction with many other similar and related instances—is, among other things, one that is optimally compatible with "doing well in school" and "growing up to be an educated, professional kind of person."

Briefly, and specifically, Gee demonstrates how this "moment" can be seen in terms of the participants interacting—indeed, *working* together, in a non-formal, playful, mutually engaging sense of "work"—around the book from the standpoint of a very particular and distinctive cultural model of reading that is highly efficacious for academic and school-based learning. The parent knows exactly what he is doing, and the child is in the process of "getting," increasingly, what this cultural model of reading is about and, simultaneously, "getting" proficient with the specific social language—mastery of classificatory questions—that that is part of a larger battery of social languages integral to the Discourse the three (child, parent, book) are playing out. This is the Discourse of being a particular kind of emergent reader: one that filters school reading ways into home reading ways long before the child is of school age. The process of "routinizing" the practice—in effect, of "institutionalizing" it within the home, so as to minimize the possibility of conflict between the child's primary Discourses and the Discourses that will advantageously confer social goods within the formal institution of school (and beyond)—involves repeated instances of interacting with the book in a particular way, which the actors in this case have "customized" to a small but very significant degree. In their enactment of the routine, the child uncovers a piece of a picture in an activity book, frames a classificatory question (for which the full picture, once revealed, provides the answer), and then gives the answer. These are the conceptual and analytic nuts and bolts of participation in a Discourse that is actively recruiting the child to being a particular kind of emergent reader. The child, in other words, is "taking on" the identity of be(com)ing a particular kind of emergent reader through this situated practice. This is an identity in the sense of "being recognized as a certain 'kind of person' in a given context" (Gee, 2004, p. 99), and instantiates Gee's idea that Discourses can be seen as "identity kits."

This "moment" can be seen as one of inducting a child into a micro-element of social order: one that will likely have him recognized by other people (e.g., teachers) within other contexts (e.g., classrooms), as being the kind of person who performs in ways that are what the institution is "on about" and, to that extent, is worthy of—or merits—obtaining a greater share of social goods than those learners who cannot or otherwise do not perform in these ways.

Elsewhere, Gee argues that "being situated selves" within particular contexts—how we are recognized and responded to, how we recognize others and respond to them, how our performances within society are interpreted and acted back on by others—is complex, because "identities are tied to the workings of historical, institutional, and sociocultural forces" (Gee, 2004, p. 100). He identifies four "perspectives" on what it means to be recognized as a particular kind of person and, thereby, on how identities are "formed and sustained" (Gee, 2004, p. 100): All or some of which may apply within a given context. When the way someone is recognized and responded to is—in some degree—a function of natural forces (e.g., the person's sex, race-ethnicity, physiology, psychology, etc.), their Nature identity (N-identity) provides an "analytic focus" for understanding and explaining what is going on within that situation in terms of identity. When it is a function of someone's institutional position, their Institution-identity (I-identity) provides an analytic focus. When it is a function of other people recognizing a trait within the process of social interaction in dialogue or discourse—such as recognizing someone as a congenial or brusque individual because there are reasons for doing so—their Discourse identity (D-identity) provides an analytic focus. When it is a function of other people (insiders) recognizing someone as being a member of an affinity or affiliation, by dint of showing allegiance to, having access to, and participating in a range of practices integral to that affinity, their Affinity identity (A-identity) provides an analytic focus.

Among other things, this framework points to the kinds of "work" involved in building up and sustaining an identity. Challenging the way one is labelled institutionally (e.g., at risk learner) may involve developing certain kinds of affinities (e.g., joining an after school club devoted to literary appreciation), or working on how one talks and writes about the novelists on the syllabus list in classroom interactions and essays). It also provides a basis for examining tensions or conflicts within or between different "forces" (Gee 2004) of identification, for example, home and school identities, ethnicity and peer group aspirations, etc.

Discourses, Identities and Social Order in the Context of Educational Change

The chapters in this book collectively address an interesting range of educational change proposals and implementations, from global to local levels, and with varying points of impact within the overall educational enterprise. Some of these are state and federal level policy changes, such as shifts in the medium of instruction associated with legislation following the passing of Proposition 227 in California in 1998, successive policy proposals in Mexico designed to align it with current international policy trends, and Mexican national curriculum initiatives as implemented in Baja California that emphasize "team work" in accordance with a purported "constructivist" approach to teaching. Global level change is represented by the "obligation" on academics everywhere to pursue publication in high-profile/high-impact journals indexed to the Web of Science (and similar indices), as well as by the far-reaching changes in formal and informal learning associated with contemporary technological change. Perhaps the most local and concrete level of change represented here involves interventions to establish charter schools with specialized missions, like preparing high-achieving low-income students of color for college.

Across this span, we are presented with diverse and interesting perspectives on, and insights into, ways in which social orderliness and hierarchy are constituted and refined within everyday processes of people being recognized as being particular kinds of persons within particular contexts. The following are typical selections from the book as a whole.

Carmen Pérez-Fragoso's account of Martha's online presence and her on- and offline interactions with peers related to her multimedia production interests points to the ways participants in affinity practices establish and refine quality standards and criteria by such means as feeding back, identifying appropriate models for emulation or as reference points for developing a personal style and so on: in effect, efforts to become certain kinds of multimedia exponents manifesting certain kinds of excellence or "cool" within domains of practice where flows of recognition and kudos are manifestly not equal. Martha's interview data documents ways in which young people recognize and respond to order in the world online, identifying kindred spirits, compatible others, experts to learn from, and higher goals and levels to pursue.

From a very different perspective and orientation, Mehan et al.'s account of low socioeconomic status (SES) college-bound students at the Preuss school shows them wrestling with the conflicting demands of competing "orders"—home, school, neighborhood—that describe intersecting parameters of their cultural universes. It reports these students' growing understandings of what these competing "orders" comprise, of what it means to "belong" to them (simultaneously) and what is involved in trying to order them into some kind of existential and emotional coherence. The rich accounts derived from interview excerpts exemplify

> the painful conflicts associated with negotiating home and school identities. On the one hand, students' recently crystallized academic identities encourage them to venture off the traditional cultural pathways traveled by peers and family members. On the other hand, students struggled with negative reactions from family members who expected them to conform to cultural norms when considering their future opportunities. These conflicts often left students pivoting between who they were and who they have become. Making the situation more difficult for students was the time and energy they invested to succeed at Preuss, while their parents, without the requisite knowledge about the arcane college-going process, did not seem to understand their struggles (p. 39).

Karen Englander's chapter on the globalized world of English language scientific publishing speaks powerfully to the hierarchical order of "national" languages (like Spanish, English, French) and social languages within the global scientific scene. Relative to institutional policies that accept the view that being a top flight researcher presupposes publishing in English language high-impact journals, the "scientific subjectivities" of researchers and scholars like Victor rank lower than their (aspiring) English language scientific subjectivities. From the standpoint of institutionally successful careers, it is becoming increasingly less tenable for scholars to identify with non-English language-based research communities and to continue developing their academic identities, reference groups and careers within these parameters. This is partly because national research systems worldwide are moving to "merit systems" that privilege publishing in ISI–[Institute for Scientific Information] referenced publications (which are overwhelming English language). More deeply, however, it is because within many academic fields

> the theoretical and methodological perspectives provided in the core theories of [a] discipline [are] delineated mostly by theorists and researchers in the Anglo-European centers (e.g., US, UK)" (Lin, 2005, cited in Oda, 2007, p. 125). Academics, whether they are within or beyond the English-language centers, apply these "global theories" (emphasis in Oda, 2007, p. 125) to local issues and places. (See p. 216)

As Englander notes, these are the global theories that researchers apply to local places and issues regardless of whether they are in English-language centers. To be recognized as a particular kind of person—"top flight scientist/researcher"—increasingly presupposes being the kind of person who is proficient in the social languages integral to research Discourses constituted by English-language scientific communities. This bespeaks a *hegemonic* order that underpins, and is reinforced and further consolidated by, institutions worldwide buying into the ideology of "high impact, ISI-referenced, English language scientific publishing."

Guadalupe López-Bonilla's discussion of the different situated meanings evoked by "team work" for high- and low-achieving students in different school cultures provides a further illuminating perspective on the intersection of discourses, identities and social order. This focus is part of a larger research purpose concerned with the kinds of social and academic participation afforded to high- and low-academic achievers within Baja California's Technological High School and General High School cultures, respectively. The policy context surrounding the research involved the recent shift to a "constructivist" approach to teaching and learning. For many teachers, this translated into placing the main burden of learning curriculum content onto students learning through "team research and collaboration." Data analysis revealed three broad patterns among students' situated meanings for team work: the meanings made by middle class students in the elite International Baccalaureate (IB) stream of a General High school; those made by low-achieving students from the Technological and General high-school cultures; and those made by high achievers across these school cultures.

The IB students (2 percent of the school's population) regarded one another respectfully as members of an esteemed group. They valued one another's academic prowess, opinions and contributions to stimulating their individual and shared learning. For this group, team work and collaboration meant "an effortless, natural, and highly valued activity" (p. 87). By stark contrast and, seemingly, independently of social class, high academic achievers in both school cultures resented having to work in teams and rejected the identity of "collaborative team member," largely because they accepted a dichotomy between "good" and "bad" students, which rationalized perceptions that *they* were doing all the work in the teams while "bad" ("irresponsible, lazy, low" achievers) were getting a "free ride." Conversely, low academic achievers valued team work and saw it creating opportunities to enact social roles and positions (leader, expert, proactive inquirer) not otherwise open to them in class.

These are, in effect, competing Discourses of teamwork, patterned by academic achievement, social class and in the case of IB students, by the contingency of team composition. High and low achievers are differentially apprenticed to these Discourses, *ordering* their experiences and perceptions of team-based work. These differences are in turn associated with very different—*hierarchical*—learning outcomes and academic trajectories. Social order begets hierarchy here.

Discourses, Identities and Learning in the Context of Educational Change

A sociocultural/practice approach to learning necessarily gives a central place to D/iscourses and identities because it shifts the emphasis in learning away from the predominance of "learning about" and toward "learning to be;" from "subject content-based learning" toward what John Seely Brown and Richard Adler (2008) call "social learning;" and, above all, to what is now commonly referred to as "situated learning". This approach to learning is based on the assumption that our understanding of concepts and processes is constructed socially in conversations about the matters in question and "through grounded [and situated] interactions, especially with others, around problems or actions" (Brown & Adler, 2008, p. 18). It shifts the emphasis from "the content of a subject to the learning activities and human interactions around which that content is situated" (p. 18)—putting the emphasis squarely on "learning to be" (Brown & Adler, 2008, p. 18; Gee, 2007, p. 172), in a sense that Gee sometimes refers to in terms of becoming "authentic professionals" (Gee, 2007, pp. 67–68). According to Seely Brown and Adler (2008, p. 19),

> mastering a field of knowledge involves not only "learning about" the subject matter but also "learning to be" a full participant in the field. This involves acquiring the practices and the norms of established practitioners in that field or acculturating into a community of practice.

We see this more clearly still in Gee's account of "deep learning," which is one of three concepts I see as central to the ideal of promoting better quality learning and more equitable academic achievement at the heart of this book.

Gee (2007, p. 172) speaks about *educational* learning as "deep learning" and defines "deep learning" in relation to learning to be, and taking on (new) identities and developing what Donald Schon calls "appreciative systems." According to Gee, deep learning is learning that can lead to real understanding, and the ability to apply one's knowledge and deploy it in innovation. In learning to be, our learning is only partly about belief but also is strongly about relating knowledge to purposes and goals. More generally, deep learning

> requires the learner being willing and able to take on a new identity in the world, to see the world and act on it in new ways. Learning a new domain, whether physics or furniture making, requires learners to see and value work and the world in new ways, in the ways in which physicists and furniture makers do. One...reason this is so is because, in any domain, if knowledge is to be used, the learner must probe the world (act on it with a goal) and then evaluate the result. Is it "good" or "bad," "adequate" or "inadequate," "useful" or "not," "improvable" or "not"? (Gee, 2007, p. 172)

This means developing value systems of the kinds that are "embedded in the identities, tools, technologies and worldviews of distinctive groups of people—who share, sustain, and transform them—groups like doctors, carpenters, physicists, etc." (Gee, 2007, p. 172). Deep learning, in other words, presupposes immersion in "mature versions of social practice" (Gee, Hull & Lankshear 2006, chapter 1), becoming insiders to their constitutive D/discourses and social languages, and taking on their distinctive identities.

Besides the concept of "deep learning," it is useful here to recognize two further concepts integral to the overall discussion of learning in this book, namely, "effective school learning" and "efficacious learning."

By "effective school learning" I mean, simply, learning that gets the kinds of results in school that accrue social goods—good grades, certification, scholarships—and result in being identified as a "good student" and a "high academic achiever." This involves such proficiencies as learning to read in more sophisticated ways than merely decoding text, such that one gets past "the fourth grade slump" (see Gee, p. 101) and succeeds in the kind of specialized reading and writing integral to school subject mastery and "disciplinary learning" (see Moje, p. 65).

For learning to be "efficacious" it is necessary that what somebody learns now is connected in meaningful and motivating ways to mature or insider versions of Discourses. This involves thinking of education and learning in terms of human lives as trajectories through diverse social practices and institutions (Gee et al., 1996, p. 4). To learn something is to progress towards a fuller understanding and fluency with doing and being in ways that are recognized as proficient relative to recognized ways of "being in the world." In this sense, for learning at particular points in time to be efficacious, it must involve doing something—and doing it in a way—that puts the learner on the right track towards becoming a competent participant in "the real thing"—whatever the Discourse, domain or practice in question might be.

In light of the overall discussion of this book, it is useful to distinguish what we might call "internal and external" and "specific and general" conceptions of efficacy. "Internal" efficacious learning might be understood in terms of successful participation in *school* discourses of learning. Hence, language lessons in the early years that get a child on track for, say, successful essay writing in high school geography, would be "internally efficacious." However, as has often been argued, school ways of knowing often comport poorly to mature versions of social practices beyond the school, where knowing something means more than knowing how to produce verbal renderings but, rather, to be able to apply the knowledge in practice, to solve problems, etc. In this sense, externally efficacious learning is learning *now* that leads in due course to *deep* learning and, furthermore, that contracts productive relationships to the kinds of situations Moje describes (chapter 3) in terms of disciplinary knowledge and practice being aspects of everyday life.

Specific and general conceptions of efficacious learning can be distinguished by comparing what Moje says about disciplinary knowledge and identities, and the themes addressed by Judith Green and Ana Inés Heras and by Guadalupe Tinajero-Villavicencio, respectively. By a more specific concept I mean where something that is learned now can be seen in relation to some relatively specific kind of engagement within a life trajectory, such as where Moje speaks of "the discourses and practices that an historian or chemist or mathematician might engage in when producing, representing, or critiquing knowledge in her or his everyday work" (p. 54). By a more general concept I mean where something that is learned now leads to broader forms of engagement within a life trajectory, such as being able to live as a bi- or multilingual person (Green and Heras, chapter 7) and/or to live bi- or interculturally (Tinajero-Villavicencio, chapter 10).

From the standpoint of the chapters in this book, ideally learning would be deeper, more academically effective, more efficacious –and access to deep, academically effective, and efficacious learning would be very much more equitable than it currently is.

Elizabeth Moje addresses the abiding issue of how best to promote disciplinary competence within school settings from the standpoint of students taking on disciplinary identities. She argues that taking on a disciplinary identity *in the first place* presupposes types and degrees of knowledge that learners often lack, prompting the question of how to design learning experiences that draw on students' extant knowledge and experience—residue of prior participation—"and also build new knowledge" that makes possible further and effective participation in disciplinary learning by taking on (new) disciplinary identities. Acknowledging the many challenges presented by the empirical realities of school ways and learner histories, and the need to regularly undertake serious "repair" work, Moje proposes an agenda for research that engages sociocultural theory and work in the New Literacy Studies more intensely with classroom settings with a view to theorizing "specific practices that might be useful under the actual conditions of schooling" while, nonetheless, "maintaining the need for structural change". (p. 68).

James Gee's chapter discusses the importance of adopting a trajectory view to early reading and language development as a *sine qua non* of effective school learning and deep learning. He argues that informal (and formal) specialized language lessons, practices built around lucidly functional language and an emphasis on *situated* rather than merely verbal understandings of terms and concepts are necessary underpinnings of a trajectory view. Importantly, he argues for the efficacy of "game-like learning," since this "leads to situated and not just verbal meanings" which, in turn, "make specialist language [of kinds inherent in academic learning] lucid, easy, and useful" (p. 114). The examples he provides of game-like learning and their take up in classrooms make a helpful contribution to the research agenda proposed by Moje, as well as pointing to important pressure points for structural change.

Alma Carrasco and Rollin Kent draw on "the new institutionalism" tradition within sociology to present a fascinating account of impediments to curriculum change in accordance with official policy discourse. These impediments are attributable to contingencies in the institutional relations among the Mexican government, Mexico's teachers' union and teachers and the ways in which the distinctive institutional educational environment in Mexico bears on teacher identity. They provide an illuminating case of how and why policy formulation is no guarantee of policy implementation and curriculum change. While the case is grounded in contingent details more or less peculiar to Mexico, readers from other countries will easily detect more localized overlaps and similarities. Carrasco and Kent focus particularly on the ways that institutional arrangements generate the potential for serious cognitive dissonance for teachers between formal policy and educational discourse, on one hand, and empirical classroom teaching and learning practice, on the other. Teachers, however, *manage* this dissonance and rationalize contradictions in ways that maintain traditional approaches and arrangements. This case provides a classic instance of social order trumping potential for enhancing learning.

Guadalupe Tinajero-Villavicencio's account of the appropriation of official policy pertaining to the indigenous school subsystem in Mexico focuses on the issue of access to academic learning outcomes for learners from minority ethnic and linguistic groups. Reporting on a study conducted in Baja California's San Quintin Valley, Tinajero-Villavicencio focuses on two recent moments in indigenous education policy discourse in Mexico: a bicultural/bilingual policy proposal facing teachers in 1994 and an intercultural/bilingual policy instituted from 1999. The deep complexities and contradictions inherent within both policy contexts—including conflicts among teachers' "natural," "institutional" and "affinity" identities, sheer linguistic diversity, lack of didactic materials and little or no visible change in the structural conditions of indigenous peoples' marginality—are discussed against the backdrop of an increasing academic attainment gap between indigenous and non-indigenous school populations.

Nonetheless, the *intercultural* orientation of the current policy is seen as progressive in important respects that are not academic, winning allegiance from teachers at the same time as they deem the policy ineffectual in terms of key objectives like promoting literacy in indigenous languages as well as in Spanish. Teachers believe the policy has helped foster a climate of greater respect for indigenous languages and cultural ways, which supports the development of intercultural life trajectories, but they do not regard it as even potentially viable in terms of realizing its specific learning objectives.

On similar terrain, Judith Green and Ana Inés Heras report some of the ways California's policy transition from bilingual to English-only instruction played out over an 8-year period with the same bilingual teacher's 5th grade classroom. Findings from this study have significance for learner life trajectories with respect to the general and external dimensions of efficacious learning described above. They also pinpoint issues of access to effective school learning on the part of students who have to learn English while studying in English. Green and Heras document in impressive detail ways in which the policy change to English Only denied *all* learners—English and non-English background alike—opportunities for certain kinds of learning and identity construction. Specifically, learners lost opportunities for learning languages besides English, for entering particular types of social relationships, for building a multilingual learning community and for seeing themselves as becoming multilingual, and for experiencing what a multilingual learning environment is like and how, within such an environment, language difference can become a resource for community building and academic success. Furthermore, by losing the opportunity to "write to think," non-English background learners ended up with incomplete records of their work.

> How is it possible to write complex ideas in a language that you have just begun to learn? [A consequence] of this for the individual is captured in the following statement from a student in 1998, *I used to know that*, which referred to the fact that he knew the comment in Spanish but did not know it in English. (p. 187)

Of course, discussing the social research/social order and educational research/learning aspects of the book in a linear way, as I have done above, tells only part of the story. Things become more interesting and complex when we look at what the chapters have to say about those points where social order and pursuit of advances in learning intersect. There is not space to go into this in any detail here, but readers will find much in the pages that follow if they attend to this dynamic.

For example, at many points and in different and often intricate ways, we find social order trumping the ideals of equitable learning and/or better quality learning. López-Bonilla's account of team work provides an interesting case in point. High-achieving students who debunk team work outright or who engage in it reluctantly maintained academic success, whereas low-achieving students who embraced team work and collaboration failed. Moreover, within the most expansive context of team work, among the middle class IB students, advances in learning made through team work confirmed and further consolidated social hierarchy. These students could appropriate team learning in ways that augmented and further consolidated their existing social advantages. In a second interesting twist, Englander's account of Victor working to bring his social language into line with English language publishing Discourses resulted in personal success. At the same time, however, the process might be seen as furthering the same facets of social order and hierarchy that created "inequity" and "disadvantage" in the first place. In another instance, institutional arrangements and lived meanings at the intersection of union membership and teaching identity worked to negate any potential that progressive policy directions and advances in educational research and theory could have for improving the quality of classroom learning. And, intriguingly, precisely opposite directions in language of instruction policy resulted in similar broad outcomes in the two contexts discussed by Green and Heras, and Tinajero-Villavicencio, respectively.

Some End Thoughts

This book is a timely reminder that in the game of educational change the odds are stacked heavily in favor of established order, structure and hierarchy. Creating conditions for more expansive and equitable learning opportunities and outcomes in classrooms presupposes unstinting efforts to address already-ordered meanings, relations, and practices in the world *beyond* the school, while addressing research, policy directions, pedagogical debate and experimentation, and other points of more direct and immediate purchase on formal teaching and learning.

It is worth remembering that the policy change pursuant to Proposition 227 began from citizen-voter action: mobilizing public opinion and action. To be sure, this activism had a lot of material and symbolic power to draw on. At the same time, however, counter-battles for progressive educational advance do not all have to be waged on a state or federal level in order for them to be effective. Most of them don't. This book contains examples of more local and specific mobilizations that have made a difference and that can be replicated, modified or otherwise extended. The book, in fact, begins and ends with such examples. As Mehan, Khalil and Morales conclude: for the hierarchy of access to be dismantled "we must witness more sustained efforts—those that are institutionalized, survive through time, and are instantiated in many different locations" (p. 46). This is informed political work that *may* take the form of establishing charter schools (or even alternative educational arrangements altogether to those of compulsory public schooling). Equally, however, it may take quite other forms, such as building support and shaping public opinion for educational change through community dialogue and mobilization. Dominant meanings, dominant Discourses, and many of the identities that institutions would recruit us to, need to be unveiled and, where necessary, contested in similar ways. The battle for progressive educational policy and practice cannot be fought solely, or even primarily, on educational terrain. It must be waged in the community and among the polity, online, offline *and* on the job.

Closer to the chalkface, a number of points occurred to me as I read the manuscript that I think provide a kind of litmus test for the prospects of progress toward the ideals and aspirations espoused in this book. To the extent that we can make progress on such fronts we might reasonably hold out hopes for the ideals. To the extent that we can't, the prospects recede. I will end by mentioning briefly just three of them here.

First, the chapters point consistently to the importance of a strong *intellectual*—conceptual, theoretical, analytic, interpretive, etc.—formation for teachers. Meanwhile, we increasingly witness teacher education programs being gutted intellectually and, instead, loaded up with classroom and behavior management "how to's," programming and assessment templates, half-assed renditions of "constructivism" and the like. If teacher education—i.e., *we*—can't start to get itself—i.e., *ourselves*—out of a rapidly descending spiral into the depths of servitude to bureaucratic performativity, how can we expect schools to enact expansive learning ideals?

Second, the concept of deep learning as involving "learning to be" raises some significant issues for teacher identities, some of which can be encapsulated crudely by such observations as "by and large science teachers are not scientists". Creating contexts for deep learning in disciplinary domains presupposes access to authentic professional identities, purposes and situations beyond those associated with being a "subject specialist teacher." Knowing how to gain or mobilize the necessary access—via simulations, online environments and spaces, resources in the community, etc.—and ground learning in the kinds of purposes authentic professionals embrace, within the limits one can negotiate for ensuring "duty of care" and the like, becomes a key ingredient of teacher formation for situated learning.

Finally, there are important issues around "curriculum time" and "timetabling". Authentic professionals do not live by the irrational constraints of time (and space) that we expect school learners and teachers to live by. Meaningful purposes are pursued on a basis close to what many young people know as "geek project time". When something is worth "geeking out" for—even academic research and writing—we find, make, or otherwise usurp the time it needs. If educational professionals cannot hold out for this, and organize their "timetabling" and "programming" accordingly, it raises serious questions about "authenticity".

Situating academic discussions of discourses and identities in contexts of educational change within the ambit of a theory of social practice along the lines articulated by Reckwitz reminds us of where and how social patterns originate, and that spaces for "agentive" action are as open and "available" as they have ever been.

References

Bourdieu, P. (1998). *Practical reason*. Stanford, CA: Stanford University Press.

Brown, J. Seely, & Adler, R. (2008). Minds on fire: Open education, the long tail and learning 2.0. *Educause Review*, Jan–Feb, 17–32.

Engeström, Y. (1990). *Learning, working and imagining: Twelve studies in activity theory*. Helsinki: Orienta-Konsultit.

Gee, J. (1996). *Social linguistics and literacies: Ideology in discourses*. (2nd edition). London: Taylor & Francis.

Gee, J. (1997). Foreword: A discourse approach to language and literacy. In C. Lankshear, *Changing literacies*. Buckingham: Open University Press, xiii–xxv.

Gee, J. (2001). Reading as situated language: A sociocognitive perspective. *Journal of Adolescent and Adult Literacy*, 44(8), 714–725.

Gee, J. (2004). Identity as an analytic lens for research in education. *Review of Research in Education*, 25, 99–125.

Gee, J. P. (2007). What *video games have to teach us about learning and literacy*. New York: Palgrave Macmillan.

Gee, J. (2008). *Social linguistics and literacies: Ideology in discourses (3rd edition)*. London: Taylor & Francis.

Gee, J., Hull, G., & Lankshear, C. (1996). *The new work order: Behind the language of the new capitalism*. Boulder, CO: Westview Press.

Latour, B. (1987). *Science in action*. Cambridge, MA: Harvard University Press.

Reckwitz, A. (2002). Toward a theory of social practices: A development in social theorizing. *European Journal of Social Theory*, 5(2), 245–265.

Schatzki, T. (1996) *Social practices. A Wittgensteinian approach to human activity and the social*. Cambridge: Cambridge University Press.

Wenger, E. (1998). *Communities of practice: Learning, meaning and identity*. Cambridge: Cambridge University Press.

Wittgenstein, L. (1953). *Philosophical investigations*. Oxford: Blackwell.

SECTION I

Educational Practices and Identities

CHAPTER TWO

Going the Distance: The Challenges of Traversing Cultural and Geographical Space between Home and School

HUGH MEHAN, NADIA KHALIL AND J. CÉSAR MORALES

Must the language and culture students learn at home be discarded to achieve academically? Or: can the academic skills learned at school be added to the language and culture of the home? The recent development of the Preuss School at University of California, San Diego (UCSD), that prepares low-income students of color for college, enables us to examine the relation between home and school identities and to expose the often painful emotional labor exhibited by students as they navigate the cultural and geographical space between home and school.

Based on 182 in-depth interviews, we report that Preuss School students see the geographical and cultural distance they travel to and from school both as an obstacle and a catalyst. On the one hand, Preuss students are encouraged to believe that they can achieve academically and obtain a college degree. On the other hand, they struggle with the need to reconcile the home and school norms and codes of conduct. We examine how students' lives are impacted by their daily navigation between different and sometimes conflicting spaces of home and school. This paper contributes to the dialogue about the academic performance of low-income black and Latino students by revealing some of the institutional arrangements that contribute to their ability to cross the border between home and school cultures.

> [Attending Preuss] helps you out, it increases your studies, you'll get smarter and all that–you know. It gives you more of a chance to go to college and stuff like that, BUT the downside to it would be that it takes a lot of hard work, a lot of hard work! Compared to other high schools, this high school is just crazy. Like we come home, you do homework, go to sleep, go to school, come, work, do homework, and wait for the weekend, and then we still have to do more homework. Other high schools, you don't do that really. (Issac, a 12th grade student)

Race-, class-, and gender-based discrimination persist; job and income inequality continue; and educational resources remain unevenly distributed in US schools. Confronting these realities, students from newly arrived immigrant families and those from underrepresented minority backgrounds face a vexing dilemma: is it necessary to give up the language and culture learned at home in order to become successful in school? Or: can the academic skills learned at school be added to the language and culture attained at home?

The recent development of the Preuss School enables us to carefully examine the relation between home and school identities and to expose the often painful emotional labor exhibited by students as they navigate the cultural and geographical space between home and school. Students reported the pain of coping with parents who did not seem to understand the fatigue induced by the 45–60 minutes it took to travel to and from school each day, the stress that difficult academic material, such as AP classes [Advanced Placement: high school classes for college-bound students], testing, and homework associated with the college-going culture being cultivated at Preuss placed on them. The students expended considerable emotional energy balancing academic requirements demanded by the school with the desires of the family to spend more time together and reconciling their newly found academic ambitions with their parents' desires that the students stay close to home when they graduate from high school.

The Preuss School is a single-track, college-preparatory public charter school on the campus of the UCSD. Developed in the aftermath of the elimination of affirmative action admissions policies in the UCSD (Rosen & Mehan, 2003), the school prepares students from underrepresented minority backgrounds to enroll in the nation's most competitive colleges and universities. Serving students from low-income backgrounds whose parents or guardians have not graduated from a 4-year college or university, the school is 15–20 miles away from the students' homes. The school has achieved a measure of success. *Newsweek* named it the 6th best high school in the United States in 2008; *US News and World Report* named it the 9th best high school in the United States in 2007. An average of 83 percent of students in the first four graduating classes (2004, 2005, 2006, 2007) have enrolled in colleges such as Berkeley, UCLA, UCSD, Harvard, MIT, Dartmouth, and Claremont (for details see McClure, Strick, Jacob-Almeida & Reichter, 2006; Reicher & McClure, 2008).

Preuss School students see the geographical and cultural distance they travel to and from school both as an obstacle and a catalyst that affords them an opportunity to succeed academically. Accompanying the opportunities, resources, and aspirations available at Preuss are the troubles and challenges of juggling home and academic lives. On the one hand, Preuss students are encouraged to believe that they can achieve academically and obtain a college degree. On the other hand, they struggle with the need to reconcile the norms and codes of conduct normally found in their homes with those demanded by the school. In the pages that follow, we specifically look at how students' lives are impacted by their daily navigation between different and sometimes conflicting spaces: the home and the school.

Research Methods

The research reported here took place at the Preuss School during the 2004–2005 school year. Data were gathered using questionnaires, interviews, and focus groups. Questionnaires were distributed to 8th, 11th, and 12th grade students who had secured parent consent forms; 77 out of 126 (61 percent) 8th grade students, 77 out of 92 (84 percent) 11th grade students, and 65 out of 75 (87 percent) 12th grade students, that is, a total of 219 students completed the questionnaire. The questionnaires were designed to obtain data about student attitudes toward their Preuss School experience and to solicit their willingness to be interviewed—and in the case of 12th grade students, also their willingness to participate in "focus groups."

Morales then conducted in-depth face-to-face interviews with the 77 8th grade students and the 75 12th grade students, while Khalil interviewed the 30 11th grade students who had indicated on their questionnaires their willingness to be interviewed; these interviews took between 30 and 60 minutes. Fifteen 12th grade students were also organized into five focus groups; these groups had an even distribution of males and females, students with high and low grade point averages (GPAs), and students with different attitudes toward the school as expressed in the questionnaires that they had completed. All student names mentioned in this chapter are pseudonyms.

The activity of conducting research is never value neutral. Researchers, especially those engaged in observational studies, shape research by their selection of topics to investigate, materials to analyze, and instances of data to interpret (Cicourel, 1964). Researchers do not simply observe and report "brute facts;" they shape materials into interpretations. The inevitable reflexive relation between researchers and objects of study was made even more complicated in this study because of the special relationship that the authors have to the school.

Khalil's access to students was facilitated by her role as a tutor, while Morales's access was facilitated by previous research he had done on the school (Morales, 2005; McClure & Morales, 2005). Mehan, who helped design the school, directs the research center (CREATE) responsible for documenting the academic performance of its students; he has written about its formation (Rosen & Mehan, 2003) and development (Alvarez & Mehan, 2006). These special relations cut two ways. On the one hand, they facilitated entrée because some degree of trust had already been established; on the other hand, reviewers can conclude that our objectivity has been clouded by these close relations. Rather than ignore these close relations, we acknowledge and make them visible in the analysis that follows. Therefore, our findings cannot be viewed as some disinterested representation of the "truth," but our most thorough and informed representations of our interpretations of data gathered during interviews of the students, interactions of the focus groups, and hours of participation at the school.

Students' Identities and Academic Performances

Identities are ways of participating in different sorts of social groups, cultures, and institutions, for example, ways of being a "good student," a "respectful daughter," a "laboratory scientist," and a "successful business person" (Gee, 2001). The appropriate use of language is crucial for participating as an accepted member of any social group. "Appropriate language use" includes speaking the right words in the right situation; it also includes using the appropriate gestures, dressing in the right clothes, displaying the right taste in food, entertainment, and friends, and using the right tools. Membership or participation in a group, culture, or institution is not solely the projection of the individual. Whether a particular person's language use (including gestures), clothing, actions, and other displays of membership or participation in a group are appropriate, is determined by the other members of the group.

Students participate in at least two social groups or institutions in their adolescent years—the home and the school. These two institutions often have unique demands, shaping students' identities within them. As a result, they may conflict. This conflict, in turn, can contribute to the academic difficulties experienced by low-income students of color. However, if home and school cultures are integrated, such integration can contribute to the academic success of the students (Khalil, 2005).

The homes or communities in which students live consist of particular practices, experiences, beliefs, ways of talking, and ways of acting—what Bourdieu (1984) calls *habitus*. The experiences, beliefs, and language adolescents experience at home constitute their *home identity*, which in turn affects how these adolescents see themselves and how they relate to the world. Home identity influences how students see themselves as members of their families, what they see as their roles within their families and communities, and what they see as their future in terms of education and the world of work. Ethnic identity often comprises a major part of this home identity, but does not necessarily comprise it entirely. The formation of home identity is influenced, certainly, by life as a teenager participating in peer culture.

In contrast, *academic identity* is formed in the interaction between school-based and home-based practices (Lareau, 2003). Parents express attitudes, beliefs, and values, which are translated into practices that set the tone for the way children—as students—interact with their school. Likewise, educators in school communicate explicit and implicit expectations for academic performance, modes of conduct, and ways of talking and writing. School-related practices include speaking in an academic register, accepting the norms of the school, such as attending regularly, acting politely, participating in lessons, and doing homework. Academic identity, then, comprises how youngsters see themselves as students, their aspirations, their attitudes toward education, and what school-related practices they adopt.

Disconnections between Home and School Identities

Many researchers assert that black, Latino, and Native American students from low-income families recognize that structures of discrimination persist in society. The "lads" in England (Willis, 1977), the "Hallway Hangers" in Boston (MacLeod, 1987), the "*vatos*" in South Texas (Foley, 1990), and the "jocks" in "Lumberville" Solomon (1992) concluded that no matter how hard they studied, they would still be relegated to low-paying jobs, or, worse, no jobs at all. In response, such students have adopted an oppositional ideology that informs a course of action that directly challenges conventional American wisdom about the relationship between academic performance and occupational success. The ideology and practice of resistance contributes to the lowly position of low-income blacks and Latinos and other low-income youth in the occupational structure because they refuse to develop the skills, the attitudes, the manners, and the speech necessary for achieving success in school and the workplace (Ogbu, 1974, 1987; Fordham & Ogbu, 1986).

When an academic and a home identity are separated and students do not actively try to maintain both, one often deteriorates. Richard Rodriguez's biography (*The Hunger of Memory*) is a searing account of his journey from being a "socially disadvantaged child" to becoming a "fully assimilated American." But his journey from the Spanish-speaking world of his family to the wider, presumably freer, public world of English was not without costs. His "American identity" was only achieved after a painful separation from his past, his family, and his life (quoted in Suárez-Orozco & Suárez-Orozco, 1997, p. 72):

> The more [Richard] Rodriguez was propelled into the public world of school and the dominant culture, the more alienated he became from his private world: family, ethnicity, and culture. His embarrassment about his parents' accent and their inability to help him even with his second-grade homework fueled his shame. When his teachers said, "Your parents must be proud of you...shyly I would smile, never betraying my sense of irony: I was not proud of my mother and father."

Rodriguez's two worlds eventually became so distinct that it became nearly impossible to bridge the gap between them.

Valenzuela (1999) calls the process by which students' home identities are excluded from the classroom *subtractive schooling*. Schools subtract resources from students by devaluing their culture and language. *Subtractive schooling* occurs when a teacher tells a student not to speak Spanish, mispronounces names, or derides cultural expressions (Valenzuela, 1999). When home experiences are not validated or are actually degraded in the classroom, students can develop deep feelings of alienation, which in turn can affect their performance at school.

The Development of Dual Identities: The Role of Institutional Arrangements

Not all low-income students of color develop an oppositional identity (Horvat & Lewis, 2003; Carter, 2006a, 2006b). Not all schools employ subtractive practices. Many students develop a dual identity: a school identity—a way of talking and acting that is appropriate for the school setting; a home identity—a way of talking and acting that is appropriate for the neighborhood. The institutional arrangements of the school can be additive, thereby fostering the development of a dual identity among students of color.

Gibson (1988, p. 431) suggests that "minority youth do better in school when they feel strongly anchored in the identities of their families, communities, and peers and when they feel supported in pursuing a strategy of selective or additive acculturation." Gibson (1988, p. 442) found that some "minority students can be successful academically without being conformists and without rejecting their ethnicity." For such students, "high academic performance need not imply conformity, nor must it entail the rejection of one's identity" (Gibson, 1988, p. 442). These students are able to maintain both an academic and a cultural identity.

Mehan, Villanueva, Hubbard, and Lintz (1996) documented how institutional agents helped foster a positive sense of academic identity in low-income underrepresented minority students without asking them to sacrifice their home identity. The Advancement via Individual Determination (AVID) program, designed to help low-achieving students with high academic potential prepare for entrance in colleges and universities, places previously low-achieving students (who are primarily from low-income and ethnic or linguistic minority backgrounds) in the same "college prep" academic program as high-achieving students (who are primarily from middle or upper-middle income and "majority" backgrounds). Recognizing that the previously low-achieving students who are placed into college-preparatory classes may not have adequate preparation, and that teachers in college-preparatory classes may not be prepared to teach this type of student, AVID has arranged a system of supports, or "scaffolds" (including explicitly teaching test-taking skills, developing strategies for engaging instructors, brokering relations with teachers, and connecting students to college admissions officers) to assist students make the transition from low-track to high-track high school classes and prepare for college (cf. Noddings, 1984; Valenzuela, 1999; Cooper, Jill, & Edward, 1999; Vasquez, Stanton-Salazar, & Mehan, 2000; Stanton-Salazar, 2001).

Academically oriented students often come from friendship groups in neighborhoods that are not always academically oriented. In such cases, many students engage in academic pursuits with their friends at school, and engage in recreational pursuits with their neighborhood friends after school and on weekends. These "border crossing" or "cultural straddling" strategies seem to be effective for Latino and African-American students and recent immigrants to the United States (Mehan et al., 1996; Gibson, 1988; Carter, 2006a, 2006b). Border crossing strategies enable students to develop enough confidence to build an academic identity and to recognize the compatibility between that identity and their neighborhood-based selves (Carter, 2006a, 2006b).

Creating a College-going Culture at Preuss

Establishing a college-going school culture is a "conditio[n] that students in educationally disadvantaged communities require for learning and successful college preparation" (Oakes, 2002, p. 2). A college-going culture develops when "teachers, administrators, and students expect students to have all the experiences they need for high achievement and college preparation.... Students believe that college is for *them* and is not reserved for the exceptional few who triumph over adversity to rise above all others" (Oakes, 2002). Elements of a college-going culture include a shared purpose shown through rituals, traditions, values, symbols, artifacts, and relationships that characterize a school's personality. A school culture is important because it "shapes the way students, teachers, and administrators think, feel, and act" (Deal & Peterson, 2002, p. 9). These elements are visible throughout Preuss.

Significant symbols that focus students on college at the Preuss School include school uniforms, the location of the school, and the daily presence of UCSD students as tutors. Preuss students wear uniforms to school that symbolize explicitly their participation in this college-preparatory school. The presence of the school on the university's campus orients students to many dimensions of college life. Some Preuss students intern on the UCSD campus giving them access to the library and professors, thereby increasing their cultural capital and connecting them to valuable social networks. UCSD students serve as role models as well as more capable peers for the students they tutor. Preuss students rotate through their eight classes on alternate days, mimicking the college Monday-Wednesday-Friday and Tuesday-Thursday class schedules. Preuss graduates who return to campus also provide insight into the college-going experience.

Rigorous Courses, Academic and Social Supports

Preuss students take only college-preparatory classes starting in 9th grade. The college-preparatory curriculum symbolizes the high expectations that the school has for each child, further emphasizing the culture of learning being instantiated at the school.

The school's educators realize that not all students are well prepared when they enter. Accordingly, the school extends its year by 18 days, which gives students more opportunities to meet the rigorous academic demands of the school. Students have an advisory teacher who serves as the advocate and counselor for the same group of students from grades 6–12. Advisory teachers observe their students in classes, communicate with parents, or conduct personal conferences. The advisory process enables students and teachers to develop relationships and to ensure that student achievement is monitored closely (Meier, 1995; Sizer, 2004).

Students' Perceptions of the College-going Culture at Preuss

The students interviewed articulated the major elements of the Preuss college-going culture; 99 percent of 8th graders, 93.4 percent of 11th graders, and 99 percent of 12th graders agreed or strongly agreed with the question "I am confident that I will continue onto university studies when I graduate from Preuss." The vast majority of students (99 percent) also said that Preuss "offers a challenging academic setting;" 97 percent of students said the school "provides enough support so that I can succeed in my studies."

Developing Dual Identities

Although "going to school" seems to be an explicitly academic task, there are many implicit social and cultural dimensions of this activity. Often called "the hidden curriculum," students need to learn when and how to talk and act as well as learn the content of math, science, and English courses. Preuss teachers helped facilitate the development of their students' academic identities when they instructed them on how to write essays in academic terms, use academic vocabulary, and present oral reports on their year's work in front of an audience composed of faculty and community members. Acquiring and activating the academic register while learning academic subjects was a particular challenge because of the cultural and physical distance that Preuss students traveled each and every day. Students encountered the task of "code switching"—knowing when and where to activate proper academic behavior and disengage from behavior considered normal in their home community each and every day.

Cultural Identities on Campus: "Never Forget How We Got Here or Where We Are from"

Preuss School students experienced their education as an additive not a subtractive process (Gibson, 1988; Valenzuela, 1999; Carter, 2006a, 2006b). "*Aunque la mona se vista de seda, mona se queda*,"[1] was the response we received from Amanda when asked if she felt comfortable expressing her cultural identity on campus. All students who we interviewed said they did not feel they had to forfeit their cultural identities in order to form their academic identities. Instead students felt that their academic identities complimented their cultural identities.

Students described the process of negotiating home and school identities as learning to express the appropriate behavior in each setting. While on campus, students understand that there is a certain way of talking required to interact properly; however, when they return home to their families and community, students reported that they do not hesitate to switch to the speech patterns and behavior expected there. When we asked Teresa if she felt she needed to act differently when on campus, she said:

> Teresa: I probably interact differently, but I still act the same just probably here because the education levels, they're different here than they are at home. So I probably have to talk more like not ghetto, but like more at their level.

---

1 Even if you dress a doll in silk, she remains a doll.

JCM: At their level, as teachers or staff?

Teresa: Yeah, well, here probably I know more educational stuff than other seniors at other high schools do, like some words that aren't even that complicated they don't even know the definition of it.

JCM: Have you ever been caught in that situation where you–

Teresa: I have. So I have to like watch out how I'm using the language, that kind of thing. Well, my mom and my dad, they at least finished high school so that they know their Spanish words very well. But like my uncles and stuff, they don't, so I need to be careful how I talk and stuff, so I won't offend them.

JCM: The academic Spanish?

Teresa: Yeah, the academic Spanish. Like *los acentos* [the accents] and all of that.

Teresa articulated the demands of maintaining two fully functioning identities. On the one hand, Teresa said she could maneuver through the challenges of the academic setting but still caught herself policing her "ghetto" self. On the other hand, she tried to taper off her academic Spanish with family and "school girl" speech with neighborhood friends.

Furthermore, Preuss students did not see the adoption of an academic identity as culture stripping in which they were asked to sacrifice their home-based cultural identity. Instead, they saw achieving in the academic setting as a normal progression. In the final analysis, students realized they were participating in two distinct worlds—one at home and the other at school. But on campus they felt as though both identities could live side by side. Latino students in particular reinforced each others' beliefs that pursuing academic success and "being Latino" was normal. Students reported that maintaining their home cultural identity was facilitated by occupying common space with classmates who shared many similar cultural beliefs, customs, and interests. It was also common to hear students converse in Spanish in hallways and on the quad.

Students also asserted a desire to overcome the typical stereotype that depicted minority students as failures. When Efrain was asked if expressing his Mexican-American identity in school ever posed any challenges, he responded, "It only comes up when it is stereotyping, that can be a challenge. Like [when people say] Mexican people, Hispanic people, they don't go to college. It is like a little challenge, 'Oh I am going to prove you wrong.'"

The Latino students we interviewed also reported that returning to neighborhoods and communities where people primarily spoke Spanish enabled them to more easily maintain a deep-rooted connection with their cultural traditions. Though as we show in the next section the costs were high, students believed they benefited from participating in two worlds. At Preuss they gained the academic preparation and social support necessary to go to college, while at home they remained intimately connected to their home culture, language, and identity. Clarisa makes it a point to not forget her roots: "Even though we come to La Jolla, we come to Preuss, we should never forget how we got here or where we are from. That is like my main focus. Don't be ashamed of who you are and where you came from! I think that it is better if you came from the bottom and come to the top than if you came from the top and always being there."

"They Just Don't Understand What I'm Going through"

Parents' participation is a crucial factor in their children's development of a college-going, academic identity (Valdés, 1996; Oakes, 2002; Lareau, 2003). Although 87 percent of 12th grade students, 88 percent of 8th grade students, and 77.6 percent of 77 11th grade students who completed our questionnaires agreed with the statement "My parents understand what it takes to succeed at the Preuss School," students participating in follow-up interviews and focus groups detailed the difficulties experienced when navigating academic and home identities. When asked to elaborate, students said their parents often did not understand the specifics of the demands placed on them at Preuss. This led to misalignments between what was expected from students at school and at home. Although their parents were not aware of details and were not prepared to assist them academically with their schoolwork, parents provided emotional support at home.

Students often used the phrase "they don't understand what I am going through" to describe parents' reactions to the tension they experienced in trying to navigate between home and school identities. They often said that it was difficult for their parents to understand the fatigue induced by the 45–60 minutes it took to travel to and from school each day. Shantell's comments represent the thoughts of the students we interviewed on this point:

> They have an idea that yeah you have to have a little something different if you want to survive in that school, but I don't think they understand the magnitude, in what it takes out of you to be at this school. I go home, I get on the bus, I come here, I'm here all day, and then I get home around 5 o'clock. And then if someone were to clean up, do chores, do this, do that, help my brothers with homework and, cook dinner and stuff like that, but, I still have homework too, and then try to maintain a social life, it's kinda' hard.

Students also felt their parents did not understand the stress associated with the difficult academic material, such as AP classes, and at Preuss:

> Jane: They don't understand that I'm taking like, right now I'm taking 3 AP classes, and they don't understand that it's hard, and they don't understand that I'm taking 8 classes, and I'm required to take higher level classes.

> Gloria: They don't realize it does get hard, because all the homework and we have more than 6 classes, then we get home late. So when we get home there's homework then we have to study for a test, then we have so many classes.

> Lizzy: Sometimes I feel like my parents do not understand how much work, even homework, they don't understand how much work I have to put into it, and they always yell at me about staying up late. They think that I stay up late for fun, when I don't.

Students especially noted that parents did not appreciate the difficulty of the testing regimen they experienced:

> Aaron: I know that my...my mom...she doesn't really understand....I tell her, oh yeah we have all these SATs, and she's like, "oh what's SATs? They're just easy, just take them." And I was like, "well it's not that easy. AP tests, they're hard."

> Gabriela: They realize it...the big things, like you guys have SAT, you guys have AP testing, you guys have to do good in your classes, but that's overall. But it's like you guys have to also realize that it's hard on me already trying to come to school, like being away all the time, like not being able to go out with my friends, and that like just being myself, just being a kid I guess you could say.

> Nicole: They don't understand that it's harder, like the whole class thing, and the long day, and the tests, and all the AP stuff, they get it but I don't think they know exactly how hard it is for me, and how stressful. Yeah, I don't think they get that.

Conflicts between Home and School Demands

Students agreed that subscribing to the school's college-going culture required them to make their academic responsibilities a top priority, a choice that at times conflicted with the desires of the family to spend more time together. Clarisa stated "The whole point about coming here, with having to stay after school, you really don't have time for other stuff. It just has to be Preuss. Your whole life is Preuss. That is how it was for me."

In her interview, Natalia echoed "the Preuss is your life" theme, an experience that demanded students fill their Monday through Friday schedule with academic activities to the exclusion of family, friends, and time for themselves. Whether it was commuting to and from school, taking college-preparatory courses, participating in academically oriented student clubs, devoting one to two hours a day to homework projects, or engaging in community service, Preuss school students worked on their "college bound" identity on a daily basis all year. Natalia described the tension created as a result of participating in two competing spaces:

> It is hard because me and my mom have a lot of fights because of that. 'Cuz most of the time my room is clean and everything, but the thing is that I don't have enough time to help out around the house more because I am doing homework and she just

> gets frustrated because I am not doing what she is telling me to do because I am trying to do what I need to do for school. Sometimes she sees me watching TV and she says, "Why aren't you doing anything?" I just need some breaks in between my homework, and she gets all mad 'cuz she thinks I am not doing anything. So it is like, "Ah, I can't relax." It is like I get home and still have all of this pressure. Sometimes it is frustrating. It builds up sometimes. I am like, "go away."

Laura faced similar disagreements with her mom:

> Yeah my mom sometimes frustrates me. Sometimes I say "I have to take this test or that test" and she is like "Ok, ok, ok...." I sometimes can't really explain it, like the college application, sometimes I couldn't really explain to her. She was like, "¿Y, ya las acabaste?" [Are you done with them?] I am "like almost." Then I would be working a lot, she'll see me lock myself up right when I get home and start doing work, and then she is like "¿Qué haces en tu cuarto encerrada all day?" [What do you do in your room closed up all day?] and I say "I am working on school work." And she says "When are you going to do the dishes, when are you going to clean up the house, when are you going to do this?"

Ricardo exemplified the special challenges faced in balancing home and school life by students whose parents worked. The time Ricardo spent with his father during the week subtracted from the time he needed to study. Ricardo lamented the absence of time spent with his father:

> I think if I went to a regular school I would see more of my dad, 'cuz he works nights and afternoons. So when I get home he is not there. If I went to regular school, I think I would still get to see him for like an hour or two. Mt. Herman [the pseudonym of the school he would attend if he was not at Preuss], they get out like at 1:30 or something, so I would be coming home at 1:30. My cousin is there and my dad picks her up from Mt. Herman, and then after that he leaves an hour later. My mom is always working, she gets home at the same time we do.

Issac also detailed how academic responsibilities often led him to isolate himself from his family. Whether it was simply locking himself up in his room for several of hours each night in an attempt to focus on school work, or missing out on family events because of his academic work load. Issac found that his relationships with parents and brother fragmented because of his absence. He felt conflicted by his desire to spend more quality time with his family and his desire to achieve academically:

> I like spending time with my family a lot. It's fun and we mess around, and then it is kind of hard 'cuz I want to be with my family, but I know I can't 'cuz I have to do homework. The only way for me to do homework is to lock myself in and isolate myself and don't pay attention to them. Yeah, I want to go kick it with my mom and go watch a movie, or kick it with my dad and go watch the game. Go see the Charger game or something, but I just can't no more. I just tell them I have to stay and do homework. An example, like for this Christmas, they want me to go to Mexico, I would go but I can't...I need my rest, I need to do my applications, I have to worry

> about school. I would be more than happy to go to Mexico, I just can't. I am trying to explain that to them but they can't understand 'cuz they are not in my shoes.

Parents often scolded the students because they were not fulfilling their responsibilities at home. Chores such as babysitting younger siblings, cleaning the house and yard often went undone because they competed with academic responsibilities. Students felt they were caught in the middle. If they fulfilled their traditional responsibilities at home, their academic responsibilities would be compromised. Or if they opted to meet their academic responsibilities they would then have to deal with disgruntled parents.

Isabel explained how frustrating it was to have her mom not give her the praise she coveted with regards to "school stuff":

> Isabel: With my mom, I would be like, "Oh this happened today at school, it was so cool," and she would be there cooking or doing something and wouldn't talk to me or anything, and I would just look at her and be like, "never mind, never mind, I am talking to myself," she would be like, "Yeah, I am hearing you, I am listening to you." So I would "say something. Like how was it?" Like my mom wasn't really involved, so I never took the time to tell her this happened today, cause she wouldn't understand. She would say "OK, *que bueno*." [Alright, how wonderful.] And she'd keep driving or doing whatever she was doing.
>
> JCM: What did that feel like?
>
> Isabel: It felt bad because it seemed like she really doesn't care, but it was because she never went to college or anything. She never had an education, so she doesn't know anything, and the times I did try to talk to her, she wouldn't know what to tell me. She'd be like, "*No sé que decirte*, good job?" [I don't know what to tell you, good job?] And so then, I found someone else telling me, "Oh, good job." Somewhere else, rather than home.

Isabel's painful experience of not obtaining coveted praise at home resonated with that of many other students we interviewed. It was common to hear that students approached their parents and neighborhood peers enthusiastically regarding school matters, but found that their desire for assistance, praise, and understanding remained unfulfilled.

Gerardo recalled the reaction he experienced when he told his mother that he had submitted an application to University of California Riverside. To his surprise, instead of praising him for his efforts, his mother questioned about how realistic it would be for him to attend that university. In her eyes, attending a school away from home only meant more expenses, something that the family could not afford:

> "Oh Mom, I sent the application," and she was like, "OK" [imitating a timid, uninterested voice]. I thought she was going to make like a bigger deal 'cuz I am the first one [to go to college]. I was like, "I might go to UC Merced," but I didn't end up applying 'cuz I didn't get the fee waiver, so I just put down UC Riverside and UC San Diego. "I put UC Riverside," and then she is like, "Are you actually going to go to

> Riverside and live over there? I mean the only way you are going to be over there is if you get accepted with a scholarship or some money that ends up paying for school." I am like OK, instead of helping out and telling me, "Oh, you're going to make it." You are here telling, "Are you actually going to go over there and study or are you just wasting money by the application and stuff." I was like OK, I am not telling them anything anymore, like whatever, I am sticking to my own stuff, telling my friends.

Teresa and Claudia appeared to have had an especially difficult time reconciling their newly found academic ambitions with their parents' expectations. For Teresa, the "battle" consisted of convincing her mother that gaining independence was a reasonable aspiration for a young woman to have, even if it meant going against her mother's deep-rooted cultural beliefs that a young girl should stay close to the immediate family:

> Teresa: I want to move out of San Diego because I want to have my own independence. That's the reason why me and my mom have a battle about this, because of that [independence]. I see that as the American dream.
>
> JCM: What's that?
>
> Teresa: Finding independence and having the independence. And my mom, she's like, "No, you and your American style." She wants me to stay at home, not leave the house until I'm married. But I'm atheist, so I'm eventually not going to marry through the church. Also, if possible, she'd like me to bring my family in with hers. And that's not happening at all! She's used to the Mexican tradition of having the grandma, the *nietos* [grandsons] and *nietas* [granddaughters], and everything. But I see myself in college, playing soccer for sure.

Claudia also encountered a resistant mother when announcing she wanted to pursue university studies on the East Coast. When scrutinizing her daughter's ambitions, Claudia's mother focused on ways her daughter could fail. First, Claudia's high objectives were beyond her reach and eventually her hopes would get crushed. Second, being away from the safety net of her home would eventually lead her to trouble:

> Claudia: Yeah, my mom thinks—I don't know. It's so weird. It's kind of sad to me in a way because she thinks I'm setting myself [up] for failure. She thinks I'm not going to make it, especially on the East Coast. She wants me to stay here.
>
> JCM: Can I ask you to clarify. What does it mean in your mind—what do you think your mom means by failure and not making it?
>
> Claudia: Getting pregnant and then giving up everything because she sees that, oh, she sees everything I want to do because my goals are super high. And she just listens to me, and sometimes I don't even like tell her anymore because I know she doesn't believe it because she still is stuck on this idea that, if I leave San Diego, if I leave home, I'm going to get pregnant, and I'm going to give up everything and get left by my partner and be a single parent and have to struggle. She's going to have to come pick up for me. That's what she thinks. I've always told her that she doesn't

> understand, and as much as I try to explain it to her, it ends up in fights and stuff. So I'm tired of that. Maybe that's why I want to get out. It's motivation. It's a bigger push for me to leave San Diego. I just need to isolate myself from that for a little while and learn about myself. Honestly, I see young girls, you know, who do get pregnant and do give everything up. I totally understand. I understand why my mom says that, but I don't understand why she expects that from me. And then I always tell her, "Mom, you think I'm going to give everything up? You think after all I've done and gone to Preuss, you think I'm going to give everything up?" I tell her, "Why did I go to Preuss, if you think that, if you think I'm going to go and get pregnant? Why would I have gone to Preuss and sacrificed everything?"
>
> JCM: Did she support you in 7th, 8th grade, 9th grade 10th grade, your being here?
>
> Claudia: Yeah, up until I had a boyfriend. I got a boyfriend here and then she wanted me to get out of this school. She really seriously did want me to get out, but I said, "No, mom. You're the one who's going to ruin it if anything, you're the one who's going to mess me up."

Students developed strategies for resolving conflicts that developed when parents felt discarded in favor of their children's academic pursuits. Amanda poignantly explained that it was often easier to simply go to her room and take care of her schoolwork than to try and resolve the resentment over the loss her mother was communicating:

> My mom *me regañaba* [she would yell at me], "You are not spending enough time with us. Sometimes you spend more time with people outside of school versus spending time with the family." She would get mad at me. I would just say I am sorry, or sometimes I would just get home and sleep. And she is like, "Oh, you don't want to talk to me." At first, even up until last year, it did affect a little bit my family relationships, especially with my sister. She would ask for help but I would have to do this [referring to Preuss] first, "Oh you never help me." It was hard for me to balance that time out. This year I've done a better job of balancing time out. I am trying to spend more time with my family. I do give myself some off-time during the weekends.

Other students resolved this dilemma by privileging activities with highest value. These students ensured that test preparation, projects, and activities most valued on college applications were completed consistently, while routine homework was completed haphazardly or not completed at all. At home, students selected family events, chores, and activities that communicated to the family they were trying to make a genuine effort to participate actively. Even this resolution of competing demands left students trying to please those around them while leaving little time for themselves.

Because students felt they could not count on their parents to guide them academically, some students often had to act alone concerning important educational matters. For example, when teachers and counselors sent home assignments to notify parents about college applications or financial aid, some students took it upon themselves to complete the forms and turn them in on time. Carlos explained the burden of being left alone to handle the process of applying to college without help from his mother:

> She doesn't really get in my business about it. And also she can't really help with any of it. For example, on Saturday we are having the financial workshop here, and they are requesting your parents come. It would be pointless for her to come because she wouldn't understand any of that stuff, 'cuz she's never gone through it. I think it would be kind of a set back because you'd have to be explaining it to her.

Sandra also detailed the need to handle her own academic matters because her parents did not understand the college application process:

> My dad has no idea about college application, SATs...He doesn't know any of that because he is always working. My mom is the one that spends more time at home and she is the one that gives me the money for the SAT scores and all of that stuff. She's just relying on me to get all of my stuff done, she doesn't know, she is just like, "You have to do what you have to do, I'll leave you alone."

These narratives exemplify the painful conflicts associated with negotiating home and school identities. On the one hand, students' recently crystallized academic identities encourage them to venture off the traditional cultural pathways traveled by peers and family members. On the other hand, students struggled with negative reactions from family members who expected them to conform to cultural norms when considering their future opportunities. These conflicts often left students pivoting between who they were and who they have become. Making the situation more difficult for students was the time and energy they invested to succeed at Preuss, while their parents, without the requisite knowledge about the arcane college-going process, did not seem to understand their struggles.

Emotional Support in Lieu of Academic Support

This is not to say parents were entirely absent from their child's experience. Nor were they uninvolved. Even though parents could not directly help with precalculus equations, physics experiments, or historical analyses, many students said their parents provided support in other ways. They cleared the dinner table for homework, shooed other siblings away, made tea and snacks. Latoya describes the value of this *emotional* support:

> Latoya: [My mom's] really supportive. I kinda feel bad for her because I'll be at home, and say I'm doing precalc homework, and I'm just lost. When I get frustrated I cry, and she hates when I cry because she can't do anything about it, and so she kind of feels sad because she can't help me. She only had a high school education, but they never had to do pre-calculus. It's things like that. She understands and she gives me my space and just lets me do my work, and every now and then comes to check on me, "Are you ok? What's going on?" she asks me about school a lot and asks me about

what I'm doing even though she knows that she can't help me. I'm a rare child. I tell my mother everything, every single thing. My mother's like my best friend. When I come home it's, "How's your day? How's school?" I tell her about school and what I learned, and if I got frustrated, or if I got into an argument, if I had a good day or a bad day, things like that.

Dora described how the entire family can provide this emotional support:

Dora: My dad and my mom and my entire, not just my parents but my entire family, know that it's a family effort. My grandparents bring me to school when I'm at my dad's house. My dad always manages, because my parents are divorced, so when he picks me up in the middle of the week, I have A days and B days, so if he picks me up in the middle of the week I don't have books for the next day. So he's willing to drive me all the way home and then all the way back here, he lives in Mira Mesa, to pick up my stuff.

Stephanie elaborated on this point:

Stephanie:...when I'm really tired and I have a lot of work to do, my mom doesn't bug me about it. She doesn't tell me, do the dishes, I just have to like....I'll go downstairs to eat and then I'll go straight up, I don't have to do anything, because my mom knows I'm tired and I just need to get my work done. She doesn't give me a hard time when like, I need to stay after school for something and it's really late, or she doesn't give me a hard time when I need to buy all this stuff for school, or yeah, they just don't bug me about like doing my chores. They just say, okay, just do it on the weekend when you have time or whatever.

The emotional support Latoya, Stephanie, and other Preuss students described has been documented in the literature (Lareau, 1989; Valdés, 1996; Mehan et al., 1996, pp. 167–185). Parents from low-income communities who have high aspirations for their children but who have not had direct experience in preparing them for higher education, often provide emotional support in the form of comfort and reductions in family responsibilities.

Whereas Preuss students genuinely appreciated their parents' general concerns and emotional support, the students lamented their parents' inability to participate fully in their new academic life. Even though parents tried mightily to stay in tune with their children's progress in school—by attending parent meetings, monitoring grades, and communicating with teachers—students felt their parents did not or could not fully understand their experiences at school.

Peer Group Interactions: "We Want to Be Somebody"

The conflicts Preuss students experienced that were associated with negotiating academic and cultural identities often led them to withdraw from their families and neighborhood friends. At such times, they turned to those who better "understood them" and their experience: Preuss School students.

65 percent of Preuss students reported on our questionnaire that they primarily associated with school peers when they were away from school. Information obtained from interviews gave us insight into the students' reasons for this choice. Preuss students said they associated more with their school peers because they were more academic and future oriented than their neighborhood peers:

> Jane: Beginning of 9th grade [when she first came to Preuss] and beginning of 10th grade I still hung out with a lot of my old middle school friends, 'cuz we lived in the same neighborhood and we kept in contact....but now I guess since we're so caught up in our own lives and school and everything and other activities that we don't really get to talk. The only thing that changed because of me going to Preuss is that I'm so caught up in school and Anjanette [her previous best friend] goes to a regular high school so she's doing the high school experience, so it's kinda' separated.
>
> NK: Do you keep in contact with friends you don't go to school with?
>
> Angelica: Not anymore. No, well I lost touch with them, because yeah they changed a lot.
>
> NK: And what kind of things are you talking about?
>
> Latoya: They want to party, and you want to party too, but you have to work hard so you really just hang out with more kids here at school.
>
> Dora: The kids in my community are going to schools that aren't as good, and they just want to hang out all the time and go to parties and stuff.

These students recapitulated the experiences related by people who shift their political, cultural, or educational orientation (Hurtado, Gurin, & Peng, 1994). They change peer and reference groups, start associating with people who share their orientations. The retreat from neighborhood friendships was not immediate for Preuss students. It was a slower process, one that developed over time, as they became more captivated by academic pursuits than their neighborhood friends, who Preuss students said, remained more focused on parties. While the development of new peer and reference group associations reinforced the college-going culture emphasized by teachers at the school, this development was not without costs. Like Richard Rodriquez, Preuss students lamented the loss of previous associations even as they valued their new ones.

A future orientation—postponing immediate gratification for gratification later in life—has been associated with the "achievement ideology" and, accordingly, a key to occupational success later in life (Turner, 1960). Mariana and Lucy articulated this belief when they said they studied hard now in preparation for the future compared to their neighborhood friends who live in the present and do not plan for the future:

Mariana: I'd have more time for my friends, but I'd have less time for me and for my future. And that's a tradeoff. And I think it's really changed me in that way.
Lucy: I guess here, my friends here, they talk more about their futures and stuff but my friends outside of school they talk, live in the present.

Gabriela thought that because students at Preuss are focused on the future, there is less peer pressure to pursue immediate pleasures:

Gabriela: At every school there's peer pressure but the thing is that at this school if you say "no" they'll just leave you alone, like say "whatever" and "fine." People are not into stuff like drugs, and I'm not saying people have boyfriends and girlfriends, it's not like they don't, but it's like we don't have the pressure of it.

NK: How come?

Gabriela: I know their parents, like Nan here, his parents are just like "it's school, school, Nam, school school"...so everybody's like thinking about the future. It's just ok why am I going to do something stupid that's gonna' give me pleasure for what, one day, two days, a week, month maybe? But if you look at it in the long run it's not going to help me out. And I guess it's just the different kids that you're around kinda' has that influence on you.

Latoya and Maria added that the lack of leisure time inhibited Preuss students from doing "stupid" things:

NK: Are Preuss students different than neighborhood students?

Latoya: When I talk to my friends from other schools a lot of kids are sexually active, or in gangs, or staying out all night, those kind of things. When it comes to us, we have to work, we don't have time to be in a gang or be doing other things that could ruin your future. So in that way I think we're a lot different than kids from other schools, because we don't have that leisure time to just, when you don't have anything to do, what are you going to do, get into trouble....Like, why we get out so late, so we don't go home and go "hey what am I going to do, go hang out with my friends and get into trouble," we don't have time to do that.

Maria: And I just feel that this school helps out by, since the hours are so long, we can't get into gangs or go make trouble. You're mainly in the house, you do homework, and I think other schools are like, you have so much time between school and the nighttime or whatever, allowing them to go do bad things. I think the school kind of prevents it.

In short, Preuss students said that they had specific aspirations for later in life: "We want to be somebody" (cf. Suárez-Orozco & Suárez-Orozco, 1997). More specifically, they want to go to college and "get ahead":

NK: Is there a typical Preuss student?

Mariana: Yes and no. Because I think we're really different, everybody here is so different, and that makes it fun that we're all different. But in a way we're all the same because we're all here for the same reason, and we all share the same mentality.

> Everybody here, they all want to go to a university, a good university or a good college or something like that. And everybody here wants to get ahead in their grades, everybody here worries about school. So I think we are the same kind of because the typical Preuss student worries about school, worries about grades, worries about their future, and how they're going to get there.

Gloria's friend Angelica also concluded that college leads you to "be something":

> Angelica: Yeah like my friend, she's my next door neighbor, she goes to Desert Sands High and she's like, "why are you working so hard?" and I tell her it's school...there's a purpose, for me to get somewhere. But she doesn't understand that. It's something that's not in her future I guess. She doesn't really want to study and do work and have a future I guess. I don't know, I guess she sees things different.

Most—but not all Preuss students (see Gloria's comment above)—"want to be somebody" and they see college as the vehicle for success later in life. In that respect, they have purchased the "achievement ideology"—hard work and effort lead to good grades, which in turn can be parlayed into access to college and good jobs.

Preuss Peers Understand What "We're Going through"

Recall that Preuss students lamented that neither their parents nor their neighborhood friends understood their life at school. By contrast, 67 percent of Preuss students feel that their school peers understand their school lives, while 66 percent said their neighborhood peers do not. This idea was reinforced in one-to-one interviews with 30 11th grade Preuss students. They think a deep level of understanding exists among students at Preuss because they all "go through" similar experiences at home and at school. The phrase "going through" appeared often in reference to their peers:

> NK: Is Preuss different socially from other high schools?
>
> Perla: I guess we interact better because we have a lot of the same classes together, we've known each other sometimes since sixth grade, so I think we mesh well together. So as opposed to other high schools, I don't think it's too much different, but I think it's just that we work better together because we are all in the same situation as far as financially, in our cultural backgrounds, what we've been through, a lot of this is the same, so I think that common ground allows us to come together more.
>
> Nicole: We've known each other for so long, and we know everything there is to know about each other kind of, we're like a family, we're not just classmates, we know each other on a deeper level I guess. And we go through the same stuff, so we relate.

> Angelica: We all know each other, we all know what we're going through, we're all going through the same thing. Unlike other schools, where you don't know what the other person is doing or going through.

Horvat and Antonio (1999, p. 332) report that the small number of black female students experienced pain and anguish at an elite boarding school centered around not belonging in that environment. They felt they had to leave a part of their identity at the door. While Preuss students did report painful experiences, they did not attribute those feelings to exclusion. Rather they felt caught in the middle between the traditional expectations of family life and the new demands of a rigorous academic life.

Conclusions

Our analysis of students' experience at the Preuss School contributes to the dialogue about the academic performance of low-income black and Latino students. The poor academic performance of low-income students of color has been attributed to their adoption of an oppositional ideology that informs a course of resistance to "the achievement ideology" (e.g., Macleod, 1987; Ogbu, 1974, 1987, 1992; Foley, 1990; Willis, 1977). They do not do well in school because they refuse to develop the skills, the attitudes, the manners, and the speech (in short, the cultural capital; Bourdieu, 1984) necessary for achieving success.

Ogbu (1974, 1987, 1992) and Fordham and Ogbu (1986) have the most developed version of this account. They assert that "involuntary minorities" (descendents of people brought to the United States through slavery, conquest, or colonization) are faced with the dilemma of adopting those attitudes and behaviors that enhance academic success (such as studying hard, pursuing good grades) but are perceived by their peers as typical of white Americans and contrary to those attitudes and behaviors that are valued by their community. Involuntary minorities resolve this dilemma more often than not by a wholesale or generalized rejection of schooling because adopting school-based attitudes and behaviors is perceived as "acting white" that is, adopting behaviors, events, symbols and meanings associated with the dominant (white) oppressive culture and undercutting their collective cultural identity (Ogbu, 1992).

Recent research (for example, Gibson, 1991; Mehan et al., 1996; Carter, 2006a, 2006b) has challenged the use of wholesale and binary categories when describing the attitudes and behaviors of ethnic and racial minority students (for example, involuntary minority vs. voluntary minority, acting black vs. acting white, assimilation vs. rejection) because this practice can obscure the variety of students' responses to subjugation, racism, and discrimination. Carter (2006b), for example identifies many forms of collective identity and orientation toward schooling among "involuntary" minorities. Most noteworthy, students who resist acting white do not adopt a *general* anti-school stance, but reject *particular* cultural dress styles and tastes, language and speech styles associated with whites.

Furthermore, the most successful students in these studies embrace the cultural codes of home and school. Our investigation of the Preuss experience reinforces this finding and reveals some of the institutional arrangements that contribute to the ability of students to cross the border between home and school cultures. The institutional arrangements of the school, most importantly, the work of creating a "college-going school culture" (Oakes, 2002) and to socialize its students in this culture helps enable Preuss students develop an academic identity and maintain a home identity. This college-going school culture is fostered through the school's college-preparatory classes supported by academic and social scaffolds, which include a longer school day, a longer school year, advisory classes, college visits, UCSD tutors, linking middle school with high school, and arranging events that connect students to Preuss graduates. Most of these activities take place in the secure and safe environment afforded by the school's presence on the UCSD campus. When the conditions of a college-going school culture are in place, students of color can learn that it is possible to develop a dual identity: a school identity—a way of talking and acting that is appropriate for the school setting; a home identity—a way of talking and acting that is appropriate for the neighborhood.

Horvat and Antonio (1999) and Stanton-Salazar (2001) report that black and Latino students are systematically marginalized in elite schools—a form of symbolic violence (Bourdieu, 1984)—in which the organization asserts the dominance of the more fortunate over the less fortunate. We did not observe this phenomenon at Preuss; nor did students report it during interviews. We surmise that the ideology of this school coupled with the density of the student population suppressed this practice. By virtue of their large numbers, students of color are insiders, not relegated to be outsiders.

This is not to say that students' development of dual identities was a smooth process. It often required a painful expenditure of emotional energy. Students faced challenges as they attempted to navigate the cultural and geographical space between school and home. They had to "go through" the material challenges induced by the longer school day, longer school year, and the long bus rides to and from school. So, too they had to navigate the cultural challenges such as the stress induced by the rigorous classes, tests, and homework associated with the college-going culture at Preuss.

Students we interviewed reported receiving mixed messages from their parents about their new, academic life. On the one hand, students received oral encouragement surrounding the theme that *una buena educación* [a good education] was the best way to avoid the troubles they experienced: earning low wages, lack of job mobility, not being able to buy desired goods. On the other hand, some parents made students feel guilty for participating in the school's time-consuming academic activities that often replaced opportunities to spend with family. Other students stated they felt as if they were caught between their parents' cultural understanding that family comes first and the school's expectations that academics are vitally important.

Students reported their parents' understood the general parameters of their school lives but not the day in and day out struggles of what they "go through." A lack of personal experience of the challenges students experienced when traversing the cultural and material distance between home and school prevented parents from participating actively in the academic dimensions of their children's experience at Preuss. In lieu of academic support, parents often provided emotional support to their children. As a result of these conflicts, Preuss students explained they developed and maintained friendships at school more often than in their neighborhoods because their Preuss peers better "understand what they were going through" both at school and at home.

The question remains: to what extent is the creation of this college-going culture, the academic success it has engendered, and the formation of dual identities a systematic modification of the power structure? One could argue—following Bourdieu (1984)—that the school's work in creating a college-going culture represents merely a crack or fissure in the hierarchy of access that is organized by class and race in the US. To be sure, a large number of low-income students of color are gaining access to higher and higher steps on the ladder of academic and economic success as a result of this concerted effort, but before we gleefully conclude that the hierarchy of access is being dismantled, we must witness more sustained efforts—those that are institutionalized, survive through time, and are instantiated in many different locations.

References

Alvarez, D., & Mehan, H. (2006). Whole school detracking: A strategy for equity and excellence. *Theory into Practice, 45*(1), 82–89.

Bourdieu, P. (1984). *Distinction.* New York & London: Routledge and Kegan Paul.

Bourdieu, P. (1986). The forms of capital. In J. G. Richardson (Ed.), *Handbook of theory and research for the sociology of education* (pp. 241–258). New York: Greenwood Press.

Carter, P. L. (2006a). *Keeping it real: School success beyond black and white.* New York: Oxford University Press.

Carter, P. L. (2006b). Straddling boundaries: Identity culture and school. *Sociology of Education, 79*, 304–328.

Cicourel, A. V. (1964). *Method and measurement in sociology.* New York: The Free Press.

Cooper, C., Jill, D., & Edward, M. L. (1999). Cultural brokers: Helping Latino children on pathways toward success. *The Future of Children, 9*(2), 51–57.

Deal, T., & Peterson, K. (2000). Eight roles of symbolic leaders. *Educational Leadership.* San

Francisco, CA: Jossey Bass, pp. 202–212.

Foley, D. E. (1990). *Learning capitalist culture: Deep in the heart of Tejas.* Philadelphia, PA: University of Pennsylvania Press.

Fordham, S., & Ogbu, J. U. (1986). Black students' school success: Coping with the burden of acting white. *The Urban Review, 8*(3), 176–206.

Gee, J. P. (2001). *An introduction to discourse analysis.* New York: Routledge.

Gibson, M. (1988). *Accommodation without assimilation: Sikh immigrants in an American high school.* New York: Cornell University Press.

Gibson, M. (1997). Complicating the immigrant/involuntary minority typology. *Anthropology and Education Quarterly, 28*, 431–454.

Horvat, E. M., & Antonio, A.L. (1999). 'Hey those shoes are out of uniform': African American girls in an elite boarding school and the importance of habitus. *Anthropology and Education Quarterly, 30*(3), 317–342.

Horvat, E. M., & Lewis, K. S. (2003). Reassessing the 'burden of acting white': The importance of peer groups in managing academic success. *Sociology of Education, 76*, 265–280.

Hurtado, A., Gurin, P., & Peng, T. (1994). Social identities: A framework for studying the adaptations of immigrants and ethnics: The adaptations of Mexicans in the United States. *Social Problems, 41*(1), 129.

Khalil, N. (2005). *Home and academic identities at the Preuss School, UCSD.* Unpublished Human Development Program Honors Thesis. La Jolla: University of California, San Diego.

Lareau, A. (1989). *Home advantage: Social class and parental intervention in elementary education.* London: Falmer.

Lareau, A. (2003). *Unequal childhoods: Class, race and family life.* Berkeley, CA: University of California Press.

MacLeod, J. (1987). *Ain't no makin' it: Leveled aspirations in a low-income neighborhood.* Boulder, CO: Westview.

McClure, L., & Morales, J. C. (2005). The Preuss School at UCSD: School characteristics and students' achievement. University of California, San Diego: CREATE. Retrieved from http://create.ucsd.edu/evaluation

McClure, L., Strick, B., Jacob-Almeida, R., & Reichter, C. (2006). The Preuss School at UCSD: School characteristics and students' achievement. University of California, San Diego: CREATE. Retrieved from http://create.ucsd.edu/evaluation

Mehan, H., Villanueva, I., Hubbard, L., & Lintz, A. (1996). *Constructing school success: The consequences of untracking low-achieving students.* New York: Cambridge University Press.

Meier, D. (1995). *The power of their ideas: Lessons for America from a small school in Harlem.* Boston. MA: Beacon.

Morales, J. C. (2005). *The question is not where they will be next year, but who will they be when they get there: A study of home and school identity.* Unpublished Latin American Studies MA Thesis. La Jolla: University of California, San Diego.

Noddings, N. (1984). *Caring: A feminine approach to ethics and moral education.* Berkeley: University of California Press.

Oakes, J. (2002). *Critical conditions for equity and diversity in college access: Informing policy and monitoring results.* Los Angeles, CA: University of California ACCORD.

Ogbu, J. U. (1974). *The next generation: An ethnography of education in an urban neighborhood.* New York: Academic Press.

Ogbu, J. U. (1987). Variability in minority performance: A problem in search of an explanation. *Anthropology & Education Quarterly, 18*(4), 312–334.

Ogbu, J. U. (1992). Understanding cultural diversity and learning. *Educational Researcher, 21*(8), 5–14.

Reicher, C., & McClure, L. (2008). The Preuss School: School characteristics and students' achievement, Class of 2007. University of California, San Diego: CREATE. Retrieved from http://create.ucsd.edu/evaluation

Rosen, L., & Mehan, H. (2003). Reconstructing equality on new political ground: The politics of representation in the charter school debate at UCSD. *American Educational Research Journal, 40*(3), 655–682.

Sizer, T. R. (2004). *The red pencil: Convictions from experience in education.* New Haven: Yale University Press.

Solomon, R. P. (1992). *Black resistance in high school: Forging a separatist culture.* Albany: SUNY.

Stanton-Salazar, R. (2001). *Manufacturing hope and despair: The school and kin support networks of U.S.-Mexican youth.* New York: Teachers College Press.

Suárez-Orozco, C., & Suárez-Orozco, M.M. (1997). *Transformations: Immigration, family life and achievement motivation among Latino students.* Stanford, CA: Stanford University Press.

Turner, R. H. (1960). Sponsored and contest mobility and the school system. *American Sociological Review, 25,* 855–867.

Valdés, G. (1996). *Con respeto: Bridging the distances between culturally diverse families and schools.* New York: Teachers College Press.

Valenzuela, A. (1999). *Subtractive schooling: U.S.-Mexican youth and the politics of caring.* Albany: SUNY Press.

Vasquez, O., Stanton-Salazar, R., & Mehan, H. (2000). Engineering success through institutional support. In S. T. Gregory (Ed.), *The academic achievement of minority students.* Lanham, NY: University Press of America.

Willis, P. (1977). *Learning to labor.* New York: Columbia University Press.

CHAPTER THREE

Developing Disciplinary Discourses, Literacies, and Identities: What's Knowledge Got to Do with It?

ELIZABETH BIRR MOJE

Approximately ten years ago, as I read Colin Lankshear's (1997), *Changing Literacies*, I was struck by an example James Gee gave on the question of what it meant to be critically literate, an argument I extend to literacy *writ large*. Gee argued that literacy requires attention to "elements-in-coordinations-in-Discourses" (Gee, in Lankshear, 1997, p. xvii), and to illustrate what he meant, he drew from Roger Lewontin's (1991) *Biology as Ideology*. Lewontin distinguished between how a medical scientist would explain the cause of the disease tuberculosis and what a social historian might label as the cause. According to Lewontin, the biologist would most likely claim that the cause of tuberculosis is the *tubercle bacillus*, whereas the social historian would more likely attribute cause to unregulated industrial capitalism in the nineteenth century. I recall being fascinated by the example at the time, not only because of how aptly it illustrated Gee's argument about elements-in-coordination-in-Discourses, but also because it reminded me that literacy is, at its core, about knowledge: comprehending, interpreting, questioning, and critiquing depend heavily on knowing something about the world and how it works. In other words, it is difficult to know how elements are coordinated in Discourses if one does not know about the requisite elements, and know them rather deeply.

The example also beautifully illustrates how knowledge and identity live in relationship to one another, and both to practices of a domain. The medical scientist's explanation for the cause of tuberculosis is a function of both her or his knowledge and her or his ways of knowing (how to explain cause and effect, for example), which stem from the identities she has developed after years of participating in practices of medical science, targeted at pinpointing sources of illness for the purpose of eradicating them. The medical scientist could not, however, begin to engage in the practices of the domain—would not even know the right questions to ask—without certain kinds of conceptual understandings of the domain—without knowledge—having been developed over time.

In this chapter, I want to extend that point about knowledge to theory and research on developing and negotiating disciplinary discourses, literacies, and identities, particularly in and with adolescents. As Lewontin's observation illustrates, learning in the disciplines is important to developing literacy and thinking skills. Furthermore, many argue that developing disciplinary identities is important to learning in the disciplines (Gee, 2001; Lave, 1996). But both seem to depend rather heavily on knowledge. And yet, in most recent sociocultural and New Literacy Studies (NLS) work on learning, discourse, and identity, knowledge seems to take a back seat, with participation in learning communities viewed as the key to developing the disciplinary identities necessary for deep learning. However, as Ford and Forman (2006) argue, "Although participation can be considered one of several learning objectives, participation itself is not 'acquired.' That is, we need to address ways in which the individual is affected by such participation and what resources he or she 'takes away' from these instructional experiences" (p. 2).

My goal then is to put knowledge—or the "residue of participation" (Moje & Lewis, 2007)—in a more prominent position in work on identity, discourse, and learning. In doing so, however, I do not wish to be read as advocating rote transfer of bits of information or of prescribing the nature and type of knowledge to be constructed, as some scholars have (Hirsch, 2006; Ravitch & Finn, 1987). Consequently, I examine theories of knowledge as dynamically produced in interaction and question the role that knowledge-in-action plays in developing a disciplinary identity and concomitant disciplinary literacy and discourse skills. Specifically, if knowledge and identity develop hand-in-hand, then what are the practices for supporting knowledge and identity development-in-action, especially in highly stressed, ethnically and racially heterogeneous classroom settings? My goal is to generate a more robust theory of the relationship among discourses, identities, and knowledge development in school contexts. I conclude that we do not yet have enough information for truly robust theorizing of domain knowledge and identity development, and I call for design experiments that draw from the principles of sociocultural and NLS theories, but translate them to actual school classrooms.

Teasing Apart the Knowledge-Identity-Discourse-Literacy Conundrum

To begin, I want to try to pull apart what appears to be a conundrum. The conundrum goes like this: Many claim that shifts in identity are both necessary for and emblematic of deep learning (Gee, 2007; Lave, 1993, 1996). Gee, for example, argued:

> All deep learning–that is, active, critical learning–is inextricably caught up with identity in a variety of ways....People cannot learn in a deep way within a semiotic domain if they are not willing to commit themselves fully to the learning in terms of time, effort, and active engagement. Such a commitment requires that they are willing to see themselves in terms of a new identity, that is, to see themselves as the *kind of person* who can learn, use, and value the new semiotic domain. (p. 54)

Furthermore, as evident in the Gee quote, it is often argued that identities are dependent on engagements in discourses and practices of a particular domain. But, as the Lewontin example illustrates, engaging in discourses and practices requires knowledge of and skill with those discourses and practices. Even in Gee's (1996) classic example of someone entering a "biker bar,[1]" the person entering the discourse community must have knowledge of the community in order to participate, to take on an identity as "biker" (or not). Thus, identity, it seems, is dependent on knowledge, which in turn helps to develop or even produce new knowledge. It is unlikely that one would be willing to see herself in a new identity about which she knows little. Those who focus on identity, me included, have done so as a way of understanding the need for people to commit to domain learning, to, in a manner of speaking, *personalize* it. We wanted to bring attention to the power of identifying (both self and other identifications) in learning. But the focus on identity may have masked the need to simultaneously develop teaching practices for developing knowledge-in-practice in formal classroom settings.

In fact, some writers have argued that in the interest in foregrounding knowledge as constructed, educators and education scholars too often neglect wholesale the knowledge that learners need to bring forward into a new learning situation. E. D. Hirsch (2006), for example, has written extensively on the need to teach "certain explicit, substantive things about history, science and literature" and, further, to "test students on such knowledge" (see also Hirsch, www.coreknowledge.org/blog, February 16, 2008). Invoking Hirsch reminds us that perspectives on knowledge development often seem to be stuck in a pendulum swing between a "banking view" (Freire, 1970), of static information delivered from expert minds into blank ones, and a radical constructivist

---

1 "Biker" refers to a person who rides motorcycles (as opposed to bicycles), and a "biker bar" is a drinking establishment frequented by or that caters to "bikers."

view (Glasersfeld, 1995), wherein the individual constructs all knowledge on the basis of the interpretation of a particular sequence of experiences. Hirsch, for his part, argues that the answer to the knowledge problem is a matter of requiring more core courses in *traditional* subjects; Hirsch's argument, however, fails to attend to the fact that core curricula are required in many states and still students fail to achieve at high levels. Indeed, the more important question that Hirsch, and other knowledge advocates, should ask is how and to what end knowledge is being taught. If taught as the simple transfer of information from one mind into another and if engaged only for the purposes of demonstrating one's knowledge on a test, then knowledge is not being taught, regardless of whether or not core curricula are employed.

Mired in the binary battle of either banking or constructing all knowledge anew, many scholars have avoided taking on the question of how knowledge and identity develop in tandem and thus support learning. The construction of knowledge, and the pedagogical practices to support knowledge construction, have of course, been theorized for years (e.g., Blumenfeld, Marx, Patrick, & Krajcik, 1997; Cobb, 1994; Cobb & Bowers, 1999; Driver, Asoko, Leach, Mortimer, & Scott, 1994). Despite attention in areas such as literacy to constructs such as *prior knowledge,* however, a number of current instructional regimes operate without attention to how knowledge, identities, or practices are developed. For example, at the secondary school level, in the literacy policy world, we see the demand for teachers to become more proficient in strategy instruction (Ford & Forman, 2006) and, in relation to disciplinary literacy, to *content literacy strategy* teaching in particular, often with little attention either to the identities young people bring to school or to the knowledge demanded to engage in the texts of different disciplinary subject-matter areas. The attention to strategy instruction is not problematic in and of itself; many cognitive strategies, tools, or practices are key to the development of strong critical literacy skills in any domain (Biancarosa & Snow, 2004; Buehl, 2002). Indeed, most cognitive reading strategies are developed on the idea that strategic reading makes links between knowledge to be learned and the knowledge and experience already constructed. In some recent initiatives, however, strategy instruction seems to be largely about providing tools to extract information from text. Strategies—absent some level of knowledge, a purpose for engaging in the literate practice, and an identification with the domain or the purpose for reading—will not take readers or writers very far.

Alternative approaches such as those offered in NLS and sociocultural theory, however, *do* acknowledge the important role of knowledge built in past participation in a community of practice (Moje & Lewis, 2007), often explaining knowledge as something that "develops" in practice as needed (Gee, 2007). These theories, unlike most sociocognitive studies (e.g., Blumenfeld, Soloway, Marx, Krajcik, Guzdial, & Palincsar, 1991; Cobb & Bowers, 1999) also address the importance of identities as an aspect of learning. But most sociocultural and NLS theories are not rooted in classroom or school practice, wherein multiple students of different backgrounds come together around topics that may or may not be of interest to them, with few resources and with teachers who may or may not know them particularly well and thus may not struggle to facilitate the development of knowledge-in-practice. As Brian Street (2003) argues, the greatest challenge to work from the NLS perspective is the question of how theories from focused studies of literate practice in everyday contexts might inform the radically different settings and contexts of schooling (i.e., institutionalized, formal teaching, and learning practices with masses of youth). The question of how knowledge gets developed in practice, in classrooms, while simultaneously developing disciplinary identities, is one example of the challenge in translating sociocultural and NLS theories to classroom practice.

Why Do We Care about Identities and What Are They?

Before moving more fully into the discussion of the relationship among knowledge, identity, discourse, and literacy development, it is worth a side trip to examine the recent *identity turn* in literacy studies (and particularly in NLS) and to offer some perspectives on identities. The increasing interest among a number of scholars, educators, and policy makers in developing disciplinary literacy skills among youth makes these questions especially important. Many educators are committed to engaging young people in deep learning in and across a variety of domains and hope to support young people's learning of literacy and other representational practices within and across those domains even as we draw from the interests, knowledges, discourses, and practices young people bring to the learning environment. As part of that quest, educators are turning their attention to issues of identity associated with proficiency in a domain of knowledge and practice, arguing that one cannot take on the skills and practices of the discipline without shifting one's identities.

What is an identity or, in keeping with current views on identity in education research, what are identities? Many different takes on the subject of identity can be uncovered in the literature, too many to review here (cf. Moje & Luke, in press, for a more comprehensive review of identity and literacy theories and research). In brief, some scholars view identities as discursive constructions, categories to which people are assigned or assign themselves (Chouliaraki, 2003); others see identities as narratives or stories that people tell about themselves and others (Sfard & Prusak, 2005), and still others see identities as enactments in particular relationships and positions (Holland & Leander, 2004; Leander, 2004; Moje, 2004; Wortham, 2001). Specifically, from my perspective, identities are enactments of self, shaped by time, space, and relationships. Because identities are embedded in relationships, they are also embedded in and, at times constitutive of, relations of power. Research on identities and literacies must take into account not only people's discursive constructions but also their enactments and other people's responses to enactments of identity.

Disciplinary identities, then, are enactments of self that reflect the habits of mind, practices, and discourses—or the ways of knowing, doing, thinking, and acting (Gee, 1996)—associated with work in the disciplines of humanities, the social sciences, and the natural sciences (Ford & Forman, 2006).[2] Disciplinary identities, in my parlance, will refer to the discourses and practices that an historian or chemist or mathematician might engage in when producing, representing, and critiquing knowledge in her or his everyday work. These identities and practices often overlap with academic identities and practices, in large part because disciplinary knowledge and practice is typically learned in formal academic settings; nonetheless, there is a specificity to disciplinary knowledge, practice, and identity that is not captured in academic knowledge, practices, and identities. A person who enacts a disciplinary identity sees herself and is seen by others as doing the things a member of the disciplines does (Bain, 2006). For example, in specifying what it means to do the work of history, Bain wrote, "Historians have long defined history as investigation, casting themselves in the role of detectives seeking plausible explanations for historical events, trends, and controversies" (p. 2080).[3] According to Bain, then, membership in the domain of history not only involves identifications (both our own self-identifications and others' identifications of us), but also particular practices, discourses, disciplinary facts and information, and conceptual frames (i.e., disciplinary *concepts*) (cf. Hobsbawm, 1997; Stevens & Hall, 1998; Stevens, O'Connor, Garrison, Jocuns, & Amos, 2008). Membership in disciplinary domains shapes opportunities to learn and, ultimately, learning itself (Stevens et al., 2008). From this perspective, one who has really learned some *conceptual* aspect of a discipline (what we often think of as *knowledge*), has also

---

2 It is useful to distinguish here between disciplinary and academic identities, although there is an important relationship between the two concepts. Academic identities are those associated with doing the work of school. These might include what Green (1983) refers to as "studenting" practices, that is, the practices of raising hands, completing assignments, speaking in certain ways, and acting within particular authority relations and roles, among many other subtle qualities of "school" practice.

3 Because much of my current work is focused in history and science, I turn often to those disciplines for examples. Any of the disciplines, and many fields of study—or subdisciplines—apply here, for the disciplines, I argue, represent groups of people who share norms and conventions for discourse and practice. In that sense, the disciplines constitute cultures.

learned the *practices* (Ford & Forman, 2006) and the *identities* of the discipline (Gee, 2007; Moje, 2008).

One important caveat is that it might be argued that disciplinary knowledge, practices, discourses, and identities are not really of central importance in the twenty-first century. Some might claim that more important knowledge is embedded in social networking systems and the "convergence" of knowledge networks (Jenkins, 2006). Others would argue that more critical than developing knowledge (regardless of how knowledge is conceptualized) is the need to develop skills for accessing, evaluating, critiquing, and producing information.

These are fair critiques. It is clear that social networking and popular cultural practices are powerful, as are skills for accessing and evaluating information that swirls about us in a knowledge and information economy. However, neither social networking nor information management operate in isolation from disciplinary knowledge, discourse, and practice, particularly if we move beyond caricatures of disciplinary knowledge as reified, stale, canonized knowledge of the disciplines. By casting disciplinary knowledge as dependent on broad and deep knowledge of world events, relationships, natural and social phenomena, people, cultures, mathematical theorems, and politics and policies that people engage in as they live, work, and act in the everyday world, we can then view disciplinary knowledge and practice as an aspect of everyday life. Such a stance topples it from a privileged position and makes it more accessible to a host of people. The toppling of disciplinary knowledge's privilege, however, requires that more people gain access to the knowledge and practices of the disciplines so that they can "speak back" to those in power. And this speaking back, of necessity, demands more than just opportunities to critique. As Bain (2006) argues in relation to classroom history teaching:

> To talk differently to the sources of classroom authority, students must not only appropriate the tools of the discipline but must also disturb their conventional interactions with classroom authority, assuming new status, role, and voice in relationship to texts and teachers. (p. 2086)

Bain uses the words "status, role, and voice," but we could replace those with identities, interpreting his point to be that one cannot critique unless one identifies with the discipline, and one cannot identify with the discipline without the tools of the discipline. Some of those tools are practices of reading and writing in particular ways (cf. Bain, 2005; Hand & Keys, 1999; Hand, Hohenshell, & Prain, 2004; Hand, Wallace, & Yang, 2004; Wineburg, 1991, 1998, 2001). Other tools are knowledge tools. That is, taking authority and/or changing status, role, and voice both require some knowledge, of the domain itself and of the larger world. Acknowledging this point, however, raises the thorny question of how teachers enable such knowledge development while also encouraging identifications.

An Example from Practice

To put a finer point on the questions raised above, I draw on an example from a co-teaching opportunity I had a few years ago. I have written about this experience extensively in Moje and Speyer (2008); here I provide just a few details of context to set the stage for the practical experience that brought many of the aforementioned concerns to light for me as a teacher, researcher, and theorist. I emphasize that these are theoretical as well as practical concerns, concerns that cannot be dismissed by simply pointing out the vagaries or problematics of school context. All teaching and learning occur in particular contexts, spaces, times, and relationships, as do all enactments of identities. If we are serious about our theories of learning, discourse, and identity, then we must acknowledge the challenges of real local and particular contexts in which a great deal of teaching and learning occurs.

This experience took place in a high school in Detroit, Michigan, USA. The high school is located in a predominantly Latino/a community, with a majority Mexican, Mexicano/a, and Mexican-American student population. I co-taught with Jennifer Speyer three classes of Grade 11 students (approximately 16–18 years of age) in a course called *Global Issues*. The course was designed to replace what used to be referred to as *world history* courses. This broad topic focus allowed for teachers to draw on historical, political, social, and cultural events, experiences, and concepts to teach young people about the larger world in which they live. In addition to the general US history and geography studies received in elementary school, all students who had attended Michigan schools in grades eight, nine, and ten had two years of upper-level US history and one year of upper-level geography. Speyer and I conceived of this unit as a kind of design experiment, testing for ourselves how we might design a focused history learning experience that drew from students' knowledge and experience and also built new knowledge via the reading and analysis of a host of primary, secondary, and tertiary (textbook) sources.

We designed a two-week unit on US immigration law throughout history. We chose immigration because many of the students are immigrants themselves, have immediate family members who are immigrants, or know extended family and friends who have immigrated. Most community members come from Mexico—across a diverse area, but with northern and southern regional divisions lived out in the community—and some youth from Central and South American nations, with the greatest number (after Mexican immigrants) from Puerto Rico and the Dominican Republic. Our hope was that the students' funds of knowledge about Latino/a immigration issues and about Latin American countries would provide a scaffold on which they could learn more about current and past immigration laws in the United States. We also sought to make an immediate connection to the imminent "May Day March," a planned protest against discriminatory immigration practices. It was widely assumed that the school would be virtually empty on that Friday, May 1, as most students would be involved in the community action activities. Thus, we established the unit's purpose for the students as the study of US immigration law historically to provide information necessary for action in the community. Activities for the two-week unit included (a) daily free writing exercises to prompts about immigration issues (e.g., *Do you think that anyone should be able to immigrate into the US at any time? Why?*), (b) primary source and other text reading (e.g., laws, journal entries, poetry, political cartoons) and discussion, (c) examination and production of visual representations of the concepts and issues of immigrations, (d) oral debates, and (e) formal essay writing (exact form to be determined by students).

The unit was progressing nicely until we encountered a stumbling block, one that revealed how lack of sophisticated domain knowledge—both conceptual and factual—can make critical disciplinary reading difficult. We had reached the point in the unit where we wanted to move beyond questions about immigration law in the United States to a study of US immigration law over time. The goal was to engage students in an analysis of any patterns to the law; our curricular goal was for students to see that the laws, regardless of time period, typically sought to exclude some groups from immigrating and to privilege others. To generate discussion and engage the students in making sense of the laws, we distributed excerpts of the written texts of key immigration laws to small groups of students and asked them to draw a representation of the law's key points. The groups set to work, and many seemed able to dive into the key points, even when reading archaic language from the laws of 1792 or 1836. This was not so true for the groups who received the Emergency Quota Act of 1921 and the Immigration Law of 1924. To illustrate, here is an excerpt of the Emergency Quota Act of 1921:

> *Emergency Quota Act of 1921*
>
> AN ACT
> *To limit the immigration of aliens into the United States. Be it enacted by the Senate and House of Representatives of the United States of America in Congress assembled...*
>
> Sec. 2. (a) That the number of aliens of any nationality who may be admitted under the immigration laws to the United States in any fiscal year shall be limited to 3 per centum of the number of foreign born persons of such nationality resident in the United States as determined by the United States census of 1910.

To put it simply, the students were stumped about how to represent this law, let alone how to take on the role of *investigator*, that is, an historian's identity, in Bain's (2006) discourse. On its surface, the text seemed to represent an equitable law that allowed anyone to immigrate into the US provided that the allowed percentage of the national group's population target had not already been met. Our students' understanding was that everyone could immigrate equally and as a consequence, they did not know what images to draw. The students found it easy to represent, for example, exclusions in prior laws because they were explicitly marked (e.g., The Chinese Exclusion Act of 1882).

What the students did not recognize, however, about the 1921 and 1924 laws was that the exclusions and privileges were encoded in strategic language of the text. By targeting the population of nationalities resident in the US in *1910*, the law effectively reduced the numbers of certain groups who could immigrate because their population numbers were lower in that year than in 1921 (the Immigration Law of 1924 took even more dramatic measures by shifting the percentage of immigrants allowed to 2 percent and the target population year to *1890*). To fully understand the implications of this law, the students would have had to know something about US immigration trends in the late 1800s and early 1900s; more specifically, they needed to know that large numbers of Eastern Europeans were immigrating, and that the number of German and English immigrants was on the decline. They would also have to know that the numbers of Eastern European immigrants were lower in 1910 and much lower in 1890, than they were in 1921.

Equally important, the students would need to know that they should be wondering about the text and asking questions of it (i.e., taking an academic identity, at the very least, and an historian's identity, at best). One might wonder, for example, what was the *emergency* that prompted the Emergency Quota Act. One might reasonably question why the law would refer to 1910 when establishing a law for 1921 or, even more surprising, for 1890, when establishing a law for 1924. This kind of questioning demands an identification with the practices of primary source reading (i.e., of historians). However, returning to Bain's conception of a disciplinary identity in history as one of investigator or "detective" who seeks "plausible explanations for historical events, trends, and controversies" (Bain, 2006, p. 2080), we wonder to what extent our students could act as investigators or detectives when they lacked the knowledge necessary to probe this text. Their lack of knowledge even made asking questions of the text rather difficult, as they did not know enough about cultural attitudes of the time period to ask why the dates in question were selected or what the emergency was.

In other words, this experience with a somewhat challenging primary source text revealed a number of different challenges to identification, challenges that revolved around a lack of knowledge of the time period and why immigration laws might be put into effect (i.e., *who* was being included and excluded with this statement, how industrialization might have mattered, how WWI mattered, questions about eugenics, etc.). The text also revealed to us what a lack of knowledge can do to hamper one's ability to identify with and engage in particular practices and discourses, or *ways of knowing*. It is difficult to take on the role of investigator, or interrogator, of history, if one has not developed either the conceptual, factual, or pragmatic knowledge necessary to recognize that something exists to be investigated, let alone to question, probe, and search for necessary information.

The solution Speyer and I developed,[4] albeit on the fly and somewhat inadequately, when facing the problem of how to engage in historical inquiry with students who lacked requisite knowledge of a relevant historical time period, was to take time to develop the necessary knowledge then and there. We did not, however, simply tell the students the information they needed. We built the knowledge by (a) presenting them with tables that represented immigration trends by nation and time, (b) showing the students images of different national groups to help them understand how race and class may have played a role in how quotas were determined, (c) presenting and analyzing political cartoons and other primary sources that shed light on the thinking of the time, (d) showing the students maps of the world so that they could visualize divisions in Europe that might seem immaterial to them, (e) defining words and showing images to make abstract concepts concrete, and (f) engaging the students in debates and essay writing designed to provide them with a meaningful space to make use of the knowledge they were building. We even taught them how to figure percentages. Thus, we built knowledge-in-practice, for use when it was needed.

This was difficult work, however. Time was limited because it was necessary to move on in the curriculum, as determined by state standards and pacing charts. As a result, we did not meet all of our learning goals, although we did "repair" (Gee, 2007) their knowledge. We label this repair work because much of the conceptual and factual knowledge about the history of immigration law should have already been learned in previous school years. As a result of stopping to do repair work, although it provided rich learning opportunities, these students—whose knowledge and identity development had already been compromised by previous miseducation—were further miseducated in the sense that they lost time to generate new understandings of immigration and to work on the writing for social action on which we had hoped to focus. Thus, despite what we considered to be a powerful learning experience, we felt that we had made significant trade-offs in providing opportunities to learn.

Other challenges included the fact that students moved in and out of the classroom as periods shifted, so ideas written on the board from brainstorming sessions had to be quickly typed in order to refer to them the next day with one class while not spoiling the activity for the next class. The presence of two teachers facilitated this kind of work, but it would probably have been impossible with only one teacher.

---

4 Described more fully in Moje & Speyer (2008).

More critical, absentee rates were high, individual students were taken from class for special activities, and at times, whole class sessions were cancelled for school assemblies or the presentations of movies and plays. Maintaining a consistent focus on the knowledge being built and on the writing we were developing was extraordinarily difficult. In addition, as Speyer and I recognized gaps in students' knowledge, we were able to fill in those gaps by using the classroom teacher's (personal) computer to search for information on US immigration databases, and we could project (on the classroom teacher's personal LCD projector) or print them (on the classroom teacher's personal printer, using his paper and ink cartridges) as needed. Not all classroom teachers, however, have the resources to supply such equipment themselves, and those resources are not always readily available to every classroom (i.e., they are often shared) in economically stressed districts. It is also worth noting that two teachers working together can more quickly access and prepare information as needed to build knowledge-in-practice both during and after class.

Finally, although we purposely chose a concept and problem in which the students were interested—the examination of patterns in US immigration law over time and the influence of race and ethnicity in the making of those laws—students' engagement varied as their own personal interests or crises trumped the more abstract question of the making of immigration law. We also noted that engagement varied with the type of activity; students were highly engaged if we debated or even when we read texts together and engaged in whole-group analyses, but enthusiasm waned when they were faced with individual reading of even average-length texts. We again attribute these points to prior miseducation and the lack of motivation to engage in the effortful processing necessary when faced with a reading task that makes strenuous demands on one's knowledge (Alexander, 2003; Alexander, Kulikowich, & Jetton, 1994).

Calling on Theory to Help Solve the Knowledge/Identity/Literacy Puzzle

Perhaps the easiest way to unlock this puzzle of the relationship among knowledge, identity, and literacy (or more generally, learning) is to take on a sociocultural perspective that sees learning as situated in people's engagements in a variety of practices with other people over time (Lave, 1988; Rogoff & Lave, 1984; Scribner & Cole, 1981; Street, 1984; Vygotsky, 1978). In this perspective, knowledge is constructed *in* practice (not prior to or as a consequence of), identities emerge and are sustained in interactions, and literate practices are learned even as they are enacted over time. More specifically, a number of sociocultural researchers (e.g., Lave & Wenger, 1991; Rogoff, 1995) demonstrated through ethnographic research in different types of communities that learning of particular skills and of cultural norms and practices occurs in *communities of practice*, in which newcomers to the community are apprenticed into sets of practices that develop the knowledge and expertise necessary to become *old-timers* in the community. As an individual becomes more knowledgeable, she or he also shifts in identity from novice to expert, from newcomer to old-timer, from outsider to member of the domain. Much of this knowledge development is implicit, with newcomers learning through repeated observation and scaffolded practice. Make no mistake, however, these theorists do not claim that all interactions between old-timers and newcomers (or masters and apprentices, experts and novices) must be implicit; within any interaction there is not only space but also necessity for explicit telling of information. The master tailor cannot afford to allow a novice to learn from the mistake of cutting material incorrectly and so provides explicit instructions to the novice on how to cut or carry out other tasks. In other words, when expediency is demanded, knowledge is passed on explicitly and directly. Still, in many cases *instruction* is implicit, sometimes carried out through modeling, sometimes through scaffolded attempts, but in all cases, knowledge—both factual and conceptual—develops in these engagements or participations in practice over time.

Despite the emphasis on learning as participation, sociocultural theories do not, however, posit knowledge as constructed anew in each moment of participation. As Cynthia Lewis and I argued in a recent volume:

> Learning, however, also leaves a residue; it makes a mark on the participant. In that sense, learning draws from and constitutes "histories of participation" (Rogers, 2002) in other spaces, at other times, and with other people. Indeed, what makes learning so complex—and more than just participation—is that people bring their histories of participation to bear on each new act or moment of participating. Thus, learning can be conceived of as always being *situated in* participation, but not necessarily synonymous with or reduced to participation. And learning obviously goes beyond the moment of participation to constitute a history and to shape a future act of participating. (Moje & Lewis, 2007, p. 16)

Ford and Forman (2006) argue in a similar vein that, "Practices have a history: They build on memories and products of the past and provide resources for the future" (p. 9). In other words, there are ideas, concepts, and memories that one draws upon to make sense of new ideas, concepts, and experiences.

Stevens and Hall (1998) offer another take on what learning leaves behind with their concept of *disciplined perception*:

> If someone can sound like a doctor, he or she can also see like one, visually and physically inspecting bodies for signs that meet doctors' criteria of "illness" or "abnormality." If someone can look like an architect, he or she can also look at things like one. This sense of discipline demands that we carefully describe visual practices, both in relation to the tasks, artifacts, and settings where they are deployed and in relation to other embodied practices (e.g., pointing and gesturing) that support them.

> We think of disciplined perception as a performance genre–a set of specific forms of embodied action. Accordingly, cognition is a property of the entire body in action, a body shaped and maintained by participation in disciplinary (and other) communities. (p. 108)

Conceived of in this way, disciplined perception depends on and produces knowledge; it is developed over time and in apprenticeship with others who practice in the discipline. Stevens further elaborates on how disciplined perceptions are produced with his notion of a triadic formation of "accountable disciplinary knowledge" (Stevens et al., 2008, p. 357), in which accountable knowledge forms position students as certain types of members of the discipline (or not) and thereby produce identities that further shape their ability to navigate the learning spaces of the discipline to access accountable knowledge forms. The triadic is thus a relationship among knowledge-in-practice; identities-in-development; and navigations through learning spaces, contexts, and relationships. As Stevens et al. (2008) argue in their study of college students learning to be engineers:

> Schools are places where successful disciplinary knowledge performances align with progressive navigation....Different students navigate differently through engineering, and these differences can be consequential not only for where they end up, but also for the duration of their undergraduate experience, the social networks they create, and the quality and substance of their identification with engineering. (p. 357)

These ideas, memories, discourses, and perceptions are brought forward into new interactions, thus raising the consequential question for formal education institutions regarding the implications for children and youth whose prior learning experiences did not afford them opportunities to develop knowledge-in-practice, with other people, over time. What residue of practice do they bring forward? How does the lack of learning residue influence future opportunities to learn?

The value of these learning theories is the emphasis they place on learning—and knowledge development—as a function of engagement in practices, embedded within communities of practice. The question that remains when working for and with these theories to design learning environments and practices, however, is that they reflect learning spaces vastly different from the typical high school classroom, and particularly the high school classrooms of disenfranchised, underserved, or impoverished communities. It is important to note that I am not offering a critique of these theories, but rather a critique of the current contexts in which we expect large numbers of young people to learn, to develop disciplinary identities, practices, and knowledge. Most ethnographic studies of learning, for example, are situated in long-term, everyday interactions (e.g., Lave, 1993; Rogoff, 1990). These studies typically focused on relatively concrete tasks that can be observed and to which learners can be apprenticed, such as the money exchanges of street vendors (e.g., Carraher,

Carraher, & Schliemann, 1985; Schliemann, 1984); the more abstract tasks of everyday life are learned over long-term participation in sustained interaction with the same experts. By contrast, formal schooling tends to focus on learning abstract concepts in short bursts. Most young people around the world attend secondary schools in fragmented blocks of time, removed from the actual world of practice in the subject matters they study.

In addition, studies of youth learning practices outside of school, such as my own study of youth in street gangs learning to write and read graffiti and tags (Moje, 2000) or studies of video and computer gaming described previously (Gee, 2007; Leander & Lovvorn, 2006), offer valuable implications for constructing learning environments that can draw in youth and support their knowledge development in practices. However, those studies assume both a motivation to engage and a sense of identity as one enters the learning space. Someone who wants to participate in a gang, for example, takes on a gang identity by attempting to engage in gang-related practices, such as dress, body movements, and graffiti writing/tagging (in my long-term study I demonstrated that gang "peewees" [young aspiring gang-connected youth] actually carried tagging notebooks where they practiced their literacy and art).

Not only are school classrooms rarely considered the "place to be" by youth, but they are also at times actively demotivating. What is more, the identities that populate advanced subject-matter courses in the secondary school—identities such as physicist, historian, author, or mathematician—are not particularly available to youth. The identities available via the popular culture are often caricatures of what the scientist or historian is.[5] Consequently, it is important to ask how we translate the learning principles generated by these findings to the learning experiences of young people required to participate in state-mandated course work, young people who cannot pick and choose points of entry. Questions of motivation, desire, and engagement seem to represent a stumbling block for translating the principles of out-of-school learning into the principles of classroom learning. Whether gamers, taggers, dancers, or musicians (some of young people's most engaged pursuits outside of school), youth come of their own volition to the activity and can choose to leave when they wish. Many students do not come willingly to classrooms, and some are understandably resentful of being forced to attend, especially those in the upper grades who have experienced years of failure and frustration. Consequently, we should also look for analyses of the development of knowledge-in-practice principles in more formalized settings.

---

[5] It is worth noting, however, that when reasonable—if not completely authentic or accurate—models of disciplinary/professional identities are offered via popular culture (e.g., forensic scientist), research with youth has documented an upswing in the numbers of youth claiming to be working toward such career goals (Moje, 2006).

One place to turn for theories that more closely approximate formal secondary school learning might be studies conducted among university students learning in the professions. Stevens et al. (2008), for example, studied the development of knowledge-in-practice in learning to be an engineer and found that professional learning happens at the intersection of constructing knowledge, identifying with a domain, and navigating different pathways toward goals. Specifically, these engineering students developed engineering knowledge in multiple sources and practices, and the knowledge itself contributed to whether and how they identified as engineering students and, ultimately, as engineers. Navigating in and out of different kinds of experiences was critical to developing both the knowledge necessary to engage in the practices associated with those experiences and the identities needed for deep engagement in the practices. The engineering students saw themselves as future engineers (i.e., they sought engineer identities even upon entering the program), because they had developed the requisite knowledge needed both for their own identifications and for the recognition by others of their future engineer identities. They had also developed knowledge that allowed them to navigate multiple experiences, which in turn produced more knowledge and stronger (or not) identifications. Stevens et al. (2008) do not attempt to solve this chicken-and-egg puzzle (i.e., which came first, the knowledge or the identity?) but instead articulate a triadic relationship in which knowledge, identity, and navigations develop one another.

It is worth noting, however, that Stevens and colleagues acknowledge that many students who possess such knowledge either struggle or simply do not succeed in becoming professional engineers. One must ask, then, how well any of these theories intervene in the kind of learning situation most youth experience, and especially in disenfranchised learning contexts. Drawing from Gee's (2007) notion of *repair work* that gamers have to do in playing video games, what are the teaching practices that might support the repair work needed for youth who have been denied opportunities to learn and, as a result, walk into subject-matter courses without the knowledge necessary to even begin to identify with the practices of the disciplines. If young people, for example, have rarely been encouraged to question or investigate in the academic disciplinary domains,[6] and if they lack background knowledge, then where do they—and their teachers—begin?

---

6 It's worth using this rather cumbersome phrase, "academic disciplinary domains," because it is the case that many youth do question and investigate disciplinary phenomena—both social and natural science phenomena—in their everyday lives (Moje, Ciechanowski, Kramer, Ellis, Carrillo, & Collazo, 2004; Stockdill & Moje, 2007), but they lack knowledge of or skill with the "academic" practices associated with investigation in the institutional disciplinary domains.

To this conceptualization, those interested in developing disciplinary literacy identities might add engagements with text as another key ingredient in the puzzle of how one develops knowledge and identities necessary both for successful navigations and for deep disciplinary learning of literacy and discourse. That is, we might argue that adolescent students learn in the disciplines by simultaneously navigating through various practices and texts of the disciplines, thus supporting the construction of knowledge-in-practice and identification with the discipline. Disciplinary texts, however, can be extremely challenging to the reader with little prior knowledge of the discipline, thus producing the conundrum mentioned previously. Even academically situated theories such as Stevens's work on the interrelationship of knowledge–identities–navigations assume relatively sophisticated levels of knowledge *and* the ability to navigate diverse domains of knowledge as one enters the domain.

Taken together, these theories and studies suggest, unsurprisingly, that learning in a disciplinary domain is a kind of "unlimited semiosis" (Witte, 1992) or spiraling progression (Vygotsky, 1986), in which opportunity to engage in practices affords opportunities to build knowledge, which in turn allows for the building of identifications and identities. The role of engagement in practices is, then, critical to building both knowledge and identities; if one precedes the other, then it seems logical to argue that engagement in domain-specific practices generates knowledge and identities. Calls for core knowledge transmission and calls for the recognition of identity, however, both fail to acknowledge the critical role of practice in generating the knowledge necessary to identify and to learn more deeply. Perhaps more problematic is that although available theories often acknowledge the limitations of school context in providing opportunities for practice that can develop both knowledge and identities, they rarely speak to strategies for intervening in those contexts.

With the exception of some NLS projects situated in formal learning institutions (e.g., Collatos, Morrell, Nuno, & Lara, 2004; Morrell & Collatos, 2003; Stevens & Hall, 1998; Stevens et al., 2008; Street, 2009) and a number of school-based design experiments inspired by theories in the learning sciences (Cobb, Confrey, diSessa, Lehrer, & Schauble, 2003; Cobb, McClain, Lamberg, & Dean, 2003; Krajcik, Blumenfeld, Marx, Bass, & Fredricks, 1998), most of our theories do not offer specific teaching tools or practices to help teachers transcend—or even work within—the structural and sociocultural constraints (as well as potential affordances) posed by formal secondary school institutions in which youth are taught *en masse*.[7] Nor do these theories distinguish as completely as they could between knowledge and practices learned from observation of concrete acts, and knowledge and practices that are more abstract. When and how are these abstractions learned? To what extent is the

---

7 A number of scholars have worked on these issues at the elementary school level (Lee & Fradd, 1998; Warren, Ballenger, Ogonowski, Rosebery, & Hudicourt-Barnes, 2001).

time involved in learning them a critically necessary component of the learning environment? In addition, many of these perspectives fail to account for the miseducation of many children and youth, which results in young people coming to new and advanced learning experiences without the requisite knowledge for learning concepts in deep and sophisticated ways. What is more, what do sociocultural and NLS studies conducted largely in contexts where individuals take up practices of their own volition tell us about how to engage children and youth who have no choice about and often—as a result of miseducation—no interest in even being in the room?

Implications: Design and Pedagogical Principles

This analysis of the role of identities and knowledge in learning the discourse and literacies of different domains offers a number of implications. These implications extend not only to structures and practices of formal schooling, but also to how sociocultural and NLS theorists might consider designing future research agendas to take into consideration the challenging contexts of formal schooling.

One of the most notable differences between the contexts typically featured in sociocultural and NLS studies and the contexts of formal schooling, especially at the secondary levels, is in the amount of time dedicated to learning activities. In both elementary and secondary schools, students are treated to short doses of instruction (except for reading instruction at the lower grades, which in the US is now often taught in 90-minute to three-hour blocks focused on stories decontextualized from any content). These short bursts are exacerbated in secondary schools where students often move from class to class in 45–55 minute periods. "Block scheduling" is the norm in some secondary schools, so that some classes are 90–120 minutes in length, but such classes then are offered only every other day. In addition, even when students are in their blocked time periods, many teachers and students face regular interruptions by public address announcements and all-school assemblies for test preparation or athletic events (Moje, Sutherland, Solomon, & van de Kerkof, 2008). These students thus have little opportunity for sustained interaction with a community of practice and learning, and teachers struggle to connect learning activities and practices over time. Add to this issues of absenteeism often noted in urban US schools, and the context appears radically different from the relatively stable and committed contexts studied in most sociocultural and NLS studies.

Furthermore, the sheer numbers of children and youth to be educated in formal learning institutions in the United States is astounding and makes for a radical departure from out-of-school contexts. One might argue that video and computer games—among the most profoundly powerful learning environments outside of school (Gee, 2007)—educate even larger numbers, as do fanfiction and other online sites (Shultz, 2009; Steinkuehler, Black, & Clinton, 2005), but these games and websites educate learners who want to be in the room, interfacing with them one at a time or bringing together groups of already-engaged youth in virtual environments. Teachers in school classrooms are responsible for educating large numbers of young people from different backgrounds, knowledge bases, skill levels, and motivations all at once and face to face. Secondary teachers may see as many as 180 of those very different youth in a single day, depending on the number of different class periods they are assigned to teach. Knowing those youth and being able to scaffold their learning, excite their interests, and connect to their lives is an enormous challenge. Building a *community* of these learners—people who sometimes dislike each other on principle—is an even greater challenge.

On a related note, unlike many out-of-school environments in which people routinely teach and learn, the reality of school learning is that youth do not all necessarily enter secondary school disciplinary classrooms excited to be learning, whether about the establishment and content of the Bill of Rights, why recombinant DNA is critical to our understanding of and raises ethical issues for the human genome, or how to derive the focus of a parabola. This potential mix of enthusiasm and disinterest walking into the context makes teaching disciplinary concepts at the secondary school level particularly challenging and requires that the contexts and tools of the contexts themselves be especially engaging. A quick look around most formal learning institutions, however, reveals less-than-motivating texts and contexts, underscoring another key difference between the contexts of sociocultural and NLS studies and formal schooling. In many economically stressed communities, in fact, teachers and students lack even sustained basic resources, let alone the technologies for new literacy engagements.

Finally, we must consider the past miseducation of youth when thinking about how they might take on disciplinary identities, practices, and knowledge. Gee (2007) acknowledges the critical need for "repair work," even among gamers, as one of the important learning principles he derived from his study of games as learning environments. And he is absolutely right; repair is necessary for all learners because it is not possible for people to know *all* they need as they develop skill and knowledge in different domains. The challenge in formal schooling, however, is that all of the differences mentioned above exist and, as a result, young people proceed through school without learning much that is meaningful or that could be applied to new settings. Children and youth are rarely taught to ask questions, to seek information, to think for themselves (in fact, in some settings, questioning and pressing for understanding is discouraged). Repair work is needed, especially for least privileged kids; as noted previously, however, if extensive time is spent repairing kids' lack of conceptual, factual, and pragmatic knowledge, opportunities to learn *new* knowledge are minimized.

Teaching Practices: A Call for a New Research Agenda

Historical analyses of education in the United States suggest that none of the constraints highlighted above will be eliminated anytime soon (Cuban, 1986). Thus, it would be useful if NLS and other sociocultural theorists interested in enhancing the development of identities and knowledge necessary for learning the discourses and identities of multiple domains could theorize specific practices that might be useful under the actual conditions of schooling (while maintaining the need for structural changes). Drawing from analyses of gaming, it is clear that young people are scaffolded in the process of searching for knowledge. Games provide tips to players, sometimes in the form of lexicons and clues, other times in the form of "cheat codes" produced by other groups, usually experienced players. Players also have access to a wide range of information sources–most critically, to one another. They work collaboratively to answer each other's questions, with old-timers to the games giving tips to newcomers. Much of what Speyer and I did in the immigration unit I describe here parallels Gee's analysis of games, in which youth were invited into an environment that allows them to construct the knowledge and develop the practices necessary to keep engaging in the practices of that environment.

A key difference, however, is that Gee also argues that the game makers offer players an identity; I argue that the identities they offer are important, but they are also taken up because the game players come to the game with knowledge and interest. It is not productive simply to offer identities in secondary school disciplinary learning without the knowledge and practices they embody and rely on. But it is also extremely difficult to do the kind of work that games and other out-of-school learning environments do for youth in our current classroom contexts. So what does it look like to develop knowledge-in-practice in classrooms? Classroom teaching can make some headway with such identity building; see, for example, my analysis of a high-school chemistry teacher who invited students to see themselves as scientists through her discourse about science and scientists (Moje, 1995). Merely offering identities, however, is meaningless without engagement in practices that allow for knowledge to be constructed in practice. Teachers can employ many different forms of representation to construct knowledge of one concept—different genres (e.g., narrative, expository, poetics, music), different symbol systems (e.g., print, graphs, tables), and different semiotic tools (image, sound, and performance). Each of these forms—now readily available through digital venues—can support the construction of knowledge necessary to access the abstract and dense print texts of the disciplines.

Still, this is complicated work. In reflecting on his work with high-school history students learning to question the authority of classroom texts, Bain (2006) has argued that young people have to learn how to talk back to texts, and the opportunity to do so rarely happens in classrooms. More to the point, if one does not identify with the practices of the discipline and does not hold extensive knowledge in the discipline, then how does one talk back? In other words, knowledge, identities, and critical literacy skill develop iteratively; this development requires scaffolding and mediation by teachers who know the content well and understand the role that language and literate practice play in producing knowledge within it. Bain models such pedagogical practices in a high-school history classroom, in which he taught students to "raise disciplined suspicions of the typical sources of scholastic authority" (p. 2082) by transforming their relationships to the texts of the classroom. He wrote:

> Students' habitual conceptions of and practices with textbooks held sway over my interventions and strategies aimed at raising their suspicions of the texts. The problem, I came to understand, was greater than sharpening their tools for critical reading, but rather involved a transformation in my students' relationships to the books, to the historical content in the books, and to the authors who wrote them. (p. 2084)

What Bain implicates here is a transformation of identities, one that requires more than simply offering students the option to "act like historians," a kind of classroom-based conception of the avatar of games and gaming. Toward that end, Bain wove together factual content knowledge in broad conceptual frames meaningful to historians. Moreover, he provided students opportunities to think about, critique, and question that content via historical problems and questions, thus transforming the students' identities as passive recipients of information or activity in the class to identities as active investigators of claims to knowledge. For Bain, this was not a question of knowledge or identity, but rather an intertwined, iterative process: "Indeed, I saw the conventional debate of 'facts versus thinking skills' as a false dichotomy; one needs content to employ thinking skills, and one could hardly learn facts without doing some thinking" (Bain, 2006, p. 2090).

Similarly, science and mathematics educators have drawn from work in the learning sciences to develop project-based approaches to learning (Blumenfeld et al., 1991; Davis & West, 2000; Marx, Blumenfeld, Krajcik, Fishman, Soloway, & Geier, 2004; Marx, Blumenfeld, Krajcik, & Soloway, 1997; Moses & Cobb, 2001; West & Davis, 2004), with some remarkable results. As these authors illustrate, however, the work is challenging and incredibly difficult to move to a large scale. Moreover, fewer projects are available in English language arts and history/social studies and—in a converse of my argument about sociocultural and NLS studies—few project-based curriculum studies explicitly acknowledge the role of *identities* in this developing disciplinary knowledge. We need, then, more design experiments in the contexts where most young people are currently educated. We need these design experiments to explicate the particulars of approaches designed to engage youth and produce deep disciplinary practices, knowledge, and identities. And, in particular, we need the experimenters to write about the challenges of time, community building, repair work, and motivation and engagement they face in developing the knowledge and identities of the domains. With these design experiments conducted in the actual contexts of schooling in hand, we may be better able to theorize how to provide children and youth the opportunities necessary to simultaneously engage in practices, build knowledge, and develop identities for deep domain learning.

References

Alexander, P. (2003). Profiling the adolescent reader: The interplay of knowledge, interest, and strategic processing. In C. Fairbanks, J. Worthy, B. Maloch, J. V. Hoffman & D. Schallert (Eds.), *53rd yearbook of the national reading conference* (pp. 47–65). Milwaukee, WI: National Reading Conference.

Alexander, P. A., Kulikowich, J. M., & Jetton, T. L. (1994). The role of subject-matter knowledge and interest in the processing of linear and nonlinear texts. *Review of Educational Research*, *64*, 201–252.

Bain, R. B. (2005). 'They thought the world was flat?' HPL principles in teaching high school history. In J. Bransford & S. Donovan (Eds.), *How students learn: History, mathematics, and science in the classroom* (pp. 179–214). Washington, DC: The National Academies Press.

Bain, R. B. (2006). Rounding up unusual suspects: Facing the authority hidden in the history classroom. *Teachers College Record*, *108*(10), 2080–2114.

Biancarosa, G., & Snow, C. E. (2004). *Reading next-A vision for action and research in middle and high school literacy: A report to the Carnegie Corporation of New York*. Washington, DC: Alliance for Excellent Education.

Blumenfeld, P., Soloway, E., Marx, R., Krajcik, J. S., Guzdial, M., & Palincsar, A. S. (1991). Motivating project-based learning: Sustaining the doing, supporting the learning. *Educational Psychologist*, *25*, 369–398.

Blumenfeld, P. C., Marx, R. W., Patrick, H., & Krajcik, J. S. (1997). Teaching for understanding. In B. J. Biddle, T. L. Good & I. F. Goodson (Eds.), *International handbook of teachers and teaching* (pp. 819–878). Dordrecht, The Netherlands: Kluwer Academic Publishers.

Buehl, D. (2002). *Classroom strategies for interactive learning*. Newark, DE: International Reading Association.

Carraher, T. N., Carraher, D. W., & Schliemann, A. D. (1985). Mathematics in the streets and in schools. *British Journal of Developmental Psychology*, *3*, 21–29.

Chouliaraki, L. (2003). Mediated experience and youth identities in a post-traditional order. In J. K. Androutsopoulos & A. Georgakopoulou (Eds.), *Discourse constructions of youth identities* (pp. 303–331). Amsterdam, the Netherlands: John Benjamins Publishing Company.

Cobb, P. (1994). Where is the mind? Constructivist and sociocultural perspectives on mathematical development. *Educational Researcher*, *23*(7), 13–20.

Cobb, P., & Bowers, J. (1999). Cognitive and situated learning perspectives in theory and practice. *Educational Researcher, 28*(2), 4–15.

Cobb, P., Confrey, J., diSessa, A., Lehrer, R., & Schauble, L. (2003). Design experiments in educational research. *Educational Researcher, 32*(1), 9–13.

Cobb, P., McClain, K., Lamberg, T. d. S., & Dean, C. (2003). Situating teachers' instructional practices in the institutional setting of the school and district. *Educational Researcher, 32*(6), 13–24.

Collatos, A., Morrell, E., Nuno, A., & Lara, R. (2004). Critical sociology in K-16 early intervention: Remaking Latino pathways to higher education. *Journal of Hispanic Higher Education, 3*, 164–180.

Cuban, L. (1986). Persistent instruction: Another look at constancy in the classroom. *Phi Delta Kappan, 68*(1), 7–11.

Davis, F. E., & West, M. M. (2000). *The impact of the algebra project on mathematics achievement.* Cambridge, MA: Program Evaluation & Research Group, Lesley College.

Driver, R., Asoko, H., Leach, J., Mortimer, E., & Scott, P. (1994). Constructing scientific knowledge in the classroom. *Educational Researcher, 23*(7), 5–12.

Ford, M. J., & Forman, E. (2006). Redefining disciplinary learning in classroom contexts. In J. Green & A. Luke (Eds.), *Review of Research in Education* (Vol. 30), Washington, DC: AERA.

Freire, P. (1970). *Pedagogy of the oppressed.* New York: Continuum.

Gee, J. P. (1996). *Social linguistics and literacies: Ideology in discourses* (2nd ed.). London: Falmer.

Gee, J. P. (2001, December). *Reading in "new times."* Paper presented at the National Reading Conference, San Antonio, TX.

Gee, J. P. (2007). *What video games have to teach us about learning and literacy.* New York: Palgrave Macmillan.

Glasersfeld, E. V. (1995). *Radical constructivism: A way of knowing and learning.* London & Washington: The Falmer Press.

Green, J. L. (1983). Exploring classroom discourse: Linguistic perspectives on teaching-learning processes. *Educational Psychologist, 18*, 180–199.

Hand, B., & Keys, C. W. (1999). Inquiry Investigation: A new approach to laboratory reports. *The Science Teacher, 66*, 27–29.

Hand, B., Hohenshell, L., & Prain, V. (2004). Exploring students' responses to conceptual questions when engaged with planned writing experiences: A study with Year 10 science students. *Journal of Research in Science Teaching, 41*, 186–210.

Hand, B., Wallace, C., & Yang, E. (2004). Using the science writing heuristic to enhance learning outcomes from laboratory activities in seventh grade science: Quantitative and qualitative aspects. *International Journal of Science Education, 26*, 131–149.

Hirsch, E. D. www.coreknowledge.org/blog, retrieved February 16, 2008.

Hirsch, E. D. (2006). *The knowledge deficit: Closing the shocking education gap for American children.* New York: Houghton Mifflin Harcourt.

Hobsbawm, E. (1997). Identity history is not enough. In E. Hobsbawm (Ed.), *On history* (pp. 266–277). New York: New Press.

Holland, D., & Leander, K. (2004). Ethnographic studies of positioning and subjectivity: An introduction. *Ethos, 32*(2), 127–139.

Jenkins, H. (2006). *Convergence culture.* New York: New York University Press.

Krajcik, J., Blumenfeld, P. C., Marx, R. W., Bass, K. M., & Fredricks, J. (1998). Inquiry in project-based science classrooms: Initial attempts by middle school students. *The Journal of the Learning Sciences, 7*, 313–350.

Lankshear, C. (1997). *Changing literacies*. Buckingham, UK: Open University Press.

Lave, J. (1988). *Cognition in practice: Mind, mathematics, and culture in everyday life*. Cambridge, UK; New York: Cambridge University Press.

Lave, J. (1993). *Understanding practice: Perspectives on activity and context*. Cambridge, UK; New York: Cambridge University Press.

Lave, J. (1996). Teaching, as learning, in practice. *Mind, Culture, and Activity: An International Journal, 3*(3), 149–164.

Lave, J., & Wenger, E. (1991). *Situated learning: Legitimate peripheral participation*. Cambridge, UK; New York, NY: Cambridge University Press.

Leander, K. M. (2004). "They took out the wrong context": Uses of time-space in the practice of positioning. *ETHOS, 32*(2), 188–213.

Leander, K. M., & Lovvorn, J. F. (2006). Literacy networks: Following the circulation of texts, bodies, and objects in the schooling and online gaming of one youth. *Cognition & Instruction, 24*, 291–340.

Lee, O., & Fradd, S. H. (1998). Science for all, including students from non-English language backgrounds. *Educational Researcher, 27*(3), 12–21.

Lewontin, R. (1991). *Biology as ideology: The doctrine of DNA*. New York: Harper.

Marx, R. W., Blumenfeld, P. C., Krajcik, J. S., Fishman, B., Soloway, E., & Geier, R. (2004). Inquiry-based science in the middle grades: Assessment of learning in urban systemic reform. *Journal of Research in Science Teaching, 41*, 1063–1080.

Marx, R. W., Blumenfeld, P. C., Krajcik, J. S., & Soloway, E. (1997). Enacting project-based science. *The Elementary School Journal, 97*, 341–358.

Moje, E. B. (1995). Talking about science: An interpretation of the effects of teacher talk in a high school classroom. *Journal of Research in Science Teaching, 32*, 349–371.

Moje, E. B. (2000). To be part of the story: The literacy practices of gangsta adolescents. *Teachers College Record, 102*, 652–690.

Moje, E. B. (2004). Powerful spaces: Tracing the out-of-school literacy spaces of Latino/a youth. In K. Leander & M. Sheehy (Eds.), *Spatializing literacy research and practice* (pp. 15–38). New York: Peter Lang.

Moje, E. B. (2006). Achieving identities: Why youth identities matter in their school achievement. In V. O. Pang & R. Jiménez (Eds.), *Race and language* (Vol. 2, pp. 133–156). Westport: Greenwood Press/Praeger.

Moje, E. B. (2008). Foregrounding the disciplines in secondary literacy teaching and learning: A call for change. *Journal of Adolescent and Adult Literacy, 52*, 96–107.

Moje, E. B., Ciechanowski, K. M., Kramer, K. E., Ellis, L. M., Carrillo, R., & Collazo, T. (2004). Working toward third space in content area literacy: An examination of everyday funds of knowledge and discourse. *Reading Research Quarterly, 39*, 38–71.

Moje, E. B., & Lewis, C. (2007). Examining opportunities to learn literacy: The role of critical sociocultural literacy research. In C. Lewis, P. Enciso & E. B. Moje (Eds.), *Reframing sociocultural research in literacy: Identity, agency, and power* (pp. 15–48). Mahwah, NJ: Erlbaum.

Moje, E. B., & Luke, A. (2009). Literacy and identity: A review of perspectives on identity and their impact on literacy studies. *Reading Research Quarterly, 44*(4), 415–437.

Moje, E. B., & Speyer, J. (2008). The reality of challenging texts in high school science and so-cial studies: How teachers can mediate comprehension. In K. Hinchman & H. Thomas (Eds.), *Best practices in adolescent literacy instruction* (pp. 185–211). New York: Guilford Press.

Moje, E. B., Sutherland, L. M., Solomon, T. C., & van de Kerkof, M. H. (2008). *Integrating literacy instruction into secondary school science inquiry: The challenges of disciplinary literacy teaching and professional development*. Unpublished manuscript.

Morrell, E., & Collatos, A. (2003, April). *Critical pedagogy in a college access program for students of color*. Paper presented at the American Educational Research Association, Chicago, IL.

Moses, R., & Cobb, C. E. (2001). *Radical equations-Civil rights from Mississippi to the algebra project*. Boston, MA: Beacon Press.

Ravitch, D., & Finn, C. E. J. (1987). *What do our 17-year-olds know? A report on the first national assessment of history and literature*. New York: Harper & Row.

Rogoff, B. (1990). *Apprenticeship in thinking: Cognitive development in social context*. New York: Oxford University Press.

Rogoff, B. (1995). Observing sociocultural activity on three planes: Participatory appropriation, guided participation, and apprenticeship. In J. V. Wertsch, P. d. Rio & A. Alvarez (Eds.), *Sociocultural studies of mind*. (pp. 139–164). Cambridge, UK: Cambridge University Press.

Rogoff, B., & Lave, J. (1984). *Everyday cognition: Its development in social context*. Cambridge, MA: Harvard University Press.

Schliemann, A. D. (1984). Mathematics among carpenters and carpenters apprentices: Implications for school teaching. In P. Damerow, M. Dunckley, B. Nebres & B. Werry (Eds.), *Mathematics for all*. UNESCO.

Scribner, S., & Cole, M. (1981). *The psychology of literacy*. Cambridge, MA: Harvard University Press.

Sfard, A., & Prusak, A. (2005). Telling identities: In search of an analytic tool for investigating learning as a culturally shaped activity. *Educational Researcher, 34*(4), 14–23.

Shultz, S. (2009). *Legitimizing and marginalizing: How the internet has shaped responses to online fan communities and practices*. Paper presented at the Conference on College Composition and Communication, San Francisco, CA.

Steinkuehler, C. A., Black, R. W., & Clinton, K. A. (2005). Researching literacy as tool, place, and way of being. *Reading Research Quarterly, 40*, 95–100.

Stevens, R., & Hall, R. (1998). Disciplined perception: Learning to see in technoscience. In M. Lampert & M. Blunk (Eds.), *Talking mathematics in school studies of teaching and learning*. (pp. 107–150). Cambridge, MA: Cambridge University Press.

Stevens, R., O'Connor, K., Garrison, L., Jocuns, A., & Amos, D. (2008). Becoming an engineer: Toward a three-dimensional view of engineering learning. *Journal of Engineering Education, 97*, 355–368.

Stockdill, D., & Moje, E. B. (2007). *Adolescents as readers of culture, history, economics, and civics: The disconnect between student interest in their world and social studies schooling*. Paper presented at the American Educational Research Association.

Street, B. V. (1984). *Literacy in theory and practice*. Cambridge, UK: Cambridge University Press.

Street, B. V. (2003). What's "new" in New Literacy Studies? Critical approaches to literacy in theory and practice. *Current Issues in Comparative Studies in Education, 5*, 77–91.

Street, B. V. (2009). *"Hidden" features of academic paper writing*. Philadelphia: University of Pennsylvania.

Vygotsky, L. S. (1978). *Mind in society*. In M. Cole, V. John-Steiner, S. Scribner & U. E. Souberman (Eds.). Cambridge, MA: Harvard University Press.

Vygotsky, L. S. (1986). *Thought and language* (A. Kozulin, Trans.). Cambridge, MA: The Massachusetts Institute of Technology.

Warren, B., Ballenger, C., Ogonowski, M., Rosebery, A., & Hudicourt-Barnes, J. (2001). Rethinking diversity in learning science: The logic of everyday languages. *Journal of Research in Science Teaching, 38*, 1–24.

West, M. M., & Davis, F. E. (2004). *The algebra project at Lanier High School, Jacson, MS: Implementation and student outcomes*. Cambridge, MA: Program Evaluation & Research Group, Lesley College.

Wineburg, S. S. (1991). On the reading of historical texts: Notes on the breach between school and the academy. *American Educational Research Journal, 28*, 495–519.

Wineburg, S. S. (1998). Reading Abraham Lincoln: An expert/expert study in the interpretation of historical texts. *Cognitive Science, 22*, 319–346.

Wineburg, S. S. (2001). *Historical thinking and other unnatural acts: Charting the future of teaching the past*. Philadelphia: Temple University Press.

Witte, S. P. (1992). Context, text, intertext: Toward a constructivist semiotic of writing. *Written Communication, 9*, 237–308.

Wortham, S. (2001). *Narratives in action: A strategy for research and analysis*. New York: Teachers College Press.

CHAPTER FOUR

"Teamwork": Conflicting Cultural Models of Gender, Class, School, and Family among High School Students

GUADALUPE LÓPEZ-BONILLA

Alicia, a straight-A high school senior in a public urban school serving lower and middle class students in Northern Mexico, was uncertain about her future after graduating. Despite her high achievements in school and her wishes to continue her studies in order to become a teacher, she felt she was not qualified enough and feared she would not gain entrance to the local public university. A year later, she was working full-time as a cook helping her parents to support her family. She had not applied to any of the local higher education institutions, yet she still longed to become a teacher. Why would a low-income student such as Alicia, one who had been academically successful throughout her education, not feel sufficiently empowered (academically, politically, and/or socially) to pursue higher education, in spite of her aspirations? The answer, I believe, resides in the kinds of social practices that Alicia had access to in and out of school, and the kinds of participation afforded to her in those practices, particularly within the school environment. It is ultimately a matter of recognition, power, and entitlement (and the lack thereof).

I interviewed Alicia at the end of her senior year. Through her reconstruction of some of the challenges she faced as a student we can learn something about the shifting identities she enacted in narrativized worlds populated by "good" and "bad" girls; "good" and "bad" students, and the kinds of rigid dichotomies that leave little or no room for negotiation or the creation of new identities. The only female in a group of 13 and the student with the highest grades in her class, Alicia's narrative provides a unique perspective about the discursive and social positioning she experienced as a female, working-class, high-achieving student.

In order to look at the kinds of social and academic participation afforded to low- and high-achieving students in two different school cultures, in this chapter I consider the institutional discourse about team collaboration introduced recently in Mexican high schools. I begin with the contextual background of the project from which this data is derived, followed by a discussion of the conceptual framework that informs this chapter. I then sketch the different situated meanings that "teamwork" evokes for low- and high-achieving students in different school cultures. Ultimately, I focus on Alicia's narrative about doing "teamwork" and identify the discourses (Foucault, 1972; Holland, Lachiotte, Skinner & Cain, 1998; Gee, 1996, 1999), cultural models or "figured worlds" (Holland & Skinner, 1987; Strauss, 1992; Holland et al., 1998; Gee, 1999), and the social languages (Bakhtin, 1981; Gee, 1999) encoded in the narrative, so that the different voices that make up Alicia's space of authoring may shed light on the challenges and unresolved conflicts students such as Alicia have to face. My intention is to provide an analytical example of how institutional discourses that overlap in moments of transition and educational change position students in paradoxical and unexpected ways. Looking at the intersection of more stable social positions such as gender and social class, with localized constructs such as "good" and "bad" students, this analysis can contribute to understanding the differentiated identities and "degrees of agencies" (Lewis, Enciso, & Moje, 2007, p. 4) afforded to students due to the cultural models and positionings available within specific school cultures.

Background

This study is part of a larger project in which I and a team of researchers and research assistants collected data over the course of three years regarding the literacy practices of four urban high schools and one peri-urban high school in selected school subjects (López Bonilla, 2008; Tinajero, López Bonilla, & Pérez, 2007; López Bonilla, Tinajero, & Pérez, 2006). Three of the schools are part of the Technological High School System (THSS), and two schools are part of the General High School System (GHSS). In addition, one of these schools offers the International Baccalaureate (IB-a program of advanced courses to university-bound students) as a separate track to selected students in their junior and senior years. Although no institutional information was available, the data we gathered through student surveys and interviews conveyed a student population of lower-/middle-class students in the THSS and one GHSS, lower-/middle-class in the GHSS track of one school, and middle-class students in the IB.

Within each system all students study a core curriculum and choose a particular track for job training. These may be as varied as fisheries, cooling systems (*refrigeración*), agriculture, food industry, accounting, and computers in technological schools; and accounting, customs legislation, computers, and communications in the general program. Regardless of the type of specialized field of study, every track enables students to apply for postsecondary education.

The study encompassed classroom observations in the subjects Language, Literature, Social Studies, and History over the course of one class generation (2004–2007). In addition, teachers, administrators, and students in each school were interviewed at different moments during the three-year period, and different textual artifacts were collected throughout the study. Due to a high percentage of student attrition, low-achieving students were interviewed during the second semester (first year), while high-achieving students were interviewed at the end of their sixth semester (senior year). For the purposes of this study, low-achieving students were categorized as those students who, by the end of the second semester, were failing one or more school subjects and therefore at risk of being prevented from enrolling the following semester;[1] whereas high achievers were students who by the end of the sixth semester had passed every school subject and had a grade point average (GPA) of 3.5 or higher. On the whole, I interviewed 15 low-achieving and 14 high-achieving students from the THSS, 12 low achievers and 14 high achievers from the GHSS, and 7 high achievers from the IB. The data for the analysis of this chapter constitutes a subset of the data collected for the study.

Our field work coincided with the initiation of a new curriculum effort that attempted to implement a "constructivist" approach to teaching, and thus substantial changes were made both to the content of instruction and the pedagogical approach. For instance, in all the technological schools we observed, individual desks were replaced by tables in every classroom in order to promote "team collaboration" and "group projects." Teachers were conceived as "facilitators" and little or no explicit instruction took place.

This curricular reform is part of a much larger international wave of innovations where a shift is being made from teacher-centered instruction to a student-centered curriculum in order to "diminish the status of knowledge structures, as well as the role of the teacher," a trend that has resulted in great uncertainty about what should be taught and how to go about it (Christie, 2007, p. 8).

Although "teamwork" has been present in Mexican schools for many years, this last reform disrupted the dominant discourse of learning and

[1] Since high school education is not compulsory in Mexico, students who fail more than two classes within a given time are not considered in "good standing" and therefore not allowed to enroll in the following semester.

instruction and has forced the agents involved (mainly teachers and students) to negotiate, conform to, and/or resist the positions this new discourse has afforded them. The balance between "teamwork" and individual activities shifted. For many teachers, "teamwork" has meant transferring the responsibility of learning curricular content solely to the students through "team research and collaboration," a discourse explicitly inscribed in curricular documents and a "hot topic" among the students I interviewed.

It is important to note, however, that these changes do not occur overnight. New discourses may take a long time to "settle in," and the new ones compete with the old. These emerging discourses coexist with other "grand" and sometimes dominant discourses (Gee, 1999). This is certainly the case in high school classrooms today in Mexico. Students are confronted with at least two distinct discourses about learning and instruction: a more traditional one that promotes rote learning and memorization (vertical knowledge, teacher-centered, fixed identities, and no room for negotiation); and a more "constructivist" one that supports peer collaboration and students' creativity. Nonetheless, testing and evaluations have remained largely unchanged, and students are rewarded, for the most part, for individual merit and not for peer collaboration.

As a result of the academic reforms, much of the work being done in high school classrooms today in Mexico is "teamwork." In many of the classes I observed, students were working in small groups doing different activities such as filling out worksheets, discussing a particular topic, finding specific information in texts, or delivering the results of a research project to the whole class. This last type of activity was recurrent in all the schools and throughout the time we visited the different classrooms. Since many of these activities were the result of assignments done at home, many questions remained about students' affiliations and identities as a "team player," as well as the kinds of positioning students experienced inside the team.

Although at first glance these activities may be perceived as "group" or "team collaborations," it is important to look carefully at the nature of the activity and the classroom cultures that enabled them in order to better comprehend the schools' and students' cultural models about "doing teamwork," and to explore how these storylines about what is "typical" or "normal" (Quinn & Holland, 1987; Holland et al., 1998; Gee, 1999) were enacted, resisted, or transformed. A case in point is Cynthia Lewis' (2001) work about the dynamics of peer-led literature discussions within a combined fifth/sixth-grade classroom. Because schools institutionalize discursively what it means to be a "good student," Lewis argues, students learn to read the discourse and position themselves (and are positioned) accordingly when working in teams.

These collaborative pedagogies also seek to empower students by allowing them to be co-constructors of their own knowledge and learning. Looking at reforms aimed at improving high school education, McQuillan (2005) distinguishes actions geared at empowering students academically, politically, and socially. Academic empowerment takes place when students are able to "participate competently in instruction as a result of having developed...appropriate school-based knowledge and interactional structures" (Cummins, 1986; as cited in McQuillan, 2005, p. 642); political empowerment is sustained when students have a voice in institutional matters, and social empowerment occurs when students are able to reflect on their learning experience, and learn to support and empower one another. It is not sufficient for students to learn academic content if they are not able to reflect on their own learning and why that learning matters; or if they don't learn the interactional skills needed to successfully communicate and collaborate with their peers, and to negotiate the different demands placed upon them by school and society.

Along with constructivist approaches for teaching and learning, working in teams has increasingly become one of the "key competences" for the social and labor demands of current society. The OECD, through the project DeSeCo (acronym for Definition and Selection of Competencies), identified three broad categories of "key competences" for students' success in life (Rychen & Salganik, 2003) and include collaborating and working in teams. Carnoy (2004) highlights the recent trends in work force organization in businesses, where the use of Information and Communication Technology (ICT) has promoted higher productivity through team collaboration and production. Similarly, Gee (2004) discusses how much of the work performed in the new capitalism in developed economies involves teams and collaboration. Due to the fast-changing nature of knowledge and the rapid pace of technological innovation, teams "can behave more smartly than any individual in it by pooling and distributing knowledge" (p. 97). Under these conditions, job security has become more volatile since team projects are temporary and team members must reassemble to engage in new projects and enact new and diversified identities.

Discourses and Agency

The seminal work of Michel Foucault analyzed discourses as systems of representation that regulate what can be done with language in a specific context. Discourses, according to Foucault, create a place for the subject and establish the possibilities for constructing knowledge. His theory of representation shows the power that discourses have over social practices, since it is through knowledge that the guidelines of what is considered legitimate behavior in specific moments and contexts are fixed. Thus, issues of subject formation, identity, and power cannot be disassociated from discourses (Foucault, 1972).

A common reading of Foucault's work suggests that, in his theory, subjects are left with no resources by which to escape subjectification (Harvey, 1996; cited in Holland et al., 1998). Theorists such as Michel Pechêux, Stuart Hall, and Judith Butler provide a theoretical framework that "corrects" Foucault's viewpoint on subject formation. Holland et al. (1998) take an alternative route that builds mainly on the work of Bakhtin and Vygotsky. Bakhtin offers the conceptual perspective to look at how "persons develop through and around the cultural forms by which they are identified, and identify themselves, in the context of their affiliation or disaffiliation with those associated with those forms and practices" (Holland et al., 1998, p. 33); while Vygotsky's work on semiotic mediation is key in understanding how people can have some control over the environment through the active construction and use of symbols.

For Bakhtin, speech is made up of different voices encoded through different social languages with particular beliefs and perspectives. A social language, in Bakhtin's terminology, is a "concrete socio-linguistic belief system that defines a distinct identity for itself within the boundaries of a language that is unitary only in the abstract" (1981, p. 356). Social languages are the living fabric of *heteroglossia*, Bakhtin's way of conceptualizing the way different languages convey "the world in words, specific world views, each characterized by its own objects, meanings and values" (1981, p. 292). Social languages can be, Bakhtin argues, juxtaposed to one another and may contradict one another as well as be dialogically interrelated. It is the interplay between one's own word and the word of others (be it externally or internally) that characterizes the dialogical nature of human language and communication. In Bakhtin's words: "The speaker strives to get a reading on his own word, within the alien conceptual system of the understanding receiver, he enters into dialogical relationships with certain aspects of this system" (1981, p. 282).

For educational theorists and researchers, a central aspect of Bakhtin's theory—a position that has not been free of controversy (Matusov, 2007)—is the distinction he makes between authoritative and internally persuasive discourse, where the first refers to a monologic, uncontestable discourse, and the second to a more open reconstruction of other people's authoritative intentions. It is this tension that enables speakers to "reaccentuate" the words of others in order to produce an authorial stance. Bakhtin describes this process as assimilation, and it involves both subjectification to alien voices as well as an active selection of those voices. The outcome of this process is "ideological becoming," which, in Bakhtin's words, entails "the process of selectively assimilating the words of others" (1981, p. 341). It is precisely this aspect of Bakhtin's theory which Holland et al. (1998) build upon to conceptualize human agency: By having to answer to the world, people orchestrate the different voices that make up their space of authoring "in order to craft a response in a time and space defined by others' standpoints...in a social field conceived as the ground of responsiveness" (p. 272), and in so doing, they improvise according to the cultural resources at their disposal. Human agency, so defined, involves the art of improvisation in a space in which others' voices are akin, according to these authors, to Vygotsky's more capable peers or adults apprenticing a neophyte in the zone of proximal development.

Figuring Out the World

Holland et al. (1998) argue that identities take shape through this improvisational activity in particular spaces of authoring within social practices. In order to understand the relationship between the private and the public domains of social practices, these authors propose to conceive identities as "practiced identities," which can be explained analytically in terms of the "figured worlds" involved, positioning and positionality, the particular space of authoring, and the making of new worlds.

A different approach for explaining identities conceived in a similar fashion is how Gee (1999) describes "socially situated identities." These involve the process of conveying, through (social) language(s), a recognizable "kind of person" performing a "certain kind of activity" (p. 13). For someone to be recognized as a certain kind of person, she/he needs to recognize and enact a distinct discourse (way of talking, thinking, acting, believing, reading, and writing); in other words, one has to participate in a community of practice and, in the process, one learns cultural models relevant to the social practice (Gee, 2004).

Cultural models are taken-for-granted storylines in which prototypical events unfold (Quinn & Holland, 1987; Strauss, 1992; Holland et al., 1998; Gee, 1999). These storylines or figured worlds are socially constructed imagined worlds populated by recognizable characters through which people make sense of social practices. For instance, in the context of high school education, figured worlds may be inhabited by "fair" or "unfair" teachers, by "popular" or "unpopular students," and each of these characters interacts in particular styles and performs certain tasks and activities.

Cultural models are social, historical phenomena, which constitute a powerful thinking device to conceptualize historical subjectivities, consciousness, and agency (Holland et al., 1998). They provide a framework that helps people establish what is relevant or irrelevant in a given situation (Gee, 2004). Because cultural models/figured worlds recruit or position people in ways in which they can recognize each other as a particular sort of agent, they also provide a means for exploring how people's identities and agency are shaped "dialectically and dialogically" in these cultural configurations (Holland et al., 1998, p. 49).

D'Andrade (as cited in Quinn & Holland, 1987) argues that cultural models of self and life are a key aspect of "vital understandings." They may constitute cultural directives that guide an individual's actions depending on the different kinds of socialization experiences. It is precisely through this process that people learn to appreciate culturally prescribed goals as desirable. Following such directives, concludes D'Andrade, is motivationally satisfying, while not achieving those goals is disappointing.

Artifacts play a crucial role in identity construction within a figured world. Holland et al. (1998) point out that, in the context of a figured world, artifacts are analogous to the way objects and symbols function in children's games as described by Vygotsky. Assigning meaning to an object and continuously recognizing such meanings through experience becomes constitutive of behaviors, thoughts, and emotions. Holland et al. (1998) provide a good example of cultural artifacts serving as mediating devices that trigger certain behaviors, feelings, and attitudes with the use that members of Alcoholic Anonymous make of poker chips as tokens of their identity as nondrinking alcoholics. In my own observations and interviews with high-achieving students, it became clear that awards of any kind (even for nonacademic activities such as punctuality) were very powerful artifacts that embodied the type of student they wanted to be recognized as being, even more so than high grades.

Participation, Positioning, and Identity Building

A central aspect of identity building is that it takes shape through participation and recognition in social and discursive practices. As a consequence of discursive positioning, a person may be recruited into a particular type or persona, which she/he may come to inhabit. This is what Holland et al. refer to as discursive, narrative, or figured identity. Participation, however, is not the same for everybody, since it is usually restricted according to a person's social position and status. Moje & Lewis (2007) point out that participation in a discourse community may depend on different characteristics such as the race, gender, sexual orientation, or economic status of potential participants, which in turn determine the access to or control of the resources and identities needed to gain entrance and participate fully in the community. Similarly, Gee (2004) stresses the political nature of social practices because "they involve social roles or positions that have implications for potential social goods, such as who is an insider and who is not to the practice (and its associated social groups)" (p. 33). Positioning, therefore, also involves inclusion or exclusion of social activities and identities. This social positioning is best understood in terms of entitlement and the lack thereof, and can be analyzed through the relational (positional) identities it engenders. In particular, episodes of positioning "leave memories laced through feelings, bodily reactions, and glances of others" (Holland & Leander, 2004, p. 131). These imperceptible yet defining marks can become significant in shaping one's self-perception at different moments, with each mark growing into layers that "thicken" through experience (Holland & Leander, 2004).

Gee (2000/2001) adds yet another dimension to the construct of identity. He distinguishes four different perspectives from which to view identity: as developed through "forces of nature" (a "natural" state or nature-identity), as a position authorized by institutions (institution-identity), as an individual trait recognized through discourse (discourse-identity), or as experiences shared with an affinity group (affinity-identity). Each of these perspectives is not to be confused with discrete categories but rather, they "are ways to focus our attention on different aspects of how identities are formed and sustained" (p. 101).

A Situated View of "Doing Teamwork"

From the students interviews and the many sessions I observed of students doing teamwork in the five schools where we conducted the study, I was able to identify a few prototypical activities of what teamwork entails: these activities were as varied as researching a particular topic in history, doing a worksheet (solving problems) in physics, or assembling a particular piece of equipment in "cooling systems" (*taller de refrigeración*). The nature of the activity depended heavily on the nature of the subject: in cooling systems, for instance, which is conceived as a workshop, the activities were primarily performing tasks; whereas in subjects such as social sciences or language, the activity consisted of a series of literacy events. Regardless of the type of activity performed by the team, team members were evaluated according to two particular expected outcomes: delivering a presentation on a particular topic for the whole class or turning in a written assignment. The literacy activities, as the students performed them, were seldom treated as collaboration. Instead, they tended to segment a textual assignment into smaller sections that were distributed to every member of the team. Each student was responsible for reading and delivering the information to the rest of the class. In most cases students read or recited what they had read to the rest of the class. In spite of the educational change and the official rhetoric on constructivism and team collaboration, activities such as this one embody local cultural models about knowledge, literacy, and learning: they position students within a monological, transmission model of learning where participation is highly restricted.

Before analyzing Alicia's cultural models about doing teamwork, I will briefly discuss the different meanings that teamwork evoked for the students I interviewed. This will provide a clearer picture of the ways that the students in each school culture figured "working in teams" and will enable me to contextualize Alicia's narrative in order to discern the different voices and positionings encoded in her narrative.

Although this was not an issue I specifically addressed in the interviews, the topic "doing teamwork" was present for both low-, and high-achieving students when asked about things they found engaging in school and the problems they had encountered. However, the patterns that emerged were consistently different for low- and high-achieving students.

Two recurring topics in the interviews of low-achieving students were access to curricular content in selected subjects (mainly chemistry and physics) and the impact of teamwork on their learning. Most students agreed that working with their peers in team projects created new opportunities to enact social positions otherwise unattainable in their classroom culture. Assuming the role of leaders and experts on particular subjects or being a proactive inquirer on difficult topics enabled students to benefit from the team. They considered this to be an empowering experience because it afforded them multiple opportunities to enact new identities depending on the nature of the activity, such as inquirer, collaborator, knower, capable peer, tutor; they felt that both work and knowledge were more distributed, and overall, they felt a strong affiliation with their team members through recognition. For instance Roberto, a student who was later expelled[2] for failing Spanish, commented on how good he felt working with his classmates in math because he was able to explain difficult procedures to them and thus help them solve a math problem.

High achievers, by contrast, resented working in teams because, as one student put it, "it is known by everyone that only a handful of students do all the work" and the rest get the credit for it. Students also complained about the roles and identities they had to assume for being perceived as a "good student." For instance, they disliked having to assume the role of the leader of the group because that implied having to assign and distribute tasks and somehow "punish" those who did not turn in their assignments.

Even though both low and high achievers were asked the same questions, it is very telling that the topic of teamwork came up at different points in the interview: for low achievers, when asked about the things they liked about school; and for high achievers, when asked to describe a past experience they found upsetting.[3] Their responses paint very different cultural models about doing teamwork, even within the same school culture. The differences seem to

---

2 Although this is officially referred to as student withdrawal, I'm using the word expel because it is actually the system that prevents students from enrolling by placing restrictions on continued enrollment.

3 Since I wanted to elicit a narrative in every interview, I asked each student to describe a particular incident at school they had found disturbing and to explain if and how they had resolved it. I also asked them to recount both a good and a bad experience.

be a result of perceived ability, social class, and school culture, as discussed below.

In technological schools, where students had to do most of the class work in teams, low achievers who were grouped together learned quickly to position themselves in novel ways that allowed them to participate and be recognized by their peers for their contribution to the team. This recognition by something close to an affinity group was not sustained by the institutional discourse that afforded the position in the first place, as suggested by the fact that none of the 27 low achieving students I interviewed was able to graduate.

On the contrary, high-achieving students positioned themselves according to a preexisting cultural model about "good" and "bad" students, where they first distance themselves from the latter through their hard work and responsibility, as Alicia's narrative will show. Being forced to work in teams most of the time, high achievers were ambivalent about these changes mainly because they felt the burden of doing all the work for the rest of the team, and some felt the teachers were not doing their share as they made students learn all the curricular content through their own research and "teamwork." The comments of Guillermo, a middle-class male, high achiever in Alicia's class, provide a good example of the kinds of positioning the changes in the pedagogical approach brought on.

At the beginning of the interview, Guillermo said without hesitation that after graduation he would study engineering at the state university, for he had no doubt he would pass the entrance exam that would take place the following week. When asked about any bad experiences or problems he had encountered while studying high school, he mentioned three times at different points in the interview a particular incident while doing a team assignment for physics (Table 1):

Table 1. Guillermo's Narrative

Spanish	English
GLB: ¿En qué es diferente la preparatoria de la secundaria?	GLB: How is high school different than middle school?
G: Pues en eso, en la secundaria era casi todo individual, todos hacían sus trabajos y ahora trabajas en equipo y ahora, como digo, varios no hacen nada y, pues tú haces el trabajo para no reprobar tú, y pues beneficias a ellos también.	G: Well like I said, in middle school almost everything was done individually, everyone did their own work and now you work in teams and now, like I said, several [people] don't do anything, and well you do the work because you don't want to fail, but they also profit from it.
...	...
GLB: ¿Me puedes contar algún problema que hayas tenido en alguna de tus clases?	GLB: Can you tell me of any problems you've had in any of your classes?

Continued on next page

Table 1 (*Continued*)

G: Pues ese que le digo en física, que pues los demás no querían hacer nada, como es en equipo, no pues dije "ya me cansé, yo tampoco voy a hacer nada, a ver qué hacemos, ahí hagan algo ustedes," "no, no vamos a hacer nada, no vamos a hacer nada" y pues no, no hicimos nada, y pues al final lo reprobamos, pero ya pasé.	G: Well like I said, in physics, the rest of them didn't want to do anything, because it is teamwork, then I said "Well, I'm tired of it, I will not do anything, let's see how we manage, now you guys do something," "No, we won't do anything, we won't do anything," so we didn't do anything so we flunked the class, but I already passed.
GLB: ¿Tú lo resolviste?	GLB: You were able to manage.
G: Sí, pues en la regularización, pues ya es individual, en las regularizaciones ya ahí ya pasé con 8, y ellos pues no, ellos no pasaron.	G: Yes, I passed the make-up exam, because it's individual, in the make-up exams I got a B+, and well, they didn't pass.

Positioning works both ways. In the interview, Guillermo had mentioned that he liked doing the work in physics because he had to research and find a solution to the problems assigned by the teacher, and this way he "was really learning." What he didn't like was the fact that his teammates were benefitting from his hard work, so instead of being positioned as the "responsible" one, he confronted his teammates and decided not to do the assignments, knowing full well the consequences for everyone involved. His thinking and behavior are testament to a traditional school cultural model that says that only a handful of "good" students are capable of working and to a middle-class cultural model that says individual merit should be rewarded. The overlapping of these two cultural models precluded for Guillermo a position from which to figure team collaboration. His problems with the new approach were not doing the work itself: he felt he was learning more and welcomed the challenge, but he had been used to working on his own and gaining/accruing the recognition granted through good grades and awards. With the change in the pedagogical approach, he resented that his teammates were receiving credit for work they had not done, and instead of trying new ways of doing things, he preferred to flunk the class[4] and find a way to show that he could succeed through his own individual effort. He was in a position to do this because he had the tools (knowledge and identities) necessary to take an alternative route to what he felt was the imposition of an unfair classroom routine (team assignments), and by passing the individual make-up exam, he retained his institutional identity of a good student. This would be an instance of the kind of improvisational work that leads to agency. Guillermo found a way to "work through the system" in a manner that allowed him to refuse the position afforded to him by the educational change, while at the same time keeping his (institutional) identity of a

[4] In many classes such as this one, team assignments were a prerequisite for taking the exam. Not turning in these assignments meant not being able to take the exams required to pass the class.

good, capable student. Therefore, it is not surprising that he expressed his confidence in gaining entrance to higher education. Guillermo's experience also shows the power some students can have over school practices where participation is essential for learning and success in school; it demonstrates that, in spite of reforms geared at team collaboration and student empowerment, schools can be good at empowering academically only a handful of students, those who already have the tools needed to participate in the first place, while the rest are left to their own devices. In the case of low achievers, although the educational change provided a real opportunity for learning through team collaboration, institutional support was insufficient for this learning to translate into actual success. One may conclude that no real efforts were made to promote academic, social, and political empowerment for every student.

Interviews with high achieving students in the IB (International Baccalaureate) portray yet another cultural model about school work and collaboration. The IB is an internationally renowned program recognized for its academic rigor and demanding curriculum. Access to the program is highly restricted, and in the case of the research site for this project, IB students comprised only 2 percent of student population.

Having experienced and met the selective institutional criteria for the program, it was not surprising that every IB student I interviewed expressed a strong affiliation with their classmates and the goals of the program. Similar to high achievers in the general and technological programs, these students admitted they craved the recognition that comes with high grades; they also commented on how they competed against each other to be recognized as "the best" at some school academic activity, something not as evident in the other schools' cultures. In the regular programs, high achievers positioned themselves in opposition to "bad students" and thus disaffiliated themselves from the rest of their class; IB students' middle-class competitive edge among themselves was apparently toned down by their strong affiliation as members of a particular and esteemed group. As one student explained, one of the things he valued about his classmates was the way they interacted with each other; he respected their opinions and recognized the role they played in his own learning. Therefore, teamwork and collaboration was an effortless, natural, and highly valued activity.

For students enrolled in this program, their identity as good students was a consequence of participation in the context of an affinity group, so defined, to a large degree, by the institutional process of selection to the program; it was also the product of the discursive recognition that came through interaction with their peers. Furthermore, given the nature of the IB program, these students experienced the institutional recognition that came not only with grades, but, most importantly, by the kinds of participation afforded through the program. As a female student commented, before entering the program she found that the way classes were taught was frustrating because the only valued sources of knowledge were the teacher and the textbooks. Conversely, in the IB program, students were encouraged to question and contribute to knowledge construction. They were, she informed me, capable of reorienting the class in new and unforeseen directions, evidence of the dialogic nature of the kind of instruction they receive. Being recognized as a "good student" by their peers (affinity group), through interaction (discursively), and by their teachers (institutionally), positioned these students in ways in which they could construct their identity as good, capable students almost as a "natural" identity. In a manner of speaking, it became *who they are*. As a consequence of the kinds of participation afforded to these students in the IB context (and, no doubt, through the cultural models learned in their middle-class homes), they became, undoubtedly, not only academically empowered but, most significantly, politically and socially empowered as well.

Alicia's Space of Authoring

A good way to look at how identities take shape and the dialogical/dialectical relationship between the self and the environment is to look at narratives of personal experience. From a Bakhtinian perspective, narratives are "multi-voiced utterances that originate from the author's internalization of past and imagined dialogues and encounters in the social world" (Skinner, Valsiner, & Holland, 2001, paragraph 2). They are, as Gee points out, "important sense-making devices [because] people often encode into narratives the problems that concern them and their attempts to make sense or resolve these problems" (1999, p. 134).

For the analysis that follows, I focus on Alicia's narrative about her experience doing teamwork at school since it was a crucial moment in the interview: one that captured different episodes of positioning and juxtaposition of the cultural models and voices she had to orchestrate in producing a more or less coherent version of herself.

At the time the interview took place, Alicia was a student in a technological school and worked part-time to contribute to her family's income. She had been an honors student throughout her education. Because of financial problems, her family came to Northern Mexico when she finished middle school, and she regretted not being able to attend a prestigious public school in Central Mexico, even though she had been accepted. She enrolled in a school that specializes in fisheries and cooling systems because she was familiar with the trade, having accompanied her father many times to do his work as a cooling systems technician. I interviewed Alicia at the end of her last year of high school. The only female in a group of 13 students, she had a GPA equivalent to 3.8 and despite her academic credentials, she was unsure if she would apply to the local university because she feared she would not be accepted.

In her narrative, Alicia answers the question of the problems she had faced at school. Similar to Guillermo's narrative, she begins by recounting a particular incident in physics where she had trouble because of her frustration doing teamwork with her peers. In spite of being "against the odds" because of her gender, she was able to overcome her problems partly because of the guidance she received from a male teacher. She finishes by wishing she could always count on someone who could encourage her to pursue her goals.

For the analysis I divided the narrative into stanzas. I followed Gee's definition of stanzas as "'clumps' of tone units that deal with a unitary topic or perspective" (1999, p. 89). After a close analysis of the narrative, I identified and coded every stanza according to the cultural models encoded in the narrative. A stanza could have one or more cultural models. By coding every utterance that revealed a particular cultural model, I was able to identify the moments of conflict between the different discourses and cultural models about doing teamwork. These sections of the narrative I coded as "moments of tension and positioning," and they voice something close to an authorial stance. I provide the full transcript of the narrative in English as well as the original in Spanish in Table 2:

Table 2. Alicia's Narrative

	Spanish	English
1	**A:** Yo creo que lo importante no es, no es que el profesor enseñe bien o enseñe mal. Parte de lo poco o de lo mucho que enseñe un profesor, el alumno debe demostrar un interés de que...el objetivo de ir a la escuela es aprender y pues, la mayoría no hace eso; no, pues no les gusta venir a la escuela.	**A:** I think the important thing isn't about whether the teacher is good or not. Regardless of how much the teacher teaches, the student has to show an interest in...the purpose of going to school is to learn, and most don't do that because they don't like going to school
2	**GLB:** ¿Qué clase te gusta menos? **A:** De plano, refrigeración, jajaja, por lo mismo de ser mujer soy la única, soy la única mujer, y pues de cierta manera indirectamente me limitan al hacer cosas que a mí me gusta hacer; que "porque soy mujer". Bueno pues, pues los dejó que hagan y yo aprendo observando y pues no hay problema; pero no me gusta porque casi no hago nada. Pero, ni modo. ¿Qué le voy a hacer?	**GLB:** Which class do you like the least? **A:** Easily refrigeration, ha ha, because I'm the only girl in the class, and they kind of limit me in a way by not letting me do things that I like to do, that: "because I'm a girl." Well then, I let them do it and I just learn through observation, so it's not a problem, but I don't like it because I rarely do anything. But, oh well. What am I going to do about it?

Continued on next page

Table 2 (*Continued*)

3	**GLB:** ¿Has tenido algún problema en la escuela? **A:** Sí, fue en el semestre pasado, en donde, de todos mis compañeros, pues son muy flojos, no les gusta trabajar, y pues siempre, en esa... siempre el nuevo aprendizaje didáctico que tenemos ahora, el nuevo modelo didáctico, y por lo mismo hacemos, puro,... pues hacemos grupos, hacemos equipos.	**GLB:** Have you had any problems in school? **A:** Yeah, it was last semester when, all my classmates, well they're very lazy, they don't like to do work, and always, always, because of the new teaching program that we have now, the teaching model, because of it we only do...well we form groups, we do teamwork.
4	Y un equipo pues, si un trabajo es en equipo pues, implica de que todos trabajen. Pero como en todo caso siempre tiene que haber alguien que haga todo por los demás	And a team, well, if there's a group project [teamwork] well, it should mean that everyone does work. But like in any case, there always has to be somebody that does all the work for everybody else
5	Pues en, en ese momento pues me agarró mucho el coraje y digo, "pues no es justo que uno tenga que hacer más que el otro; si todos van a trabajar que trabajen"; y ahí fue donde yo no, pues, "sí lo quieren hacer que lo hagan". Dejé de hacer mis trabajos, siempre este... distrayéndome.	Well at, at that point well I got very angry and I go, "well it's not fair that one has to do more than the others; if everyone's going to do work then they should," and that was when I, well, "if they want to do it let them." I stopped doing my assignments; always uhh, getting distracted.
6	Porque, porque...nuestra...economía familiar no es nada fácil, pues se trabaja en la casa, se trabaja...cada quien trabaja por su lado; que "hay que trabajar en la casa". que "hay que ayudar a mamá a vender", y pues, trabajan todos en casa y pues, cada quien ya sabe lo que tiene que hacer	Because, because...our family finances are not easy, well, you work at home, you work...everyone works on their own; "you have to work at home," "you have to help your mom sell," and well, everyone works at home and each one knows what they have to do
7	Principalmente todos esos factores me estaban influyendo mucho. Y hubo un momento en el que el profesor se acercó a mí, y me preguntó que qué me pasaba, ya ni para exponer podía, podía expresarme bien y pues, me preguntó que qué me pasaba	Mainly all these factors were influencing me a lot. And there was a moment when my teacher came to me and asked me what was going on, I couldn't even express myself well when presenting a project, and he asked me what was wrong
8	Le digo "es que no sé"; le digo "tengo un dolor de cabeza, que no aguanto"; le digo "tengo problemas en la casa, hay que trabajar, ya son miles de cosas, no puedo dedicarle más tiempo al estudio",	I tell him "well I don't know"; I say "I have a headache that I can't take any longer"; I say "I have problems at home, I have to work, it's a ton of things, I don't have any time left for my studies,"

Continued on next page

Table 2 (*Continued*)

9	Pues me dice "y luego, pero por qué me lo dices"; dice "pues porque tus compañeros trabajan normalmente mal, pero tú trabajabas normalmente bien y ahora estás trabajando mal, te estás yendo con todos ellos". Le digo "pues, tiene razón"	And he says to me, "why are you telling me this?" He says, "because your classmates normally work poorly, but you normally work well and now you're working poorly; you're going with all of them." I say to him "well, you're right"
10	Me dice, este, "todos son hombres" dice; "y tú como mujer, tienes...."	He says to me "they're all guys" he says, "and you as a girl have to...."
	[interrupción]	[Interruption]
11	Yo creía pues decía: "no, pues, esta mujer qué va, qué va a hacer acá". No, pues, ya voy en sexto semestre y con primeros lugares; pero no, ahora, ya se les hace raro porque en tantos semestres he salido bien y luego tener conflicto....	I used to think because I said [to myself]: "No, well, what is this girl going to do here." But I'm already in sixth semester and with honors. But now they think it's weird because in so many semesters I've been doing well and then to have a conflict....
12	Y dice, "no pues es que esta mujer, el problema así contra la corriente". "Si ellos no trabajan, pues trabaja". Y, y dice "sí, es muy difícil porque como mujer tienes que darles, tienes que darles primero, decirles que darte a respetar ante los hombres, porque los hombres son muy llevados, y es muy difícil darte, darte a respetar con ellos, y no les des confianza y sé muy estricta con ellos"	And he says, "no, because this girl here, the problem is going against the current." "If they don't work, then you work." And, and he says "yes, it is very difficult because you, as a girl, have to, first you have to, you have to make yourself be respected by guys because boys are very brazen, and it's very hard to make yourself, to make yourself be respected by them. And don't get familiar with them and be very strict with them"
13	**E:** ¿Y cómo resolviste esa situación? **A:** Pues ya aunque, haga de cuenta que antes de darme un zapotazo en el piso pues ya, abrí los ojos, me desperté y pues luego luego, a trabajar a trabajar, me puse al corriente con mis trabajos, el profe me ayudó, me esforcé mucho y sí, pude obtener mi diez que quería.	**GLB:** And how did you resolve this situation? **A:** Well like, before I hit rock bottom, I opened my eyes, I woke up and I started working and working, I caught up on my schoolwork. The teacher helped me, I really tried hard and yes, I eventually got my A that I wanted.
14	Pues ya, me dicen, "ay pues, es que eres la única mujer y porque traes falda". Pues bueno, pues yo, "ahí están mis trabajos y están las pruebas de que, tengo una calificación por lo que yo hice, no por lo que...."	Well now they tell me: "ha, that's because you're the only girl, and because you wear a skirt." Well ok, but I go "there's my schoolwork and there's the evidence that, that I got my grades based on my own merit and not because of...."

Continued on next page

Table 2 (*Continued*)

Lo que más me gustaría es que siempre hubiera alguien que me aliente, siempre. La última vez creo que, como nadie me decía nada, pues yo ya, me estaba desviando, pero antes de que me llamaran la atención y me dijeron: "oye", que "tú estás bien", que "no hagas esto" que "está muy mal; tú échale ganas, eres muy inteligente", pues ahora sí que eso me, me aviva y me hace que, que termine un objetivo que tenga por cumplir.	What I would like the most would be to always have someone who would encourage me, always. The last time, I think that since no one told me anything, I was getting sidetracked; but before I was admonished and they called me on it: "listen, you're ok and don't do this because it's wrong; get to it, you're very intelligent," well now that kind of uh, it wakes me up and makes me finish the goal I have to accomplish.

There are at least three social practices and several episodes of positioning captured in Alicia's narrative: Doing shop (cooling systems), doing team assignments in physics, and working both in and outside of the home. I will concentrate first on the social practice identified as doing shop.

Alicia was the only female student working in a clearly male-dominated environment due to the technical field she had chosen. As explained earlier, Alicia conveyed her disappointment for not being able to attend a prestigious public high school to which she had been admitted before moving out of the area. Not knowing her new environment, she enrolled in a technical high school that offered a field she was familiar with and of which she was somewhat knowledgeable. In spite of her previous experience and knowledge, she was not allowed by her male classmates to perform any of the tasks assigned by the teacher. This is an episode of positioning where she is denied participation in the practice due to her gender (Stanza 2). These actions reveal a gendered cultural model about girls in shop class that contradicted Alicia's home experience, where her father apprenticed her in his own trade. Although she seems to accept it, she expressed her frustration and helplessness at the situation: "Well then, I let them do it and I just learn through observation, so it's not a problem, but I don't like it because I rarely do anything" (Stanza 2).

In her recollection, however, Alicia's discourse manifests its double-voicedness when quoting her classmates' reasons for excluding her: "that 'because I'm a girl.'" This would be something close to what Bakhtin refers to as a hybrid construction; it captures an alien voice that expresses a dominant cultural model about girls in shop class, as well as Alicia's own intentions in a refracted way through the use of the conjunction "that." It is a case of authoritative discourse which, for Alicia, is not internally persuasive. I will get back to this episode of positioning in Alicia's narrative, but for now I just want to point out once more that these experiences tend to leave marks in a person that may resurface at different times as layers in a laminate.

Turning now to the social practice of working in teams when doing physics assignments, we can find similarities between Guillermo's and Alicia's narrative. She, like him, resents the educational change that was brought on with the routinization of teamwork. In Stanza 3, she recounts the problems when faced with having to do the work for her male teammates because, as she put it, her classmates "are very lazy, they don't like to work." Alicia describes a cultural model about "good" and "bad students" learned, no doubt, throughout her education. This cultural model is best captured in the first stanza, where she voices very strong opinions about the role teachers and students should play at school. She takes up this cultural model in Stanzas 3 and 4, and again in Stanzas 8 and 9. This figured world about school goes something like this: teachers and students enact very rigid identities; students are categorized as either good (hard-workers, motivated, responsible) or bad (lazy, unmotivated, irresponsible). Teachers deserve respect regardless of what they do because they represent an institution where learning takes place. Students are responsible for their own learning, but most students are too lazy to be involved. Because students are lazy, they make poor teammates and leave all the work to "good" and responsible students, who are few and therefore have to work harder.

This is the same cultural model evoked in Guillermo's narrative. Both Alicia and Guillermo have learned through years of schooling what was expected of them and to position themselves accordingly when "working" in teams; but they also knew that it was their individual effort that would be rewarded and recognized. What is different in Alicia's narrative are her reasons for resisting the position offered to her by the new school discourse, as the analysis of the following stanzas will show.

Stanza 4 is interesting in that it juxtaposes two cultural models about doing teamwork. In the first sentence she illustrates an espoused cultural model that says everyone should share the responsibility when working in a group. It is stated in a rather argumentative manner by expressing a thesis: "and a team...should mean that everyone does work." This argument is taken up again in Stanza 5 ("it's not fair that one has to do more than the others"), and exemplified in Stanza 6 through hers and her family's commitments and responsibilities ("you work at home, everyone works on their own...everyone works at home and each one knows what they have to do"). Using direct speech, she captures the voice of authority (her father, perhaps) indicating what she has do to contribute to the family income. This episode illustrates a cultural model predominant in some working-class families in Mexico where, even though each member of the group may be working on their own, they share collectively the responsibility of bringing home the family income. It is through this shared understanding that she is able to express her rejection of the identities assigned to her by her peers and the school culture (and discourse).

In her narrative, she juxtaposes precisely this cultural model of teamwork to her school culture's envisioning of work in a group. She parodies this (school) "common knowledge" about what working in a team entails: "But like in any case, there always has to be somebody that does all the work for everybody else." Once again we hear the double-voicedness in Alicia's narrative, a truly dialogic instance of the words of others ("common sense," a cultural model about teamwork that is not internally persuasive for Alicia) and her own voice refracted through her parodic style ("like in any case"). This stanza is revealing in that it captures a moment of ideological becoming for Alicia, one that leads to agency.

Stanza 5 describes Alicia taking a stand against her teammates ("if everyone's going to do work then they should"). These are the same (male) classmates that had refused to let her participate in activities in shop class she enjoyed and was good at. Positioning, in this second instance, is due to her perceived ability as a good, responsible student, but it also resonates with the exercise of power due to a gendered model that says that women (girls) should do the work for men (boys), and that has been evidenced in studies exploring gender roles in collaborative school assignments in mathematics (Barnes, 1998). Layering one episode upon another "thickens" and resonates in Alicia's narrative providing the "impetus" she needs to refuse this identity.

It is interesting to note that, in her narrative, the reasons she utters for rejecting this identity are quite different than those of Guillermo: whereas his motives were for rather individualistic, middle-class values (his teammates profiting from his own work), Alicia rejected this cultural model due to an internally persuasive discourse about shared responsibility and working-class ethic. However, unlike Guillermo, who confronted his classmates directly and strategically opted for a different route, Alicia was unable to voice her dissatisfaction and stopped doing her work altogether, even to the point of losing the social academic language needed to succeed in her classes, as she reveals in Stanza 7.

Social Positions, Figured Identities, and Agency

It is important to note the roles that key authority male figures play in Alicia's narrative: her father and her decision to enter a technical high school, her father telling her what to do at home, and her male teacher urging her not only to work harder but to stay away from her male classmates.

When she starts performing poorly in her physics class, she is confronted by her male teacher who acknowledges that she is "going against the current" in her school environment: not only is this because she is the only girl in class, but also because she works the hardest. This is the third episode of positioning in Alicia's narrative. In her space of authoring, however, she cannot find a voice or a position from which to convey her frustration with an institutional discourse she finds unfair, and instead she replies with the voice not of the good, committed student she has always been, but with that of a working-class girl struggling to find the time and energy to continue studying.

Bakthin (1981) describes authoritative discourse as a "prior discourse" ("the word of a father, of adults and teachers") that "demands that we acknowledge it, that we make it our own" (p. 342). In this episode of positioning, Alicia's teacher disregards her standpoint and utters the kind of authoritative discourse that finds internal persuasiveness for Alicia through the directive force of the figured worlds they evoke: the figured identity of a "good," hardworking female student being led astray by her male, "bad" student teammates (Stanza 9 in Table 2), and the figured identity of a "good" girl for whom interaction and collaboration with her male peers is prohibited if she wants to be respected (Stanza 12). Thus, Alicia's relational identities and possibilities for improvising and enacting new ways of being (the "making of new worlds" in Holland et al.,1998, terminology) loses impetus by being recruited back into the kinds of rigid, figured personae she has come to learn and desire.

In her narrative she re-voices not only her teacher's discourse but also that of her classmates, whose cultural model about female students depicts girls as being treated differently and benefiting from their gender (and implied actions). This cultural model takes shape in a highly dialogized social language. Alicia uses direct speech to capture the voices of the male characters (students and teacher); while she decenters herself in Stanza 11, an image that is echoed in her teacher's quasidirect speech (Stanza 11). These are the voices she has to orchestrate and the resources she possesses to convey her authorial stance.

The help Alicia receives from her teacher to catch up in her work and the high marks she's able to obtain provide a new edge to Alicia's cultural model about school; the story in Alicia's figured world ends up something like this: Sometimes "bad" students influence the "good" ones, but because teachers can distinguish the "good" from the "bad" through their actions, misguided "good" students can depend on "good" teachers to get them back on track. In the end, "good" students' hard work is honored and rewarded.

Alicia captures this episode as a kind of epiphany ("before I hit rock bottom, I opened my eyes and started working and working," Stanza 13), a discourse that to a certain degree shows that her ideological becoming about authoritative school and gender discourses has been lessened. She's able to retain her good student identity and to graduate successfully, but she also learns to mistrust her own decisions and reasoning, as evidenced in her last stanza. In it, she speaks of her need and dependency on others' voices and glances (an institutional and authoritative discourse, since it's the only kind of recognition she's been granted) to find the motivation for achieving the goals she needs to accomplish.

Final Remarks

By analyzing the cultural models in Alicia's narrative, I was able to identify the moments of tension between the different cultural models, identities, and voices in Alicia's recounting of a personal experience and her negotiation and positioning of the different identities she had to enact. In Stanza 2 (Table 2) she expresses the tension about what she likes to do at school (work and learn) and the social rules for girls in a male-dominated environment. In Stanza 4 she expresses the tension between a cultural model of shared responsibility of work at home and a cultural model of teamwork at school. In Stanza 11 Alicia encodes the tension between how others perceive her (gender and good grades) and about what she knows she has done (earned her grades through hard work).

Alicia resists the cultural model of what being "a good student" entails in this school culture in Stanza 5. However, it is through her teacher's authoritative discourse that she gets recruited back into the identity of a hardworking "good student" when she realizes she's losing the social language that enabled her to assume that identity.

Her multivoiced, heteroglossic narrative shows the frailty of her good, capable student identity: it is not supported by her male classmates who exercise power over her because of her gender; it is not recognized discursively since she has no one she can talk to; and it is only recognized institutionally when and if she conforms to the authoritative discourse that created the position she begins to question. Furthermore, her working-class social conditions seem to deny her an identity of a student at all, let alone a "good" student with all the hard work and dedication it requires.

If learning entails "changing patterns of participation in specific social practices" and transforms socially situated identities (Gee, 2004, p. 38), this recent institutional discourse on teamwork should afford students opportunities to forge new identities. However, because the new educational discourse is still partial, incomplete, and superficial, students may begin to forge new identities, but this does not warrant access to the social languages necessary to succeed in school. Students are confronted with a very much entrenched school discourse that rewards individual merit and institutionalizes rigid identities of "good" and "bad" students. For some students, it is through "teamwork" that alliances are forged and new identities enacted, but this may not be sufficient to stay in the game of traditional school. For others, especially disadvantaged students such as Alicia who value and depend on school's recognition, the consequences of playing by the rules and accepting the dominant cultural models of school and society may come at a very high cost: the loss of agency to forge new alliances, identities, and new possibilities for learning.

References

Bakhtin, M. M. (1981). *The dialogic imagination: Four essays by* M. M. *Bakhtin*. In M. E. Holquist (Ed.). Austin: University of Texas Press.

Barnes, M. (1998). Analysing power relationships in collaborative groups in mathematics. *Conference proceedings of the mathematics education and society international conference*. University of Nottingham, 6th–11th September.

Carnoy, M. (2004). *ICT in education: Possibilities and challenges*. Inaugural lecture of the Universitat Oberta de Catalunya 2004–2005 academic year. Retrieved October 15, 2008, from http://www.uoc.edu/inaugural04/eng/carnoy1004.pdf.

Christie, F. (2007). Ongoing dialogue: Functional linguistic and Bernsteinian sociological perspectives on education. In F. Christie & J. R. Martin (Eds.), *Language, knowledge and pedagogy. Functional linguistic and sociological perspectives*. (pp. 156–183). New York: Continuum

Foucault, M. (1972). *The archeology of knowledge*. Translated by A. M Sheridan Smith, New York: Pantheon Books.

Gee, J. P. (1996). *Social linguistics and literacies: Ideology in discourses* (2nd Edition). London: Taylor & Francis.

Gee, J. P. (1999). *An introduction to discourse analysis. Theory and method*. London and New York: Routledge.

Gee, J. P. (2000/2001). Identity as an analytic lens for research in education. *Review of Research in Education, 25*, 99–125.

Gee, J. P. (2004). Discourse analysis: What makes it critical? In R. Rogers (Ed.), *An introduction to critical discourse analysis in education* (pp. 19-50). Mahwah, NJ: Lawrence Erlbaum Associates.

Holland, D., Lachicotte, W., Skinner, D., & Cain, C. (1998). *Identity and agency in cultural worlds*. Cambridge, MA: Harvard University Press.

Holland, D., & Leander, K. (2004). Ethnographic studies of positioning and subjectivity: An introduction. *Ethos, 32*(2) 127–139.

Holland, D., & Skinner, D. (1987). Prestige and intimacy: The cultural models behind American's talk about gender types. In D. Holland & N. Quinn (Eds.), *Cultural models in language and thought* (pp. 78–11). New York: Cambridge University Press.

Lewis, C. (2001). *Literary practices as social acts*. Mahwah, NJ: Lawrence Erlbaum.

Lewis, C., Enciso, P., & Moje, E. B. (2007). Introduction: Reframing sociocultural research. In C. Lewis, P. Enciso & E. B. Moje (Eds.), *Reframing sociocultural research on literacy* (pp. 1–11). Mahwah, NJ: Lawrence Erlbaum Associates.

López Bonilla, G. (2008). Teachers' D/discourses and situated identities: Literacy practices in a Mexican high school. In L. I. Bartolomé (Ed.), *Ideology in education: Unmasking the trap of teachers' neutrality* (pp. 73–94). New York: Peter Lang.

López Bonilla, G., Tinajero, G., & Pérez, C. (2006). Jóvenes, currículo y competencia literaria. *Redie. Revista Electrónica de Investigación Educativa*, 8(2). Retrieved from http://redie.uabc.mx/vol8no2/contenido-bonilla.html.

Matusov, E. (2007). Applying Bakhtin scholarship on discourse in education: A critical review essay. *Educational Theory, 56*, 215–237.

McQuillan, P. J. (2005). Possibilities and pitfalls: A comparative analysis of student empowerment. *American Educational Research Journal, 42*(4) 639–670.

Moje, E. B. & Lewis, C. (2007). Examining opportunities to learn literacy: The role of critical sociocultural literacy research. In C. Lewis, P. Enciso & E. B. Moje (Eds.), *Reframing sociocultural research on literacy* (pp. 15–48). Mahwah, NJ: Lawrence Erlbaum.

Quinn, N. & Holland, D. (1987). Culture and cognition. In D. Holland & N. Quinn (Eds.), *Cultural models in language and thought*. New York: Cambridge University Press.

Rychen, D. S. & Salganik, H. (2003). *Key competencies for a successful life and a well functioning society*. Göttingen, Germany: Hogrefe & Huber Publishers.

Skinner, D., Valsiner, J., & Holland, D. (2001, September). Discerning the dialogical self: A theoretical and methodological examination of a Nepali adolescent's narrative [34 paragraphs]. Forum Qualitative Sozialforschung / Forum: *Qualitative Social Research, 2*(3). Retrieved May 30, 2008, from http://www.qualitative-research.net/fqs-eng.html

Strauss, C. (1992). Models and motives. In R.G. D'Andrade & C. Strauss (Eds.), *Human motives and cultural models* (pp. 1–20). Cambridge: Cambridge University Press.

Tinajero, G., López Bonilla, G., & Pérez, C. (2007). Cambio curricular en el bachillerato tecnológico mexicano: El caso de ciencia, tecnología, sociedad y valores. Archivos Analíticos de Políticas Educativas, *15*(4). Retrieved from http://epaa.asu.edu/epaa/

SECTION II

Literacy, Youth Cultures and Virtual Spaces

CHAPTER FIVE

Reading, Language Development, Video Games, and Learning in the Twenty-first Century

JAMES PAUL GEE

Reading: A Trajectory Approach

Consider the situation of a child learning to read. What should our goal for this child be? On the face of it, the goal would seem to be that the child learns to decode print and assign basic or literal meanings to that print. But the situation is not that simple. We know from the now well-studied phenomenon of the "fourth-grade slump" (the phenomenon whereby many children, especially poorer children, pass early reading tests, but cannot read well enough to learn academic content later on in school) that the goal of early reading instruction has to be more forward looking than simple decoding and literal comprehension (American Educator, 2003; Chall, Jacobs, & Baldwin, 1990; Gee, 2008; Snow, Burns, & Griffin, 1998). The goal has to be that children learn to read early on in such a way that this learning creates a successful trajectory throughout the school years and beyond. Such a trajectory is based, more than anything else, on the child being able to handle ever increasingly complex language, especially in the content areas (e.g., science and math), as school progresses. Children need to get ready for these increasing language demands as early as possible. It is as if school were more and more conducted in Greek as the grades increased: surely it would be better to be exposed to Greek as early as possible and not wait until school becomes the equivalent of advanced Greek.

Let's call this a "trajectory approach" to early reading. Such an approach has to look not only forwards, but backwards, as well. Early phonemic awareness and early home-based practice with literacy are the most important correlates with success in first grade, especially success in learning to read in the "decode and literally comprehend" sense (Dickinson & Neuman, 2006). However, the child's early home-based oral vocabulary and early skills with complex oral language are the most important correlates for school success—not just in reading, but in the content areas—past the first grade, essentially for the rest of schooling (Dickinson & Neuman, 2006; Gee, 2004; Senechal, Ouellette, & Rodney, 2006). Thus, a child's oral language development is critical to a successful trajectory approach to reading, that is, an approach that seeks to make a long-term school-based reader of academic content (and that's what's in the high school biology textbook, for example). It is the key to avoiding, even eradicating the fourth-grade slump.

However, we must pause here, for two reasons. First, I am aware that some people consider the sort of academic language that is in biology textbooks simply to be exclusionary jargon attempting to colonize people's everyday cultural identities in the name of a rationalist positivism. I am as interested as any one in the politics of schooling and science (Gee, 1990/1996/2007), but in this paper my concern is with the fate of children who get to high school and cannot cope with their textbooks and related language practices. In my view, it does no good to rail against the language of the textbook, but, nonetheless, to leave the textbook and other instances of academic language behind as the litmus test of school success—the "revolution" had better be total or children will suffer for adults' politics. For the record, while I fully concede that aspects of academic language have been used historically for little more than exclusion and the creation of status—and that textbooks should be replaced with texts more specially tied to activities and practices—by and large I believe that specialist varieties of language, when used appropriately, are critically and integrally tied to the functioning (workings) of specialist domains (whether this be an academic area or real-time-strategy video games) and access to these domains is severely limited without such language and related representational systems.

Second, I must pause because we are on the brink of what could be a major misunderstanding. Decades of research in linguistics have shown that every normal child's early language and language development are just fine (Chomsky, 1986; Labov, 1979; Pinker, 1994). Every child, under normal conditions, develops a perfectly complex and adequate oral language, the child's "native language" (and, of course, sometimes children develop more than one native language). It never happens, under normal conditions—and normal here covers a very wide array of variation—that, in acquiring English, say, little Janie develops relative clauses, but little Johnnie just cannot master them. That is, of course, in a way, a surprising fact, showing that the acquisition of one's native language is not particularly a matter of ability or skill.

But, when I say, that children's early oral language—vocabulary and skills with complex language—are crucial correlates of success in school, correlates that show up especially after the child has learned to decode in first grade (one hopes)—I am not talking about children's everyday language, the sort of language that is equal for everyone. I am talking about their early preparation for language that is not "everyday," for language that is "technical" or "specialist" or "academic" (Gee, 2004; Schleppegrell, 2004). I will refer to people's "everyday" language—the way they speak when they are not speaking technically or as specialists of some sort—as their "vernacular style." I will refer to their language when they are speaking technically or as a specialist as a "specialist style" (people eventually can have a number of different specialist styles, connected to different technical, specialist, or academic concerns).

An Example

Let me give an example of what I am talking about, both in terms of specialist language and in terms of getting ready for later complex specialist language demands early on in life. Kevin Crowley has talked insightfully about quite young children developing what he calls "islands of expertise." Crowley and Jacobs (2002, p. 333) define an island of expertise as "any topic in which children happen to become interested and in which they develop relatively deep and rich knowledge." They provide several examples of such islands, including a boy who develops relatively deep content knowledge and a "sophisticated conversational space" (p. 335) about trains and related topics after he is given a *Thomas the Tank Engine* book.

Now consider a mother talking to her four-year-old son, who has an island of expertise around dinosaurs (the transcript below is adapted from Crowley & Jacobs, 2002, pp. 343–344). The mother and child are looking at a replica fossil dinosaur and a replica fossil dinosaur egg. The mother has a little card in front of her that says:

- Replica of a Dinosaur Egg
- From the Oviraptor
- Cretaceous Period
- Approximately 65 to 135 million years ago
- The actual fossil, of which this is a replica, was found in the Gobi desert of Mongolia

In the transcript below, "M" stands for the mother's turns and "C" for the child's:

C: This looks like this is a egg.

M: Ok well this....That's exactly what it is! How did you know?

C: Because it looks like it.

M: That's what it says, see look egg, egg....Replica of a dinosaur egg. From the oviraptor.

M: Do you have a....You have an oviraptor on your game! You know the egg game on your computer? That's what it is, an oviraptor.

M: And that's from the Cretaceous period. And that was a really, really long time ago.

M: And this is....the hind claw. What's a hind claw? (pause) A claw from the back leg from a velociraptor. And you know what....

C: Hey! Hey! A velociraptor!! I had that one my [inaudible] dinosaur.

M: I know, I know and that was the little one. And remember they have those, remember in your book, it said something about the claws....

C No, I know, they, they....

M: Your dinosaur book, what they use them....

C: Have so great claws so they can eat and kill....

M: They use their claws to cut open their prey, right.

C: Yeah.

This is a language lesson, but not primarily a lesson on vernacular language, though, of course, it thoroughly mixes vernacular and specialist language. It is a lesson on specialist language. It is early preparation for the sorts of academic (school-based) language children see ever more increasingly, in talk and in texts, as they move on in school. It is also replete with "moves," which are successful language teaching strategies, though the mother is no expert on language development.

Let's look at some of the features this interaction has as an informal language lesson. First, it contains elements of nonvernacular, specialist language, for example: "*replica* of a dinosaur egg," "from the *oviraptor*," "from the *Cretaceous period*," "the *hind claw*," and "their *prey*." The specialist elements here are largely vocabulary, though such interactions soon come to involve elements of syntax and discourse associated with specialist ways with words as well.

Second, the mother asks the child the basis of his knowledge: Mother: "How did you know? Child: Because it looks like it." Specialist domains are almost always "expert" domains that involve claims to know and evidence for such claims. They are in Shaffer's (2005) sense "epistemic games."

Third, the mother publicly displays reading of the technical text, even though the child cannot yet read: "That's what it says, see look *egg, egg*....Replica of a dinosaur *egg*. From the oviraptor." This reading also uses print to confirm the child's claim to know, showing one way this type of print (descriptive information on the card) can be used in an epistemic game of confirmation.

Fourth, the mother relates the current talk and text to other texts the child is familiar with: "You have an oviraptor on your game! You know the egg game on your computer? That's what it is, an oviraptor;" "And remember they have those, remember in your book, it said something about the claws." This sort of intertextuality creates a network of texts and modalities (books, games, and computers), situating the child's new knowledge not just in a known background, but in a system the child is building in his head.

Fifth, the mother offers a technical-like definition: "And this is...the hind claw. What's a hind claw? (pause) A claw from the back leg from a velociraptor." This demonstrates a common language move in specialist domains, that is, giving relatively formal and explicit definitions (not just examples of use).

Sixth, the mother points to and explicates hard concepts: "And that's from the Cretaceous period. And that was a really, really long time ago." This signals to the child that "Cretaceous period" is a technical term and displays how to explicate such terms in the vernacular (this is a different move than offering a more formal definition).

Seventh, she offers technical vocabulary for a slot the child has left open: Child: "Have so great claws so they can eat and kill...."Mother: "They use their claws to cut open their *prey*, right." This slot and filler move co-constructs language with the child, allowing the child to use language "above his head" in ways in line with Vygotsky's concept of a "zone of proximal development" (Vygotsky, 1978).

Informal Specialist-Language Lessons

So, let's be clear about two things. This is an informal language lesson. And such lessons involve more than language and language learning. They involve teaching and learning cognitive (knowledge) and interactional moves in specialist domains. Finally, they involve teaching and learning identities, the identity of being the sort of person who is comfortable with specialist, technical knowing, learning, and language. Of course, even formal language lessons—in learning a second language, for instance, in school—should involve language, knowledge, interaction, and identity. But this is not formal teaching it is informal teaching, the teaching equivalent of informal learning. Let's call such informal language lessons, with the sort of features I have just discussed, "informal specialist-language lessons" (ironically, they are informal formal-language lessons!).

Along with all we know about "emergent literacy" at home (Dickinson & Neuman, 2006; Emergent Literacy Project, n.d.; Gee, 2004), informal specialist language lessons are crucial if one wants to take a trajectory view of reading development. They are preschool pre-reading activities that lead to early reading instruction that avoids the fourth-grade slump. Of course, the reading instruction the child receives at school must continue these language lessons, informally and formally. It must place reading from the get-go in the context of learning specialist styles of language, just as this mother has done. This, however, raises the issue of what happens to children who come to school without such informal specialist language teaching, and, often, too, without other important aspects of emergent literacy. My view is that this cannot be ignored. We cannot just move on to reading instruction of the "decode and literally comprehend" sort as if it just doesn't matter that these children have missed out on early specialist language learning. For these children language teaching needs to start, start with a vengeance and sustain itself throughout the course of reading instruction. And, again, remember, this claim has nothing to do with teaching "standard" English or ESL (English as a second language), *per se*: it is a claim that even native speakers of vernacular standard English need language learning to prepare for specialist varieties of language.

Specialist Language in Popular Culture

There are other things beyond such informal specialist-language lessons that can prepare children for the increasing language demands of school in the content areas. And we can see one of these if we look, oddly enough, at young people's popular culture today. Something very interesting has happened in children's popular culture. It has become very complex and it contains a great many practices that involve highly specialist styles of language (Gee 2004, 2007). Young children often engage with these practices socially with each other in informal peer learning groups. And, some parents recruit these practices to accelerate their children's specialist-language skills (with their concomitant thinking and interactional skills).

For example, consider the text below, which appears on a *Yu-Gi-Oh* card. *Yu-Gi-Oh* is a card game involving quite complex rules. It is often played face-to-face with one or more players, sometimes in formal competitions, more often informally, though it can be played as a video game, as well.

Armed Ninja
Card-Type: Effect Monster
Attribute: Earth | **Level:** 1

Type: Warrior
ATK: 300 | **DEF:** 300
Description: FLIP: Destroys 1 Magic Card on the field. If this card's target is face-down, flip it face-up. If the card is a Magic Card, it is destroyed. If not, it is returned to its face-down position. The flipped card is not activated.
Rarity: Rare

The "description" is really a rule. It states what moves in the game the card allows. This text has little specialist vocabulary (though it has some, e.g., "activated"), unlike the interaction we saw between mother and child above, but it contains complex specialist syntax. It contains, for instance, three straight conditional clauses (the "if" clauses). Note how complex this meaning is: First, if the target is face down, flip it over. Now check to see if it is a magic card. If it is, destroy it. If it isn't, return it to its face-down position. Finally, you are told that even though you flipped over your opponent's card, which in some circumstances would activate its powers, in this case, the card's powers are not activated. This is "logic talk," a matter, really, of multiple related "either-or," and "if-then" propositions.

Note, too, that the card contains a bunch of classificatory information (e.g., type, attack power, defense power, rarity). All of these linguistic indicators lead the child to place the card in the whole network or system of *Yu-Gi-Oh* cards—and there are over 10, 000 of them—and the rule system of the game itself. This is complex system thinking with a vengeance.

Consider, also, the *Yu-Gi-Oh* card below:

Cyber Raider
Card-Type: Effect Monster
Attribute: Dark | **Level:** 4
Type: Machine
ATK: 1400 | **DEF:** 1000
Description: When this card is Normal Summoned, Flip Summoned, or Special Summoned successfully, select and activate 1 of the following effects: Select 1 equipped Equip Spell Card and destroy it. Select 1 equipped Equip Spell Card and equip it to this card.
Rarity: Common

This card—and remember it is one of 10,000—contains nearly nothing but words and phrases that are technical, specialist terms in *Yu-Gi-Oh*. Few texts children see in school will be this saturated with such technical language.

I have watched seven-year-old children play *Yu-Gi-Oh* with great expertise. They must read each of the cards. They endlessly debate the powers of each card by constant contrast and comparison with other cards when they are trading them. They discuss and argue over the rules and, in doing so, use lots of specialist vocabulary, syntactic structures, and discourse features. They can go to web sites to learn more or to settle their disputes. If and when they do so, here is the sort of thing they will see:

> **8-CLAWS SCORPION** Even if "8-Claws Scorpion" is equipped with an Equip Spell Card, its ATK is 2400 when it attacks a face-down Defense Position monster.
>
> The effect of "8-Claws Scorpion" is a Trigger Effect that is applied if the condition is correct on activation ("8-Claws Scorpion" declared an attack against a face-down Defense Position monster). The target monster does not have to be in face-down Defense Position when the effect of "8-Claws Scorpion" is resolved. So if "Final Attack Orders" is active, or "Ceasefire" flips the monster face-up, "8-Claws Scorpion" still gets its 2400 ATK.
>
> The ATK of "8-Claws Scorpion" becomes 2400 during damage calculation. You cannot chain "Rush Recklessly" or "Blast with Chain" to this effect. If these cards were activated before damage calculation, then the ATK of "8-Claws Scorpion" becomes 2400 during damage calculation so those cards have no effect on its ATK.
>
> http://www.upperdeckentertainment.com/yugioh/en/faq_card_rulings.aspx?first=A &last=C

I do not really think I have to say much about this text. It is, in every way, a specialist text. In fact, in complexity, it is far above the language many young children will see in their school books, until they get to middle school at best and, perhaps, even high school. But, seven-year-old children deal and deal well with this language (though *Yu-Gi-Oh* cards—and, thus, their language—are often banned at school).

Let's consider for a moment what *Yu-Gi-Oh* involves. First and foremost it involves what I will call "lucidly functional language." What do I mean by this? The language on *Yu-Gi-Oh* cards, web sites, and in children's discussions and debates is quite complex, as we have seen, but it relates piece by piece to the rules of the game, to the specific moves or actions one takes in the domain. Here language—complex specialist language—is married closely to specific and connected actions. The relationship between language and meaning (where meaning here is the rules and the actions connected to them) is clear and lucid. The *Yu-Gi-Oh* company has designed such lucid functionality because it allows them to sell 10, 000 cards connected to a fully esoteric language and practice. It directly banks on children's love of mastery and expertise. If only that schools did the same. If only the language of science in the early years of school were taught in this lucidly functional way. It rarely is.

So we can add "lucidly functional language" to our informal specialist-language lessons as another foundation for specialist-language learning, one currently better represented in popular culture than in school. And, note here, too, that such lucidly functional language is practiced socially in groups of kids as they discuss, debate, and trade, with more advanced peers often playing a major educative role. They learn to relate oral and written language of a specialist sort, a key skill for specialist domains, including academic ones at school. At the same time, many parents (usually, but not always, more privileged parents) have come to know how to use such lucidly functional language practices—like *Yu-Gi-Oh* or *Pokemon*, and, as well as we will see below, digital technologies like video games—to engage their children in informal specialist-language lessons.

My thirteen-year-old son Sam recently told me that he felt he had learned to read by playing *Pokemon*, another card and video game. He was referring to the games on the Nintendo Game Boy, games he played before he could read when he was five. His mother or I sat with him and read for him—the game requires a lot of reading. In a real sense, Sam did learn to read by playing *Pokemon*. But he learned to read, then, in a context that was also early preparation for dealing with complex specialist language, a type of language he would see later in school, though, for the most part, only after the first couple of grades. Of course, he learned other sorts of reading in other activities, as well. I am not arguing for early literacy that is focused on only specialist languages.

Of course, the sorts of lucidly functional language practices and informal specialist-language lessons that exist around *Yu-Gi-Oh* or *Pokemon* could exist in school—even as early as first grade—to teach school-valued content. But they don't. Here the creativity of capitalists has far outrun that of educators.

Situated Meaning and Video Games

So far we have talked about two underpinnings of a trajectory view of reading: informal (and later formal) specialized-language lessons and practices built around lucidly functional language. Why are these underpinnings for reading, in a trajectory sense? Because they place reading development in the context of specialized-language development, which is the basis for being able to keep up with the ever increasing demands for learning content in school via complex technical and academic varieties of language (and, indeed, other sorts of technical representations used in areas like science and math).

Now we move to a third underpinning of a trajectory view of reading development. Lots of research has shown, for years now that in areas like science, a good many students with good grades and passing test scores cannot actually use their knowledge to solve problems (Gardner, 1991). For example, many students who can write down for a test Newton's Laws of Motion cannot correctly say how many forces are acting on a coin when it is tossed into the air and at the top of its trajectory—and, ironically, this is something that can be deduced from Newton's Laws (Chi, Feltovich, & Glaser, 1981). They cannot apply their knowledge, because they don't see how it applies—they don't see the physical world and the language of physics (which includes mathematics) in such a way that it is clear to them how that language applies to that physical world.

There are two ways to understand words. I will call one way "verbal" and the other way "situated" (Gee, 2004, 2007). A situated understanding of a concept or word implies the ability to use the word or understand the concept in ways that are customizable to different specific situations of use (Brown, Collins, & Dugid, 1989; Clark 1997; Gee, 2004, 2007). A general or verbal understanding implies an ability to explicate one's comprehension of a concept or word in terms of other words or general principles but not necessarily an ability to apply this knowledge to actual situations. Thus, while verbal or general understanding may facilitate passing certain sorts of information-focused tests, they do not necessarily facilitate actual problem solving.

Let me quickly point out that, in fact, all human understandings are, in reality, situated. What I am calling verbal understandings are, of course, situated in terms of other words and, in a larger sense, the total linguistic, cultural, and domain knowledge a person has. But they are not necessarily situated in terms of ways of applying these words to actual situations of use and varying their applications across different contexts of use. Thus, I will continue to contrast verbal understanding to situated ones, where the latter implies the ability to do and not just say.

Situated understandings are, of course, the norm in everyday life and in vernacular language. Even the most mundane words take on different meanings in different contexts of use. Indeed, people must be able to build these meanings on the spot in real time as they construe the contexts around them. For instance, people construct different meanings for a word like "coffee" when they hear something like "The coffee spilled, get the mop" versus "The coffee spilled, get a broom" versus "The coffee spilled, stack it again." Indeed, such examples have been a staple of connectionist work on human understanding (Clark, 1993).

Verbal and general understandings are top-down. They start with the general, that is with a definition-like understanding of a word or a general principle associated with a concept. Less abstract meanings follow as special cases of the definition or principle. Situated understandings generally work in the other direction; understanding starts with a relatively concrete case and gradually rises to higher levels of abstraction through the consideration of additional cases.

The perspective I am developing here, one that stresses knowledge as tied to activity and experiences in the world before knowledge as facts and information, and knowledge as situated as opposed to verbal understandings, has many implications for the nature of learning and teaching, as well as for the assessment of learning and teaching (Gee, 2003a). Recently, researchers in several different areas have raised the possibility that what we might call "game-like" learning through digital technologies can facilitate situated understandings in the context of activity and experience grounded in perception (Games-to-Teach Team, 2003; Gee, 2003b, 2005; McFarlane, Sparrowhawk, & Heald, 2002; Squire, 2003).

Before I discuss game-like learning in some depth, let me point out a phenomenon that all gamers are well aware of. This phenomenon gets to the heart and soul of what situated meanings are and why they are important: Written texts associated with video games are not very meaningful, certainly not very lucid, unless and until one has played the game. Let me take the small booklet that comes with the innovative shooter game *Deus Ex* to use as an example of what I mean by saying this. In the 20 pages of this booklet, there are 199 bolded references that represent headings and subheadings (to take one small randomly chosen stretch of headings and subheadings that appears at the end of page 5 and the beginning of page 6: *Passive Readouts, Damage Monitor, Active Augmentation & Device Icons, Items-at-Hand, Information Screens, Note, Inventory, Inventory Management, Stacks, Nanokey ring, Ammunition*). Each of these 199 headings and subheadings is followed by text that gives information relevant to the topic and relates it to other information throughout the booklet. In addition, the booklet gives 53 keys on the computer keyboard an assignment to some function in the game, and these 53 keys are mentioned 82 times in the booklet in relation to the information contained in the 199 headings and subheadings. So, though the booklet is small, it is just packed with concise and relatively technical information.

Here is a typical piece of language from this booklet:

> Your internal nano-processors keep a very detailed record of your condition, equipment and recent history. You can access this data at any time during play by hitting F1 to get to the Inventory screen or F2 to get to the Goals/Notes screen. Once you have accessed your information screens, you can move between the screens by clicking on the tabs at the top of the screen. You can map other information screens to hotkeys using Settings, Keyboard/Mouse (p. 5).

This makes perfect sense at a literal level, but that just goes to show how worthless the literal level is. When you understand this sort of passage at only a literal level, you have only an illusion of understanding, one that quickly disappears as you try to relate the information in this passage to the hundreds of other important details in the booklet. Such literal understandings are precisely what children who fuel the fourth-grade slump have. First of all, this passage means nothing real to you if you have no situated idea about what "nanoprocessors," "condition," "equipment," "history," "F1," "Inventory screen," "F2," "Goals/Notes screen" (and, of course, "Goals" and "Notes"), "information screens," "clicking," "tabs," "map," "hotkeys," and "Settings, Keyboard/Mouse" mean in and for playing games like *Deus Ex*.

Second, though you know literally what each sentence means, they raise a plethora of questions if you have no situated understandings of this game or games like it. For instance: Is the same data (condition, equipment, and history) on both the Inventory screen and the Goals/Notes screen? If so, why is it on two different screens? If not, which type of information is on which screen and why? The fact that I can move between the screens by clicking on the tabs (but what do these tabs look like, will I recognize them?) suggests that some of this information is on one screen and some on the other. But, then, is my "condition" part of my Inventory or my Goals/Notes—does not seem to be either, but, then, what is my "condition" anyway? If I can map other information screens (and what are these?) to hotkeys using "Setting, Keyboard/Mouse," does this mean there is no other way to access them? How will I access them in the first place to assign them to my own chosen hotkeys? Can I click between them and the Inventory screen and the Goals/Notes screens by pressing on "tabs"? And so on and so forth—20 pages is beginning to seem like a lot—remember there are 199 different headings under which information like this is given at a brisk pace through the booklet.

Of course, all these terms and questions can be defined and answered if you closely check and cross-check information over and over again through the little booklet. You can constantly turn the pages backwards and forwards. But once you have one set of links relating various items and actions in mind, another drops out just as you need it and you are back to turning pages. Is the booklet poorly written? Not at all. It is written just as well or poorly, in fact, just like any of a myriad of school-based texts in the content areas. It is, outside the practices in the domain from which it comes, just as meaningless, however much one could garner literal meanings from it with which to verbally repeat things or pass tests.

And, of course, too, you can utter something like "Oh, yea, you click on F1 (function key 1) to get to the Inventory screen and F2 to get to the Goals/Notes screen" and sound like you know something. The trouble is this: in the actual game, you can click on F2 and meditate on the screen you see at your leisure. Nothing bad will happen to you. However, you very often have to click on F1 and do something quickly in the midst of a heated battle. There's no "at your leisure" here. The two commands really don't function the same way in the game—they actually mean different things in terms of embodied and situated action—and they never really *just* mean "click F1, get screen." That is their general meaning, the one with which you can't really do anything useful until you know how to spell it out further in situation-specific terms in the game.

When you can spell out such information in situation-specific terms in the game, then the relationships of this information to the other hundreds of pieces of information in the booklet become clear and meaningful. And, of course, it is these relationships that are what really count if you are to understand the game as a system and, thus, play it at all well. *Now* you can read the book if you need to piece in missing bits of information, check on your understandings, or solve a particular problem, or answer a particular question you have.

When I first read this booklet before playing *Deus Ex* (and at that time I had played only one other shooter game before, a very different one)—yes, I, an overly academic baby boomer, made the mistake of trying to read the book first, despite my own theories about reading—I was sorely tempted to put the game on a shelf and forget about it. I was simply overwhelmed with details, questions, and confusions. When I started the game, I kept trying to look up stuff in the booklet. But none of it was understood well enough to be found easily without continually re-searching for the same information. In the end, you have to just actively play the game and explore and try everything. Then, at last, the booklet makes good sense, but, then too, you don't need it all that much anymore.

So now I would make just the same claim about any school content domain as I have just said about the video game *Deus Ex*: specialist language in any domain—games or science—has no situated meaning—thus no lucid or applicable meaning—unless and until one has "played the game," in this case the game of science, or, better put, a specific game connected to a specific science. Such "games"("science games") involve seeing the language and representations associated with some part of science in terms of activities I have done, experiences I have had, images I have formed from these, and interactional dialogue I have heard from and had with peers and mentors outside and inside the science activities. School is too often about reading the manual before you get to play the game, if you ever do. This is not harmful for kids who have already played the game at home but is disastrous for those who have not.

Good video games do not just support situated meanings for the written materials associated with them in manuals and on fan web sites—and these are copious—but also for all the language within the game. The meaning of such language is always associated with actions, experiences, images, and dialogue. Furthermore, players get verbal information "just in time," when they can apply it or see it apply, or "on demand," when they feel the need for it and are ready for it—and then, in some cases, games will give the player walls of print (e.g., in *Civilization IV*).

So my claim: what I will call "game-like learning" leads to situated and not just verbal meanings. In turn, situated meanings make specialist language lucid, easy, and useful. In order to demonstrate what I am talking about—and what I mean by "game-like learning"—I will turn first to an application of what I consider game-like learning that uses no real game, then to a game made explicitly to enhance school-based learning, then to a game-like simulation, built into an overall learning system.

Game-like Learning: Andy diSessa

Andy diSessa's (2000) work is a good example, in science education, of building on and from specific cases to teach situated understandings. DiSessa has successfully taught children in sixth grade and beyond the algebra behind Galileo's principles of motion by teaching them a specific computer programming language called Boxer.

The students write into the computer a set of discrete steps in the programming language. For example, the first command in a little program meant to represent uniform motion might tell the computer to set the speed of a moving object at one meter per second. The second step might tell the computer to move the object. And a third step might tell the computer to repeat the second step over and over again. Once the program starts running, the student will see a graphical object move one meter each second repeatedly, a form of uniform motion.

Now the student can elaborate the model in various ways. For example, the student might add a fourth step that tells the computer to add the value *a* to the speed of the moving object after each movement the object has taken (let us just say, for convenience, that *a* adds one more meter per second at each step). So now, after the first movement on the screen (when the object has moved at the speed of one meter per second), the computer will set the speed of the object at two meters per second (adding one meter), and, then, on the next movement, the object will move at the speed of two meters per second. After this, the computer will add another meter per second to the speed and on the next movement the object will move at the speed of three meters per second. And so forth forever, unless the student has added a step that tells the computer when to stop repeating the movements. This process is obviously modeling the concept of acceleration. And, of course, you can set *a* to be a negative number instead of a positive one and watch what happens to the moving object over time instead.

The student can keep elaborating the program and watch what happens at every stage. In this process, the student, with the guidance of a good teacher, can discover a good deal about Galileo's principles of motion through his or her actions in writing the program, watching what happens and changing the program. What the student is doing here is seeing in an embodied way, tied to action, how a representational system that is less abstract than algebra or calculus (namely, the computer programming language, which is actually composed of a set of boxes) "cashes out" in terms of motion in a virtual world on the computer screen.

An algebraic representation of Galileo's principles is more general than what diSessa's students have been exposed to; basically it is a set of numbers and variables that do not directly tie to actions or movements as material things. As diSessa points out, algebra does not distinguish effectively "among motion ($d = rt$), converting meters to inches ($i = 39.37 \times m$), defining coordinates of a straight line ($y = mx$), or a host of other conceptually varied situations." They all just look alike. He goes on to point out that "[d]istinguishing these contexts is critical in learning, although it is probably nearly irrelevant in fluid, routine work for experts," who, of course, have already had many embodied experiences in using algebra for a variety of different purposes of their own.

Once learners have experienced the meanings of Galileo's principles about motion in a situated and embodied way, they have understood one of the situated meanings for the algebraic equations that capture these principles at a more abstract level. Now these equations are beginning to take on a real meaning in terms of embodied understandings. As learners see algebra spelled out in more such specific material situations, they will come to master it in an active and critical way, not just as a set of symbols to be repeated in a passive and rote manner on tests.

DiSessa does not actually refer to his work with Boxer as game-like learning, though some people pushing the design of actual games for learning have been inspired, in part, by his approach to learning and science education (Gee, 2003b). And, indeed, Boxer produces simulations that are, in many respects, game-like and certainly can entice from learners the sort of flexible consideration of possibilities that play can inspire. However, I turn now to an actual game designed to enhance situated learning that goes beyond verbal understandings.

Supercharged!

Kurt Squire and his colleagues (Squire, Barnett, Grant, & Higginbotham, 2004; Squire, 2003, 2006, 2007) have worked on a computer game called "*Supercharged!*" to help students learn physics. Players use the game to explore electromagnetic mazes, placing charged particles and controlling a ship, which navigates by altering its charge. The game play consists of two phases: planning and playing. Each time players encounter a new level, they are given a limited set of charges that they can place throughout the environment, enabling them to shape the trajectory of their ship.

Each level contains obstacles common to electromagnetism texts. These include points of charge, planes of charge, magnetic planes, solid magnets, and electric currents. Each of these obstacles affects the player's movement according to laws of electromagnetism. The goal of the game is to help learners build stronger *intuitions* for electromagnetic concepts based on perceptual and embodied experiences in a virtual world where these concepts are instantiated in a fairly concrete way.

Squire et al., (2004) report some results that are part of a larger design experiment examining the pedagogical potential of *Supercharged!* in three urban middle school science classrooms with a good deal of cultural diversity. In this study, the experimental group outperformed the control group on conceptual exam questions. Post-interviews revealed that both experimental and control students had improved their understanding of basic electrostatics. However, there were some qualitative differences between the two groups. The most striking differences were in students' descriptions of electric fields and the influence of distance on the forces that charges experience. For example, one girl during her post interview described an electric field as:

> The electric[ity] goes from the positive charge to the negative charge like this [drawing a curved line from a positive charge to a negative charge]. I know this because this is what it looked like in the game and it was hard to move away or toward it because the two charges are close together so they sort of cancel each other out. (p. 510)

It appears that students in the experimental group were recalling experiences and challenges that were a part of the game play of *Supercharged!*, whereas students in the control group relied more on their ability to memorize information. Playing *Supercharged!* enabled some students to confront their everyday (mis)conceptions of electrostatics as they played through levels that contradicted these conceptions.

But Squire and his colleagues also acknowledge that the teachers came to realize that students were initially playing *Supercharged!* without a good deal of critical reflection on their play. The teachers then created log sheets for their students to record their actions and make predictions, which reinforced the purpose of the activity and encouraged students to detect patterns in their play. Later the teachers provided even more structure, using the projector to display game levels, encouraging the class to interpret the events happening on screen and make predictions about how they thought the simulation would behave. This added structure added more focus to students' play and allowed the teacher to prompt deeper reflection on game play.

So we see, here, then a good example of what I would call a "post-progressive pedagogy" (Gee, 2004), a well-integrated combination of embodied immersion in rich experience (the game wherein the learner virtually enters an electromagnetic field) and scaffolding and guidance, both through the design of the game itself as a learning resource and through teachers making the game part of a larger coherent learning activity system. The argument is not for games in and of themselves, but as part and parcel of a well-designed learning activity system.

Augmented by Reality: Madison 2020

In their Madison 2020 project, David Shaffer and Kelly Beckett at the University of Wisconsin have developed, implemented, and assessed a game-like simulation that simulates some of the activities of professional urban planners (Beckett & Shaffer, 2004; see also Shaffer, Squire, Halverson, & Gee, 2005; see Shaffer 2007 for a definitive discussion of his "epistemic games"). I call this a "game" because learners are using a simulation and role-playing new identities, but, of course, it is not a "game" in any traditional sense.

Shaffer and Beckett's game is not a stand-alone entity but is used as part of a larger learning system. Shaffer and Beckett call their approach to game-like learning "augmented by reality," since a virtual reality—that is, the game simulation—is augmented or supplemented by real-world activities, in this case further activities of the sort in which urban planners engage. Minority high-school students in a summer enrichment program engaged with Shaffer and Beckett's urban planning simulation game and, as they did so, their problem-solving work in the game was guided by real-world tools and practices taken from the domain of professional urban planners.

As in the game *SimCity*, in Shaffer and Beckett's game, students make land use decisions and consider the complex results of their decisions. However, unlike in *SimCity*, they use real-world data and authentic planning practices to inform those decisions. The game and the learning environment in which it is embedded is based on David Shaffer's theory of *pedagogical praxis*, a theory that argues that modeling learning environments on authentic professional practices—in this case, the practices of urban planners—enables young people to develop deeper understandings of important domains of inquiry (Shaffer, 2005).

Shaffer and Beckett argue that the environmental dependencies in urban areas have the potential to become a fruitful context for innovative learning in ecological education. While ecology is, of course, a broader domain than the study of interdependent urban relationships, cities are examples of complex systems that students can view and with which they are familiar. Thus, concepts in ecology can be made tangible and relevant.

Cities are comprised of simple components, but the interactions among those components are complex. Altering one variable affects all the others, reflecting the interdependent, ecological relationships present in any modern city. For example, consider the relationships among industrial sites, air pollution, and land property values: increasing industrial sites can lead to pollution that, in turn, lowers property values, changing the dynamics of the city's neighborhoods in the process.

Shaffer and Beckett's Madison 2020 project situated student experience at a micro level by focusing on a single street in their own city (Madison, Wisconsin):

> Instead of the fast-paced action required to plan and maintain virtual urban environments such as *SimCity*, this project focused only on an initial planning stage, which involved the development of a land use plan for this one street. And instead of using only a technological simulation [i.e., the game, JPG], the learning environment here was orchestrated by authentic urban planning practices. These professional practices situated the planning tool in a realistic context and provided a framework within which students constructed solutions to the problem. (pp. 11–12)

The middle-school students Shaffer and Beckett worked with had volunteered for a ten-hour workshop (run over two weekend days) focused on city planning and community service. At the beginning of the workshop, the students were given an urban planning challenge. They were asked to create a detailed redesign plan for State Street, a major pedestrian thoroughfare in Madison, and a street quite familiar to all the students in the workshop. Professional urban planners must formulate plans that meet the social, economic, and physical needs of their communities. To align with this practice, students received an informational packet addressed to them as city planners. The packet contained a project directive from the mayor, a city budget plan, and letters from concerned citizens providing input about how they wished to see the city redesigned. The directive asked the student city planners to develop a plan that, in the end, would have to be presented to a representative from the planning department at the end of the workshop.

Students then watched a video about State Street, featuring interviews with people who expressed concerns about the street's redevelopment aligned with the issues in the informational packet (e.g., affordable housing). During the planning phase, students walked to State Street and conducted a site assessment. Following the walk, they worked in teams to develop a land use plan using a custom-designed interactive geographic information system (GIS) called "MadMod." MadMod is a model built using Excel and ArcMap (ESRI, 2003) that lets students assess the ramifications of proposed land use changes.

MadMod—which is the "game" in the learning system—allows students to see a virtual representation of State Street. It has two components, a decision space and a constraint table. The decision space displays address and zoning information about State Street using official two-, or three-letter zoning codes to designate changes in land use for property parcels on the street. As students made decisions about changes they wished to make, they received immediate feedback about the consequences of changes in the constraint table. The constraint table showed the effects of changes on six planning issues raised in the original information packet and the video: crime, revenue, jobs, waste, car trips, and housing. Following the professional practices of urban planners, in the final phase of the workshop, students presented their plans to a representative from the city planning office.

MadMod functions in Shaffer and Beckett's curriculum as a game in much the same way as *SimCity* does. In my view, video games are simulations that have "win states" in terms of goals players have set for themselves. In this case, the students have certain goals and the game lets them see how close or far they are from attaining those goals. At the same time, the game is embedded in a learning system that ensures that those goals and the procedures used to reach them are instantiations of the professional practices and ways of knowing or urban planners.

Shaffer and Beckett show, through a pre-interview/post-interview design, that students in the workshop were able to provide more extensive and explicit definitions of the term "ecology" after the workshop than before it. The students' explanations of ecological issues in the post-interview were more specific about how ecological issues are interdependent or interconnected than in the pre-interview. Concept maps the students drew showed an increased awareness of the complexities present in an urban ecosystem. Thus, students appear to have developed a richer understanding of urban ecology through their work in the project.

One hundred percent of the students said that the workshop changed the way they thought about cities and most said the experience changed the things they paid attention to when walking down a city street in their neighborhood. Better yet, perhaps, Shaffer and Beckett were able to show transfer. Students' responses to novel, hypothetical urban planning problems showed increased awareness of the interconnections among urban ecological issues. All these effects suggest, as Shaffer and Beckett argue, "That students were able to mobilize understanding developed in the context of the redesign of one local street to think more deeply about novel urban ecological issues" (Beckett & Shaffer, 2004, p. 21).

Video Games and Situated Learning

Just as children today often see complex specialist language in their popular culture activities like *Yu-Gi-Oh*, they also see complex and deep learning in their commercial video games. Modern video games set up a learning situation that is situated in the sense that meanings are situated, as we have just seen, and in the sense that skills and concepts are learned in an embodied way that leads to real understanding. There is a reason for this: games place language and learning in a setting that fits very well with how the human mind is built to learn and think. Schools sometimes do not. This is why I have stressed game-like learning above in my discussions of diSessa's work, *Supercharged!*, and *Madison 2020*. Let me explicate what I mean.

Video games are a relatively new technology replete with important, and not yet fully understood, implications (Gee, 2003b). Scholars have often viewed the human mind through the lens of a technology, which they thought worked like the mind. Locke and Hume, for example, argued that the mind was like a blank slate on which experience wrote ideas, taking the technology of literacy as their guide. Much later, modern cognitive scientists argued that the mind worked like a digital computer, calculating generalizations and deductions via a logic-like rule system (Newell & Simon, 1972). More recently, some cognitive scientists, inspired by distributed parallel-processing computers and complex adaptive networks, have argued that the mind works by storing records of actual experiences and constructing intricate patterns of connections among them (Clark, 1989; Gee, 1992). So we get different pictures of the mind: mind as a slate waiting to be written on, mind as software, and mind as a network of connections.

Human societies get better through history at building technologies that more closely capture some of what the human mind can do and getting these technologies to do mental work publicly. Writing, digital computers, and networks each allow us to externalize some functions of the mind. Though they are not commonly thought of in these terms, video games are a new technology in this same line. They are a new tool with which to think about the mind and through which we can externalize some of its functions. Video games of the sort I am concerned with—games like *Half-Life 2*, *Rise of Nations*, *Full Spectrum Warrior*, *Morrowinds: The Elder Scrolls*, and *World of WarCraft*—are what I would call "action-and-goal-directed preparations for, and simulations of, embodied experience." A mouthful, indeed, but an important one.

To make clear what I mean by the claim that games act like the human mind and are a good place to study and produce human thinking and learning, let me first briefly summarize some recent research in cognitive science, (Bransford, Brown, & Cocking, 2000). Consider, for instance, the remarks below [in the quotes below, the word "comprehension" means "understanding words, actions, events, or things"]:

> ...comprehension is grounded in perceptual simulations that prepare agents for situated action. (Barsalou, 1999, p. 77)

> ...to a particular person, the meaning of an object, event, or sentence is what that person can do with the object, event, or sentence. (Glenberg, 1997, p. 3)

What these remarks mean is this: human understanding is not primarily a matter of storing general concepts in the head or applying abstract rules to experience. Rather, humans think and understand best when they can imagine (simulate) an experience in such a way that the simulation prepares them for actions they need and want to take in order to accomplish their goals (Barsalou, 1999; Clark, 1997; Glenberg, 1997).

Video games turn out to be the perfect metaphor for what this view of the mind amounts to, just as slates and computers were good metaphors for earlier views of the mind. To see this, let me now turn to a characterization of video games, and then I will put my remarks about the mind and games together.

Video games usually involve a visual and auditory world in which the player manipulates a virtual character (or characters). They often come with editors or other sorts of software with which the player can make changes to the game world or even build a new game world. The player can make a new landscape, a new set of buildings, or new characters. The player can set up the world so that certain sorts of actions are allowed or disallowed. The player is building a new world but is doing so by using and modifying the original visual images (really the code for them) that came with the game. One simple example of this is the way in which players can build new skateboard parks in a game like *Tony Hawk Pro Skater*. The player must place ramps, trees, grass, poles, and other things in the space available in such a way that players can manipulate their virtual characters to skate the park in a fun and challenging way.

Even when players are not modifying games, they play them with goals in mind, the achievement of which counts as their "win state" (and it's the existence of such win states that, in part, distinguishes games from simulations). These goals are set by the player, but, of course, in collaboration with the world the game designers have created (and, at least in more open-ended games, players don't just accept developers' goals, they make real choices of their own). Players must carefully consider the design of the world and consider how it will or will not facilitate specific actions they want to take to accomplish their goals.

One technical way that psychologists have talked about this sort of situation is through the notion of "affordances" (Gibson, 1979). An "affordance" is a feature of the world (real or virtual) that will allow for a certain action to be taken, but only if it is matched by an ability in an actor who has the wherewithal to carry out such an action. For example, in the massive multiplayer game *World of WarCraft* stags can be killed and skinned (for making leather), but only by characters that have learned the Skinning skill. So a stag is an affordance for skinning for such a player, but not for one who has no such skill. The large spiders in the game are not an affordance for skinning for any players, since they cannot be skinned at all. Affordances are relationships between the world and actors.

Playing *World of WarCraft*, or any other video game, is all about such affordances. The player must learn to *see* the game world—designed by the developers but set in motion in particular directions by the players, and, thus, co-designed by them—in terms of such affordances (Gee, 2005). Broadly speaking, players must think in terms of "What are the features of this world that can enable the actions I am capable of carrying out and that I want to carry out in order to achieve my goals?"

So now, after our brief bit about the mind and about games, let's put the two together. The view of the mind I have sketched, in fact, argues, as far as I am concerned, that the mind works rather like a video game. For humans, effective thinking is more like running a simulation than it is about forming abstract generalizations cut off from experiential realities. Effective thinking is about perceiving the world such that the human actor sees how the world, at a specific time and place (as it is given, but also modifiable), can afford the opportunity for actions that will lead to a successful accomplishment of the actor's goals. Generalizations are formed, when they are, bottom-up from experience and imagination of experience. Video games externalize the search for affordances, for a match between the character (actor) and the world, but this is just the heart and soul of effective human thinking and learning in any situation.

As a game player you learn to see the world of each different game you play in quite different ways. But in each case you see the world in terms of how it will afford the sorts of embodied actions you (and your virtual character, your surrogate body in the game) need to take to accomplish your goals (to win in the short and long run). For example, you see the world in *Full Spectrum Warrior* as routes (for your squad) between cover (e.g., corner-to-corner, house-to-house) because this prepares you for the actions you need to take, namely attacking without being vulnerable to attack yourself. You see the world of *Thief* in terms of light and dark, illumination and shadows, because this prepares you for the different actions you need to take in this world, namely hiding, disappearing into the shadows, sneaking, and otherwise moving unseen toward your goal.

When we sense such a match, in a virtual world or the real world, between our way of seeing the world, at a particular time and place, and our action goals—and we have the skills to carry these actions out—then we feel great power and satisfaction. Things click, the world looks as if it were made for us. While commercial games often stress a match between worlds and characters like soldiers or thieves, there is no reason why other games could not let players experience such a match between the world and the way a particular type of scientist, for instance, sees and acts on the world (Gee, 2004). Such games would involve facing the sorts of problems and challenges that that type of scientist faces, and living and playing by the rules that that type of scientist uses. Winning in such a game would give a student just what it gives a scientist: the feeling of a sense of accomplishment through the production of knowledge to solve deep problems.

I have argued for the importance of video games as "action-and-goal-directed preparations for, and simulations of, embodied experience." They are the new technological arena—just as were literacy and computers earlier—around which we can study the mind and externalize some of its most important features to improve human thinking and learning. But games have two other features that suit them to be good models for human thinking and learning externalized out in the world. These two additional features are: (a) they distribute intelligence via the creation of smart tools, and (b) they allow for the creation of "cross functional affiliation," a particularly important form of collaboration in the modern world.

Consider first how good games distribute intelligence (Brown, Collins, & Dugid, 1989). In *Full Spectrum Warrior*, the player uses the buttons on the controller to give orders to two squads of soldiers. The instruction manual that comes with the game makes it clear from the outset that players, in order to play the game successfully, must take on the values, identities, and ways of thinking of a professional soldier: "Everything about your squad," the manual explains, "is the result of careful planning and years of experience on the battlefield. Respect that experience, soldier, since it's what will keep your soldiers alive." In the game, that experience—the skills and knowledge of professional military expertise—is distributed between the virtual soldiers and the real-world player. The soldiers in the player's squads have been trained in movement formations; the role of the player is to select the best position for them on the field. The virtual characters (the soldiers) know part of the task (various movement formations) and the player must come to know another part (when and where to engage in such formations). This kind of distribution holds for every aspect of military knowledge in the game.

By distributing knowledge and skills this way—between the virtual characters (smart tools) and the real-world player—the player is guided and supported by the knowledge built into the virtual soldiers. This offloads some of the cognitive burden from the learner, placing it in smart tools that can do more than the learner is currently capable of doing by himself or herself. It allows the player to begin to act, with some degree of effectiveness, before being really competent—"performance before competence." The player thereby eventually comes to gain competence through trial, error, and feedback, not by wading through a lot of text before being able to engage in activity. Such distribution also allows players to internalize not only the knowledge and skills of a professional (a professional soldier in this case), but also the concomitant values ("doctrine" as the military says) that shape and explain how and why that knowledge is developed and applied in the world. There is no reason why other professions—scientists, doctors, government officials, urban planners (Shaffer, 2004)—could not be modeled and distributed in this fashion as a deep form of value-laden learning (and, in turn, learners could compare and contrast different value systems as they play different games).

Finally, let me turn to the creation of "cross-functional affiliation." Consider a small group partying (hunting and questing) together in a massive multiplayer game like *World of WarCraft*. The group might well be composed of a Hunter, Warrior, Druid, and Priest. Each of these types of characters has quite different skills and plays the game in a different way. Each group member (player) must learn to be good at his or her special skills and also learn to integrate these skills as a team member within the group as a whole. Each team member must also share some common knowledge about the game and game play with all the other members of the group—including some understanding of the specialist skills of other player types—in order to achieve a successful integration. Each member of the group must have specialist knowledge (intensive knowledge) and general common knowledge (extensive knowledge), including knowledge of the other members' functions.

Players—who are interacting with each other, in the game and via a chat system—orient to each other not in terms of their real-world race, class, culture, or gender (these may very well be unknown or, if communicated, made up as fictions). They must orient to each other, first and foremost, through their identities as game players and players of *World of WarCraft* in particular. They can, in turn, use their real-world race, class, culture, and gender as strategic resources if and when they please, and the group can draw on the differential real-world resources of each player, but in ways that do not force anyone into preset racial, gender, cultural, or class categories.

This form of affiliation—what I will call cross-functional affiliation—has been argued to be crucial for the workplace teams in modern "new capitalist" workplaces, as well as in modern forms of social activism (Beck, 1999; Gee, 2004; Gee, Hull, & Lankshear, 1996). People specialize, but integrate and share, organized around a primary affiliation to their common goals and using their cultural and social differences as strategic resources, not as barriers.

So video games, though a part of popular culture, are, like literacy and computers, sites where we can study and exercise the human mind in ways that may give us deeper insights into human thinking and learning, as well as new ways to engage students in deep and engaged learning. What we see here—and it's the same message we saw with *Yu-Gi-Oh* and *Pokemon* before—is that areas of popular culture are beginning to organize thinking and learning in efficacious ways. The practices they recruit—lucidly functional language, situated meanings, and embodied understandings leveraging experiences to build simulations (in the mind and outside it), distributed intelligence, and cross-functional collaborations—are all ones that do not need to be restricted to military games. They are key to deep understanding in any specialist domain, whether in school or at work.

Conclusions

I have argued that learning to read, if a child is not to be a victim of the fourth-grade slump, must involve early preparation for specialist, technical, and academic forms of language, forms that will be seen more and more both in speech and, most characteristically, in writing as school progresses. I have discussed some of the underpinnings of effective early preparation for such styles of language. These underpinnings have included "informal specialist-language lessons," "lucidly functional language" practices, and practices that facilitate "situated meanings." These practices are common in certain homes and in some of the popular cultural practices of children. They are, perhaps, less common in the early years of schooling. More generally, I have argued that a game-like approach to learning—by which I mean, not "having fun," but thinking inside of and with simulations in a situated and embodied way, an approach well represented even in commercial video games—holds out a good deal of potential as a foundation for learning that leads to problem solving and not just passing a paper and pencil test.

References

American Educator (2003). The fourth-grade plunge: The cause. The cure. *American Educator.* Special issue, Spring.

Barsalou, L. W. (1999). Language comprehension: Archival memory or preparation for situated action. *Discourse Processes, 28*, 61–80.

Beck, U. (1999). *World risk society*. Oxford, UK: Blackwell.

Beckett, K. L., & Shaffer, D. W. (2004). Augmented by reality: The pedagogical praxis of urban planning as a pathway to ecological thinking. University of Wisconsin-Madison. Available at: http://www.academiccolab.org/initiatives/gapps.html.

Bransford, J., Brown, A. L., & Cocking, R. R. (2000). *How people learn: Brain, mind, experience, and school: Expanded edition.* Washington, DC: National Academy Press.

Brown, S. L., Collins, A., & Dugid. (1989). Situated cognition and the culture of learning. *Educational Researcher, 18*, 32–42.

Chall, J. S., Jacobs, V., & Baldwin, L. (1990). *The reading crisis: Why poor children fall behind.* Cambridge: Harvard University Press.

Chi, M., Feltovich, P., & Glaser, R. (1981). Categorization and representation of physics problems by experts and novices. *Cognitive Science, 5*(2), 121–152.

Chomsky, N. (1986). *Knowledge of language*. New York: Praeger.

Clark, A. (1989). *Microcognition: Philosophy, cognitive science, and parallel distributed processing.* Cambridge, MA: The MIT Press.

Clark, A. (1993). *Associative engines: Connectionism, concepts, and representational change.* Cambridge, MA: Cambridge University Press.

Clark, A. (1997). *Being there: Putting brain, body, and world together again.* Cambridge, MA: The MIT Press.

Crowley, K., & Jacobs, M. (2002). Islands of expertise and the development of family scientific literacy. In G. Leinhardt, K. Crowley, & K. Knutson (Eds.), *Learning conversations in museums* (pp. 333–356.). Mahwah, NJ: Lawrence Erlbaum.

Dickinson, D. K., & Neuman, S. B. (Eds.). (2006). *Handbook of early literacy research: Volume 2.* New York: Guilford Press.

diSessa, A. A. (2000). *Changing minds: Computers, learning, and literacy.* Cambridge, MA: The MIT Press.

Emergent Literacy Project. (n.d.). *What is emergent literacy?* Available at: http://idahocdhd.org/cdhd /emerlit/facts.asp.

Games-to-Teach Team. (2003). Design principles of next-generation digital gaming for education. *Educational Technology, 43*(5), 17–33.

Gardner, H. (1991). The unschooled mind: How children think and how schools should teach. New York, NY: Basic Books.

Gee, J. P. (1990/1996/2007). *Sociolinguistics and literacies: Ideology in discourses.* London: Taylor & Francis (Second Edition, 2007).

Gee, J. P. (1992). The social mind: Language, ideology, and social practice. New York: Bergin & Garvey.

Gee, J. P. (2003a). Opportunity to learn: A language-based perspective on assessment. *Assessment in Education, 10*(1), 25–44.

Gee, J. P. (2003b). *What video games have to teach us about learning and literacy.* New York: Palgrave/Macmillan.

Gee, J. P. (2004). *Situated language and learning: A critique of traditional schooling.* London: Routledge.

Gee, J. P. (2005). *Why video games are good for your soul: Pleasure and learning.* Melbourne: Common Ground.

Gee, J. P. (2007). *Good video games and good learning: Collected essays on video games, learning, and literacy.* New York: Peter Lang.

Gee, J. P. (2008). *Getting over the slump: Innovation strategies to promote children's learning.* New York: The Joan Ganz Cooney Center at Sesame Workshop.

Gee, J. P., Hull, G., & Lankshear, C. (1996). *The new work order: Behind the language of the new capitalism.* Boulder, CO: Westview.

Gibson, J. J. (1979). *The ecological approach to visual perception.* Boston, MA: Houghton Mifflin.

Glenberg, A. M. (1997). What is memory for. *Behavioral and Brain Sciences, 20,* 1–55.

Labov, W. (1979). The logic of nonstandard English. In P.Giglioli (Ed.), *Language and social context* (pp. 179–215). Middlesex, UK: Penguin Books.

McFarlane, A., Sparrowhawk, A., & Heald, Y. (2002). *Report on the educational use of games: An exploration by TEEM of the contribution which games can make to the education process.* Cambridge, UK: Cambridge University Press.

Newell, A. and Simon, H. A. (1972). *Human problem solving.* Englewood Cliffs, NJ: Prentice Hall.

Pinker, S. (1994). *The language instinct: How the mind creates language.* New York: William Morrow.

Schleppegrell, M. (2004). Language of schooling: A functional linguistics perspective. Mahwah. NJ: Lawrence Erlbaum.

Senechal, M., Ouellette, G., & Rodney D. (2006). The misunderstood giant: Predictive role of early vocabulary to future reading. In D. K. Dickinson & S. B. Neuman, (Eds.), *Handbook of early literacy research: Volume 2.* (pp. 173–182). New York: Guilford Press.

Shaffer, D. W. (2005). Epistemic games. *Innovate 1*(6). Available at: http://www.innovateonline.info/index.php?view=article&id=81

Shaffer, D. W. (2007). *How computer games help children learn*. New York: Palgrave/Macmillan.

Shaffer, D.W., Squire, K.D., Halverson, R., & Gee, J.P. (2005). Video games and the future of learning. *Phi Delta Kappan, 87*(2), 105–111.

Snow, C. E., Burns, M. S., & Griffin, P., (Eds.). (1998). *Preventing reading difficulties in young children*. Washington: National Academy Press.

Squire, K. (2003). Video games in education. *International Journal of Intelligent Games and Simulation, 2*(1). Retrieved November 1, 2003, from http://www.scit.wlv.ac.uk/~cm1822/ijkurt.pdf.

Squire, K.D. (2006). From content to context: Video games as designed experience. *Educational Researcher, 35*(8), 19–29.

Squire, K. (2007). Games, learning, and society: Building a field. *Educational Technology, 4*(5), 51–54.

Squire, K., Barnett, M., Grant, J. M., & Higginbotham, T., (2004). Electromagnetism Supercharged! Learning physics with digital simulation games. In Y. B. Kafai, W. A. Sandoval, N. Enyedy, A. S. Nixon & F. Herrera (Eds.), *Proceedings of the sixth international conference of the learning sciences* (pp. 513–520). Mahwah, NJ: Lawrence Erlbaum.

Vygotsky, L. S. (1978). *Mind in society: The development of higher psychological processes*. Cambridge, MA: Harvard University Press.

CHAPTER SIX

Between Physical and Virtual Spaces: The Literacy Practices of High School Students

CARMEN PÉREZ-FRAGOSO[1]

History shows that young people have been in the vanguard in the use of technologies, and the current era is no exception (McPherson, 2008). What makes the difference today is the diversity and the level of complexity of the available tools, creating a situation in which, "for the first time in the history of humanity, a new generation is trained to use the technology better than their parents" (Eio, cited in Balardini, 2004, p. 109). As Livingstone (2008) notes, only on rare occasions have children achieved levels of command greater than their parents in relation to skills that have a high social value. This is the case of children of immigrants who learn the language of the new country faster than their parents. In terms of skills in the use of Information and Communication Technologies (ICTs), young people not only have a greater command but stand out in terms of the creativity and professionalism of their productions.

The amount of textual, video, animation, audio, and multimedia productions that we find in cyberspace has increased in proportions unthinkable several years ago, and a good number of the authors of these works are very young people, most of them self-taught. McPherson (2008) explains that currently, around the world, the majority of learning occurs outside of school. The enormous amount of information to which we have access through technologies is far greater than the amount of information communicated

1 I sincerely thank Tania Elisabet Zavala Martinez and Sara Alicia Villavicencio Aguilar, both college students majoring in education sciences and project fellows, for their participation in this study.

through formal instruction and textbooks. Jenkins (2004) confirms this and shows evidence that some of the best teaching—the most influential—occurs outside of the classroom, through participation in online communities.

Before beginning, it is important to clarify that our interest is not in sanctifying or condemning technologies but rather recognizing their role as companions of specific social practices, carried out in specific contexts with defined objectives. We do not seek to minimize the multiple dimensions of the problems of the digital divide and the inequalities in access and use of ICTs. We are aware that they make evident the prevalent exclusions in society. We believe, as Granjon (2004) notes, that the inequalities related to ICTs do not reveal new social divisions, but rather are the expressions of inequalities that preceded the dissemination of ICTs. At the same time, though it appears contradictory, we also agree with DiMaggio and Hargittai (2001) who state that the growing penetration of the Internet shows that the division, in terms of access, is reduced for a greater part of the population. On the other hand, we also eschew a sentimental vision of young people's use of ICTs. Moje (2007) prevents us from falling into the "romanticism" of this media and our amazement and surprise at the wonders that some young people create with certain technologies. Herring (2008) criticizes the tendency of adults to consider young people's use of technologies as exotic, encouraging us to focus on the communication needs of young people more than in the media that they use.

Terrero (1997) indicates that as a social phenomenon, the profusion of video apparatuses, from television to iPhones, tends to construct cultural formations centered on the continual presence of image-sound. This creates a new modality of technological integration and interaction with information and entertainment networks for households. She notes that the diversity of available technologies on the market makes visible, through consumerism, both social inequality and sociocultural differences in terms of access and use, as well as showing the tendency towards universalism. She also states that this tendency has allowed us to "verify shared modalities, collective uses of the media, ways of appropriation that involve all social classes, ways of circulating products, ideas, stories, forms, representations that are generalized in a culture that tends to universalize and that cuts across all sectors and individuals, becoming the axis of a common culture and of a new way of creating social relationships."

The objective of this study, from which we take this case, was to identify the use of ICTs among a group of young public high school students from low-income families. We were particularly interested in examining: (1) if (and to what extent) the restricted access of some technologies and material goods limited the skills, and as a result the practices, of these young people in computer and Internet use, and (2) if (and how) new forms of cultural and social relationships are expressed.

According to Levinson (2007), a correlation does not necessarily exist between formal literacy (acquired in school) and social and economic empowerment; there are other variables that carry more weight in explaining the relationship between meaningful literacies for people and their economic and/or social success. Further, as Selwyn (2007) indicates, effective access to ICTs is contingent on diverse types of resources, beyond the material resources necessary for the equipment and service. The social and cultural resources of ICT users allows them to position themselves and obtain greater possibilities for better paying jobs (Seiter, 2008). These resources, as Moje, Overby, Tysvaer, and Morris (2008, p. 27) state, have a continual feedback relationship in which, "social capital provides access to social networks, and social networks provide opportunities to build social capital." The literacy promoted in schools must also build this social capital. Digital literacies must be fostered within school as these skills are central to people's labor, civic, and artistic performance in the twenty-first century (Black, 2005).

In order to analyze the case and discuss literacy practices we have taken concepts from New Literacy Studies (NLS) and studies on youth cultures. From the former, we will use concepts of literacy, practice, and event, exploring their roots and supporting our arguments in the theory and discourse outlined by James Paul Gee, among others, on D/discourse (with capital D and lower case d), social languages, identity kits, and affinity spaces. By locating the NLS concepts in youth culture studies, we support our arguments with the work of Elizabeth Moje who considers that youth cultures are multiple, dynamic, changing, and complex, where young people test, consolidate, accept, and reject new identities. In this section we will review the theoretical proposals on adolescence and early youth regarding the formation of identities as well as young people's literacy practices in their physical and virtual spaces.

D/discourse and New Literacy Studies

According to Gee (2001), "Meaning in language is tied to people's experiences of situated action in the material and social world" (p. 715). In other words, meaning is always situated in a particular context. The context, for Gee (1999), does not only refer to the words, actions, and artifacts that surround conversations, but also includes the objectives, values, and intentions of the actions and interactions of the participants in communication events.

Gee (2001) argues that language is not uniform, but rather it is comprised of a wide variety of different styles, registers, and social languages. Each social language is related to a specific type of social activity and with a specific socially situated identity. Therefore, Gee makes a distinction between the two levels of discourse. The first, with a capital D, refers to the social languages that allow speakers to actively participate in a specific community, while discourse (in lower case) refers to the language in use. With this distinction, Gee emphasizes the interrelation between social relationships and identities, and the contexts and the specific situations of language use (McKay, 2003). Discourses involve more than language: "A Discourse integrates ways of talking, listening, writing, reading, acting, interacting, believing, valuing, and feeling (and using various objects, symbols, images, tools, and technologies) in the service of enacting meaningful socially situated identities and activities" (Gee, 2001, p.719). These Discourses can be seen as sets of tools or *identity kits* inasmuch as they constitute the elements that permit the display of a specific identity and participation in the activities associated to that identity in such a way that the enacted social role is recognized by others (Gee, 1996). In other words, the command of these identity kits (ways of talking, dressing, thinking, etc.) "can be used to identify oneself as a member of a socially meaningful group or 'social network'" (Gee, 1996, p. 131).

The debate on the formation of identities acquires special importance in this day and age. As Buckingham (2008) states, globalization and the disappearance of the Welfare State, among other factors, contributes to the creation of a sense of uncertainty and fragmentation in which the traditional resources for the formation of identity are more opaque and difficult to access. In express reference to the youth population, Martín Barbero (2003) indicates that "there is no longer only one reference map for their identity since there are multiple references for their ways of belonging and therefore they are identified in different environments with different spaces, experiences and roles" (p. 21). He adds that today's young people find themselves trapped in a paradox, where society simultaneously demands that they take responsibility for themselves, but without providing clarity about their work, professional, and moral future.

Referring again to Gee's proposals in this complex scenario, identities are neither innate nor arise in a vacuum; instead, they are constructed through social interactions with members of specific discursive communities. The majority of social languages are not acquired through direct instruction, but rather through a process of socialization. In order to have command over them, that is, recognize and produce them, immersion in the meaningful practices of the specific group or community is necessary (Gee, 2001). The theoretical tools of the NLS share with Gee a sociocultural perspective whereby the use of language and its expressions are considered social practices. In this way, literacy is seen as plural, and literacies are associated with distinct social practices, in the same way that Gee argues that one cannot speak of a single Discourse, but rather Discourses (Trier, 2006).

For Gee, Discourses and literacies are inseparable. To be recognized as a member of a discursive community—of a Discourse—requires evidence of the command of the tools (vocabulary, forms of oral and written expression, dress, ideology, etc.) that allow one to talk and act appropriately in order to assume and represent a determined role or identity.

From the perspective of the NLS, Barton & Hamilton (2000) state that literacy practices involve not only the observable activities of people when they read or write, but additionally and most importantly, they involve the non-observable aspects such as their knowledge, feelings, intentions, etcetera. The NLS conceive literacy practices as social practices that go much farther than traditional written texts. Street (2003) says that literacy practices should not be seen as a group of neutral competencies, but instead, as ideological practices, as a complex grouping of practices and values always involved in power relations, inseparable from the cultural meanings and practices in which they are expressed. Therefore, research from the perspective of the NLS analyzes the ways in which literacy practices are situated in specific social, cultural, and political contexts.

Literary practices, as the central concept of the NLS, can only be studied through the analysis of literacy events and the texts involved in those events, given that the practices can only be inferred from the events mediated by the texts. The NLS researchers use the metaphor of an iceberg in order to signal that what we see, the events, is only the tip, a part of the specific individual contribution in a determined time and space, but that the base, the largest part and what gives them social substance and meaning, remains hidden, impossible to observe but only inferred. Current or new literacy practices are derived from traditional or conventional literacy practices. Likewise, on an individual scale, the way in which people produce meanings depends on one's own life story, and one's life story is affected by their literacy practices. As Barton and Hamilton (2000, p. 13) state, "Literacy practices are as fluid, dynamic and changing as the lives and societies of which they are a part." Thus, an historical approach is needed for an understanding of the ideology, culture, and traditions on which current practices are based, at the global scale as literacy practices and at the individual scale, in the history of a person's life.

One of the NLS' most important contributions is the repositioning of literacy as originating from individual observable activities carried out with isolated texts to positioning it in broadly dispersed and complex practices whose analysis requires locating their meaning in a social dimension as cultural practices sustained in power relationships in different contexts and cultures. The analysis of these practices makes evident two levels: a social collective level where literacy practices are seen as ideological, always and everywhere, and an individual level where the identity work of the participants is reflected, acting as coconstructors of identities (Leander & Johnson, 2002).

The Discourse and Literacy Practices of Young People

The different Discourses and their literacy practices can be considered as subcultures existing within one broad culture or society (McCarthey & Moje, 2002; McKay, 2003; Moje, 2007). In this way, a person can belong simultaneously to various subcultures, in other words, participate in different Discourses. For example, Moje (2007) identifies aspects of overlap, hybridization, and complement in family, ethnic, and religious cultures, in groups of young people from different social backgrounds.

Adolescence and early youth are periods in which individuals are confronted with the task of defining their identity (Coleman, 2008; Stern, 2008). The general theories on adolescent identity assume that adolescence is a critical period of identity formation, and therefore, a period of intense experimentation (Coleman, 2008; Stern, 2008; Valkenburg, Schouten, & Peter, 2005). The studies of youth cultures show that adolescence and early youth, as stages of life, are complex periods in which young people seek new experiences in order to test, consolidate, accept, and reject new identities; it is a period in which their actions always have a purpose, a well-defined intention.

Moje starts from the premise that young people's lives provide them with multiple types of texts and sources of information, different forms of contact with people from varied geographic and socioeconomic origins and very diverse experiences. This, Moje (2002) explains, is because young people are immersed in many environments: between childhood and adulthood, between play and work, between home and school and friends, between romance and sex, between classes of diverse disciplines (history, biology, mathematics), between cartoons, magazines and the Internet, between the local community and the global market, etcetera. Precisely because of their age, young people have opportunities to make interesting choices among texts, experiences, and practices. The unstructured way in which these opportunities are presented makes young people confront obstacles in developing themselves, and they are obliged to negotiate different experiences, frequently disconnected. These experiences can empower young people and prepare them for the challenges of the future labor market in the current changing world.

Moje (2007) conducted a literature review of the research on youth culture(s) and found four basic assumptions regarding the concept, which are:

1. A plurality of youth cultures
2. A distinction (and overlap) between youth and popular cultures
3. A distinction (and overlap) between youth and ethnic cultures
4. The recognition of the influence of social class and socioeconomic status on the generation and maintenance of youth cultures

In regard to the first point, Moje (2007) explains that some research mentions youth culture as a unitary construct, in spite of the fact that the concept of culture is considered a dynamic, changing, and plural concept; it is not possible to speak of a homogenous youth culture, as there are multiple cultures. In her work, Moje has verified that young people especially derive meanings from what happens in the world, in accordance with their affinity groups, lifestyles, and youth cultures. In this sense, Moje (2007) argues that popular cultures and youth cultures are closely related; one depends on the other and gives life to the other. This relationship is well documented, both in physical spaces (i.e., Moje, 2004) as well as virtual spaces (i.e., Black, 2005, 2007). The latter, because of their very nature, allow for greater diversity of expressions and fusions, as in the case of memes[2] (Knobel & Lankshear, 2007) or collective texts of characters in popular books or television programs-*fan fiction* (Black, 2005, 2007). Children (i.e., Kendrick, 2005) and adolescents (i.e., Black, 2007) use popular cultural resources to position themselves in their social, physical, and virtual networks. In regards to the aspects of overlap between youth and family cultures, especially in relation to ethnic origins, Moje (2002, 2007) has observed that young people do not necessarily reject the values, experiences, and practices of their parents, but instead articulate and inject the values and interweave the practices of adults in their families in other spaces and social relationships in their daily lives. Among others, Moje (2007) and Moje et al. (2008) state that the way in which youth cultures position themselves in society is closely related to young people's economic resources and social networks.

Finally, social networks bring us to another central concept in order to understand the literacy practices in virtual spaces, the concept of affinity spaces. According to Gee (2004), shared spaces are arising, above all, in video-games, which cannot be explained with the concept of communities of practice, and instead, he names these spaces, affinity spaces. The difference between them and communities of practice are clear: affinity spaces do not require group membership, or feelings of belonging. In virtual spaces, people are geographically disperse and affiliated around a topic or cause, and with the exception of this shared interest, do not have other things in common (Stone, 2007). People act and relate to one another in order to fulfill joint tasks in regards to an issue or activity of mutual interest. The affiliation to one group, defined in this way, emphasizes the precedence for the group that the activities of shared interest have over social class, gender, and ethnic questions. The socio-demographic variables of the participants continue to be present, but are relegated to a second plane, highlighting the affinity for common interests, the

---

2 "Memes are contagious patterns of cultural information that are passed from mind to mind and propagate key actions and mindset of a social group... "They include melodies, icons, phrases, and fashion statements" (Lankshear & Knobel 2006, p. 211).

delight for something, or the common project (Black, 2007). These spaces are structured around informal leaderships, where experts and amateurs share and value different forms of knowledge.

Literacy Practices in Young People's Physical and Virtual Spaces

The literacy practices that ICTs use are not isolated, but rather, are related to the social structures that give them form and that they help to form within physical as well as virtual spaces (McCarthey & Moje, 2002; Cammack, 2005; McGinnis, Goodstein-Stolzenberg, & Costa Saliani, 2007). These ICT literacy practices are mutually reinforcing. This argument stems from the fact that online literacy practices are sustained in complex ways by practices offline that are not easy to separate or to rigidly categorize as on or offline (Cammack, 2005). The intention behind the practices is central. Myers (2006) warns of the risks in separating literacy practices carried out with traditional tools from those carried out with new tools. Myers says that literacy practices should be considered as social practices in evolution that combine the use of new and old tools in order to achieve the objectives of the users in a better way.

Similarly, Leander, & Johnson (2002) conceive literacy practices (both on and offline) as dynamic and relational, without considering either as primary or independent of the other. Given the conditions of contemporary life, where digital media modifies our sense of time and space, the traditional boundaries between times and spaces, and public and private are erased. For adults, this means that they can work from home, socialize from work, shop or carry out banking transactions at night; all are activities inconceivable when the baby boom generation entered into the adult world. For young people, the fact that these possibilities have been present since their infancy makes the activities carried out through digital media as real as those carried out in their immediate physical world. This blurring of what is real and what is virtual, according to Leander and Johnson (2002) involves a change in the sense of what it means to have an experience and an evolution in the meaning of what is authentic in an interaction. In other words, the experiences in both physical and virtual spaces are equally valuable and meaningful, and together they form the living world.

Another characteristic of virtual spaces is that they provide young people with spaces for choices to test, reject or reaffirm their identities and form and consolidate their identity tools for the future (Moje, 2002). In these spaces of socialization between peers, perceived by them as safe, horizontal, and equitable, young people share and generate their visions of the world. As Guichard (2001) says, media space is a space of liberty, which users explore with different intentions and projects. The contents that they produce and to which they have access are of their own choosing, in their free time, practiced intermittently, recognized, and validated by them and their peers. Boyd (2006, 2007) observes that young people consider these online spaces to be private, to be "youth spaces" (Boyd, 2006, p. 5). Similarly, Stern (2008) reports that many young people consider communication that is not seen or heard by people who know them in their immediate environment as private, regardless of the number of people who know of it, giving a different meaning to what we consider as private.

We cannot isolate the virtual practices from the contexts and physical spaces in which they are generated. As Moje (2004) indicates, all spaces, physical and virtual, are spaces of identity representation, and these representations give form and are formed by literacy practices. Moje also observes that young people carry out their literacy practices in order to establish, reclaim, or construct new spaces and specific identities. Young people navigate between physical and virtual spaces effortlessly, as part of their daily social practices. As Moje (2002) notes, it is the movement between these spaces in which new forms—new texts and new literacies—of cultural production emerge.

Literacy Practices in Different Contexts: The Case of Martha

The case of Martha (a pseudonym) forms part of a broader study on the uses of ICTs by high school students. This study began four years ago and includes, in addition to the analysis of interviews and interviewee productions, the analysis of electronic registries of high school students' user sessions with different technologies, including a public chat, a private chat, bulletin boards, and weblogs. The interviews with Martha were carried out between June 2007 and June 2008. In order to discuss this case we have selected several aspects that we think contribute to the discussion of the production of young people's identities in virtual spaces. Specifically, we are interested in highlighting the role of family and school in the development of digital literacy practices, the importance of recognition of identities by peers, the search for professional models and the hybridization of identities, and lastly, the navigation between physical and virtual spaces.

We met Martha when she was 18 and in her last semester of high school. She lives with her parents and twin brother in a mobile home in a semi-urban zone, "in a trailer," in her own words (expressions and comments by Martha are indicated by quotations). At home, her family has a telephone and a television that gets the public television channels but cable services are not available in their somewhat isolated area. She has a personal computer but it does not work, a "stereo" for listening to music, and a digital camera ("without a lot of memory"). They do not have Internet and she does not have a cell phone.

This lack of electronic equipment is an indicator of her family's lower working-class economic status. She attends high school in the same area during the mornings. The school has 45 computers for student use (one computer for every 20 students). During the academic year 2006–2007 the school had an enrollment of 875 students. Since the time of our first interviews, Martha entered graphic design studies in a prestigious private local university where she receives a full scholarship.

Returning to the time of our first interview, it became evident that Martha is someone inclined towards the visual arts and she likes to experiment and produce works that integrate images (fixed and in movement) and sound. Her literacy activities and practices on and offline are directed primarily at developing her visual art skills. She is interested in "photography, painting, drawing in general, and computer drawing in particular."

Her offline activities consist primarily of pencil drawing, modifying photographs on the computer, making Movie Maker presentations, and modifying songs. The computer programs that she uses most are Corel (and Corel Trace to trace her images in ink in order to paint them more easily), OpenCanvas (for painting), PhotoFiltre and Photopaint (to edit her photographs), and My MP3 (to record and edit audio). She suspended her use of Audacity because the version that she downloaded had a virus. One of her favorite programs is SUPER, which she primarily uses to extract audio from videos. In high school she was taught to use the Office package but she almost never uses Excel or Access. When she got a virus while using Office she obtained Open Office, which she used for a time but found it to be limiting for what she wanted to do. Before her home computer got a fatal virus, she would spend about four hours a day working on it.

Without Internet access at home, Martha concentrates her activities while paying for access at Internet cafes. She told us, "When I get a chance to go to an Internet café I grab two hours." She has used it on many occasions for school research but, "I realize that sometimes it is more satisfying to find information at the library because sometimes I find a lot of pages [online] that aren't what I am looking for, and I waste time, then I go to the library and get the book that I want and there it is." She uses the Internet primarily for researching questions that arise from her recreational reading, "For example, when I am in my house reading a magazine, there is always something that interests me and if it isn't fully explained then I go to the Internet and I resolve the doubts I have." Likewise, when she goes to Internet cafes, Martha has a "passion for looking at photographs on the Internet, visiting blogs, I like that a lot." But what she most appreciates about the Internet is, "making friends from other parts, getting to know their culture or listening to what they say to me about where they live or things like that." Her productions include drawings and photographs as well as songs that she has composed (she uploads the words and also sings them). "I like that they tell me that they like the words, regardless of the music or my singing."

Martha moves between her physical and virtual spaces in a natural and continuous way, knowledgeable of the possibilities and limitations of each one. Some extracts from the interviews with Martha reveal this level of consciousness, "I have found that my pastimes and the things that I like aren't things that people around here like. It's difficult to find compatibility with people in my environment, for example, ...and sometimes on the Internet I go and look for someone with my same interests and I find them, since it's what I like most, that way I can find out things more easily."

Martha is conscious of the limitations for meeting young people with her same interests in her immediate physical social environment and, she turns to electronic media as a way to solve this. For her, this is not a disadvantage; it is simply an easy and accessible way to find people she can relate to.

The Role of Family and School

The role of the family is central to Martha's computer access. She explained that when her computer got a fatal virus, she began to save her wages from her work in an Internet café, which she later left because it interfered with her studies. "I thought about working more time there in order to buy a computer. I was going to buy it at Elektra [a local department store], but my father, who came with me, had made some notes from a magazine about the kind of computer that someone who studies graphics design needs, and we went to check them out and [the computers that the store had available] didn't have the capacity. They weren't good enough and they were very expensive...so I need to wait."

The above experience coincides with Livingstone's (2008) findings that in order to engage in a creative and meaningful use of technologies, young people not only need economic resources and time, but more importantly, the support of their family. In Martha's case, her comments about her family's dynamics demonstrate that she feels understood and supported.

Another form of interaction with her family is based on her ability to help her parents with their computational skills. For example,

> In my house, my mother says to me: "ah, I wish you cooked more often," since I don't do it very often, but for example she likes to sing [and says], "ah I want to go somewhere so they can record me and make a track,..." It was like her dream or something like that. So, at that time I had a small computer and I told her to set up a [physical] space and we closed the room so I could record her voice while she put on

> the audio phones, and then later I edited her voice on the track....It's something simple, but she doesn't know how to do it and they would have charged her like 2,000 pesos to make a CD with 14 songs, and here it was free. So these are things that motivate me and her also. Or for example, my father said, "Ah, I want a magazine but I missed a certain number, could you go online and get it?" And then, "I want to print it with Adobe," and he doesn't know how, things like that, and so I look it up online for him.

Her comments related to her twin brother show her admiration and affection for him. "He works, he doesn't study, but we have a similar life....He hasn't become involved with the computer, but he knows more than me about other things."

As much as Martha feels support from her family, difficulties within the family have their consequences as well. When family problems come up, she feels them intensely and they affect her performance. For example, when her mother lost her job, Martha's grade point average fell. "It was a situation that I didn't expect and it lowered my morale and, I don't know, I didn't make the same effort, but I also didn't give up, I didn't fail that bad."

Martha assigns an important role to her achievements at school, "When I was studying at [name of the high school], they gave me the opportunity to demonstrate my skills, for example in painting competitions, and that is when I made some paintings, and some were good, so I applied for a talent scholarship from [name of the university] and they gave me a full scholarship." However, Martha considers that her perseverance was the most important factor in obtaining the scholarship: "What I attribute this most to was to my persistence." She went to the university frequently for information on the requirements and exams needed to qualify for a scholarship.

Martha also credits her school with her developing artistic abilities. "In terms of my drawings, I always demand a lot of myself. The truth is that I think I have developed myself well, at least since I was in high school, when I was very influenced by *manga*.[3] Now I have separated myself a little and have tried to find my own style and [thanks to] school and the people that I know, I think I have acquired a style. It's hard to say because it isn't easy to find your own style, but there are people that tell me that my work is professional and that motivates me a lot."

---

3 *Manga* is an artistic genre distinguished by its stylized characters, which have exaggerated eyes and simplified features. The genre comes from Japan, but the term, coined in 1814, consists of two Chinese ideograms: "Man," meaning involuntary or in spite of oneself, and Ga, meaning "pictures" (Gravett, 2004).

Peer Recognition

The value that Martha assigns to recognition by her peers and her authorship is apparent in the following extract: "Now that YouTube is very fashionable I spend time meeting people and I give them my email and that's it. For example, I haven't painted a lot recently because you can upload videos and people communicate with you through this format, through YouTube. They leave comments there, or whatever you like."

For young people, such as Martha, it is not enough to simply upload their texts, because what they seek is recognition by their peers, expressed by their comments and the social relationships that can be derived from them. In her identities production, Martha has tested different formats of text and different media discontinuing the ones that she does not like. She tells us, "I wrote poems or stuff like that you could say, but I don't know, in the end I wrote things that occurred to me and I uploaded them, but later I regretted it. I don't know why, I feel like I'm not very good at these things." She added, "There is always an age when you want to do everything, but you stay with what most satisfies you."

For many young people, as in Martha's case, only through comments that denote recognition (approval or criticism) of other members of the group do they feel that it is worthwhile to participate in specific spaces and activities. The satisfactions derived from their efforts (literary, photographic, and musical) are not rooted in the publication itself, but rather in the response that the publication generates. In this sense, having an online presence in certain spaces ("being seen") is not what is most significant for these young people, but rather the recognition ("being recognized") that they obtain, which is what motivates them to continue experimenting with different media. Gee (2000) confirms the importance of recognition of identities by others. It is not enough that a person assumes a given identity; it must be recognized to be considered as part of the person. The comments that the young people receive also help them to learn about themselves. According to Thomas (2007), young people informally learn to see their strengths and weaknesses as producers of texts (and of meanings) through their peers' feedback. For example, about her songs, Martha explains, "I uploaded two songs, nothing more. I only have five songs that I like. Maybe I will make more, but these five can be heard without people laughing at me. People made some comments on them, some very good, some very bad."

Martha reacts to the comments in different ways, but says: "What I don't like for them to say is, 'you're wasting your time,' or things like that, because they are things that you like to do." She feels highly motivated when she receives positive comments. "There was someone named Salomon who is Spanish and his comments made me feel really happy because he said that my drawings were so good that he thought some publishers might be interested in me." When she receives hostile comments she simply ignores them: "For example, one time someone said to me, 'I don't like you,' and I said...'Why? What did I do?' and anyway, but it doesn't bother me too much... I didn't answer anything bad; I told them that I didn't care, something like that. It was in English, '*I don't like you*' and I said, '*I don't mind*,' and then they responded with something worse and I didn't say anything because, they have their own problems over there that they have to solve, right?" The way in which she responds to hostile remarks coincides with other studies that show that young people are not as susceptible to comments received online, nor as vulnerable to the dangers of the Internet as we adults many times imagine (Cassell & Cramer, 2008).

The recognition by their physical and virtual peers is very important. Apparently, for them, there is no difference in the value they ascribe to their real and virtual peers. Another student mentioned that he plays with his "real neighbors" to clarify to the researcher that his peers are not virtual, and Martha refers to her "meat and bone friendships." In the virtual spaces, Martha likes to receive comments from strangers. She pays attention to comments "from those that I don't know, because it is more fun. Those that I know generally give me comments in person and never put comments for me there." Contrary to the majority of the participants in our study, Martha is very selective in choosing her online peers, "I don't have a lot of contacts, and generally if I don't like them, or if I don't think that they are interesting or if there isn't compatibility online, then I eliminate them from the list."

Martha created her own system for using the available communications tools. Besides her blog in YouTube for her photographs and videos, she has another on Blogger because "it is a little more serious, so when they see something a little more serious they take you more seriously." Martha maintains three electronic mail accounts. Her Yahoo account is for correspondence, her Hotmail account is for MSN chat, and her Gmail account is for saving personal documents that she wants to save for herself or does not want to upload on a blog or publish elsewhere. "I send myself the information that I want to save for myself, for my own use, and that is the way that I use the [Gmail] account. The only one that I use to send email is the Yahoo account. No one is connected and I don't even know how to enter the Chat rooms there, nor does it interest me, I don't know, it's like the design is weird. Hotmail is cooler. I am more familiar with it than with the others."

It is interesting to note the times in which Martha checks her different accounts, which is in direct proportion to her interests. She checks YouTube daily "since there is almost always something that I want to see," meanwhile she checks Blogger, "one or two times a week because I don't draw that much so every time that I upload a drawing maybe one person a week will leave me a comment." She checks her e-mail every three days, "because I get impatient when I send e-mails so I'd check every day, but it feels a little weird to not have anything there so I only check it every three days because I know that every three days I'll have e-mail."

Martha clearly designates her digital literacy practices and her digital media intentions: she has knowledge about the tools and she optimizes them for her own purposes. Her comments about the design of Hotmail and Blogger show her inclinations, analysis, and utilization of the various media/mediums.

The Search for Models and the Hybridization of Identities

The identities constructed by young people give form to their literacy practices and their literacy practices are converted into vehicles for representing the identities that they assume (McCarthey & Moje, 2002). Martha's discussion on the origin of the characters in her art shows how she refers to the cultural and identity resources within her reach in order to position her productions online. It shows on the one hand, her search for models, and on the other, her search for recognition, given that her creativity is a central aspect of her identity. Like every creator, she needs the recognition of the others in order to make sense of her creations.

> I really like the work of the artist Tim Burton, though I like it because it is original. I am not such a fan of him [...but] I would like to cause the impact that he has created, so I compare myself with him. You could say that I want to be like him or better, so I feel motivated to give it my best shot. I don't think of how the character is going to look but how much I want the character to last in people's minds.

The search for desirable models or characteristics for production online and for the construction of identities (Stern, 2008) is evident. The need to define one's own style, as well as the growing capacity of young people to propose increasingly higher goals (Stern, 2008) converts online spaces into ideal places for experimentation and self-knowledge. Moje et al. (2008) found that young people read and write as a form of self-expression in order to resolve problems, find information, or identify models that can help them to develop themselves in their homes, schools, and communities. This is evident in Martha's discourse. She shows the interrelationship between her personal identity resources and cultural resources that are part of popular youth culture, such as the works of Tim Burton, which drive her to seek out models beyond her immediate social environment. Her goals are very high and she demands a great deal of her productions, reflecting on the audience and the effect that she would like her characters to have.

In regard to the personality of her characters, Martha, like many other creators, uses her personal experiences and identity resources. According to the literature, it is common for young people to create characters based on themselves (Thomas, 2007).

> I think of a story where I could be the primary character....For example, the character that I have liked the best is one that I named Margot. She is a girl about 17 years old that dresses Punk but the story in which I placed her is a little gothic. This was because I had a boyfriend...that liked these things, so I made the character of him and me, but we don't look anything like them. We don't look anything like the drawing, but we are a little alike in personality or something like that. [I gave them these characteristics] and I liked it, since it wasn't exactly him and me, but this opposite personality. This made it so that the character took a personality of her own, a distinctive one, and I only thought, "it has to have original eyes. They don't have to be like *manga*," though they almost look like *manga*, but anyway, the girl is out there now. First she looked like "Emily the Strange" but later I said, "no, she can't be like her," and then I made another that looked *anime*,[4] and then Margot alive and I said: "eh, Margot." I gave her the name Margot because it is a name that sounds strong, like weird.

The interrelationship between the use of cultural resources and one's own resources is also evident in the research carried out with children. From a young age, popular culture, such as music, television programs, and videogames, form part of children's repertoire of valuable and meaningful textual tools (Kendrick, 2005). Among other authors, Dyson (2001) has noted the importance of cultural symbols and practices through which children construct their own childhoods. She observes that the ways of reconfiguring, rearticulating, and stretching these resources are central aspects for the learning and development of literacy practices in the current world. Likewise, in her work with adolescents and young people, Moje (2007) remarks on the interrelationship between youth cultures and popular cultures, documenting young people's uses of cultural texts for their own means, aside from the purposes imagined by the producers of the texts.

From the literature on the producers of *fanfiction* we learn that the authors frequently create hybrid identities that are represented in their texts (Black, 2005). The phenomenon of inserting versions of themselves in their characters is called identity fusion (Black, 2004, in Thomas, 2007). Although Martha is the sole creator of her characters (unlike the producers of *fanfiction*), she also has imbued her characters with some of her own personal traits. As a creator, she is putting herself and transforming herself in her texts; she based what she considers her favorite character on herself and her ex-boyfriend. In an imaginative way, she has used the qualities of both of them to imbue her character with life and make her stronger. This form of projecting themselves as authors on their characters, allows them to imagine the same possibilities for themselves in their real lives (Thomas, 2007). In some cases, for the producers of

---

4 *Anime* refers to Japanese animation and dates from about 1917 (Lubich, 1995).

fanfiction one finds a mix of authentic and idealized personal characteristics in the characters (Black, 2005). Therefore, the production of digital texts can be associated with the expansion of identities inasmuch as the production of the text can be accompanied by a transformation in the identities of the producer of the text (Kress, 2003, in Rowsell, & Pahl, 2007).

The Navigation between Physical and Virtual Spaces

According to the available literature, virtual spaces provide young people with valuable opportunities for experimenting with diverse identities. Electronic spaces provide young people with the opportunity to show the best facet of their persona, which is particularly important during adolescence as Stern (2008) indicates, given that they are discovering their capacity to imagine the variety of responses that they can receive from others. These spaces do not present social limits to the participants (Beach & Lundell, 1998). People can mask their identity and simulate situations, emotions, or beliefs that they do not possess in reality. As Anolli, Villani, & Riva (2005, p. 93) explain, referring to the chat room dynamics, "It acts like an enormous theater in which, in each scenario and on each occasion, people can take on different roles." However, the same anonymous condition can guarantee users the necessary safety to show themselves just as they are, without fears or anxieties.

People make decisions about the personal characteristics that they want to show by acting in all types of spaces, both on and offline. The decisions about how people present themselves to others are not coincidental, explains Stern (2008); rather they deliberately adapt them to the audience and the way in which they want to be received. Given that in this stage of life peers are very important, young people learn how to give the impression that they want in different social groups by experimenting with identities and peer feedback (Boyd, 2007). In this way, introducing oneself in virtual spaces allows young people to exhibit their interests, perspectives, concerns, and the image of themselves that they want to show in cyberspace.

Martha conceives the computer as "a means for sharing things with your friends." Her productions help her to strengthen the connections with her friends from school and form new connections with like-minded people. She is conscious of her skills in the use of technologies and derives great satisfaction in doing things for her friends (like sending songs and videos to their cell phones). She has developed a critical sense of herself and of her own and others' digital texts. For example, in regards to videogames she says, "I really like to watch them in order to appreciate the image that the companies create for us, because I am always trying to understand the people that do these types of things. Sometimes the stories they invent surprise me, but also how they innovate and stuff like that, with their technology...these are things that I like to observe." She does not play a lot, "I really like the game, the story and the effects and the image and everything, maybe I'll try them, but generally with games I don't get fixated. I prefer the ones with fighting or something like that to play with other people. I don't like the games where I have to carry out a mission or something like that, they seem very impersonal to me."

It is not possible to separate online activities from the physical spaces where they are produced. Though they are social activities, and destined in some cases for personal enjoyment, the context permeates and defines their meaning, making evident the author's identity production. As the above comment demonstrates, in Martha's case, her sociable nature and interest in graphic design permeates her activities on and offline.

Conclusions

Based on the results of this study, we can draw several conclusions. First, the scarcity of material goods, technologies in this case, does not prevent young people from developing skills for, and from participating in, complex and multimodal literacy practices. It is obvious that we have no way of knowing what their skills and practices would be if they had the most up-to-date technology, but we do know that young people use the technologies that they have within their reach, though not necessarily within their ownership, in different ways, according to the objectives that they set for themselves.

The results indicate that the relationship between possession and use of technologies is not lineal. As we saw in the case of Martha, there are other factors that have most likely had an influence on the development of her literacy practices. For example, she had considerable freedom to explore digital tools without restrictions as well as with the encouragement of her family, which probably supported the development of her digital competencies.

As Livingstone (2008) states, the possibility of working with digital tools at home from a young age does not guarantee the development of complex digital skills. In order for these skills to be developed, young people need freedom and the support of their parents. This support certainly seems to be evident in Martha's case.

Based on the results, we can confirm that young people take advantage of the potential of ICTs in order to reach their objectives and develop their creative, social, and technical skills. In Martha's case, her inclinations for the visual arts are enriched, reinforced, and complemented by her actions, both in her physical and virtual spaces. In regard to the development of her identities, her work online is essential. Given the limitations within her immediate social environment, it is through the comments that her productions receive online that she reaffirms her interests and constructs her social capital in order to achieve her future goals.

According to Stern (2008), young people learn effective ways of introducing themselves through different media. Young authors gradually learn how to create the identities and images that they want others to see. They learn to use cultural symbols for their own purposes and, at the same time, they learn the technological skills necessary to create these representations. This is very important. In Martha's case, the computer tools that she uses are in English; therefore she not only develops her technological skills but also learns another language. As Moje et al., (2008) observe, the development of these skills, generally self-taught and in collaboration with peers, feed young people's motivations and they choose challenges that are increasingly more complex in order to position themselves before diverse groups of their interest.

In reality, the need to get to know and to be in contact with other young people has not changed; what has changed is the opportunity for today's young people to socialize by using the technologies within their reach, which surpass the barriers of geography, social class, and religion. As Herring (2008) and others have shown, young people conceptualize and use technology depending on their cultural, economic, and family contexts. However, the appearance of new affinity spaces (Gee, 2004) and of new virtual sites and projects show that the social networks of the next generations of young people, regardless of their socio-demographic conditions, is broader and more diverse than their parents. The case presented here is an example of this. We do not claim that Martha's case is representative of the public high school student population in Mexico, but neither is it the exception. In this case, her creativity and determination have more weight than her economic disadvantages, and they motivate her to do her creative work.

In regards to the tendency towards universalizing literacy practices using technologies, it is interesting to highlight the participation of the mass media. The interest in novels and *manga* movies, in the pictorial style of *anime* characters, and in creators and creations from different countries, shows that young people share interests and common practices with groups of other young people of different nationalities. In Martha's case, her search and participation in virtual affinity spaces has brought her to demand more of herself and improve her skills in order to prepare and publish her artistic expressions in anticipation of comments from people around the world.

The use of ICTs by the young people studied, from which Martha's case is derived, shows that the traditional meaning of dichotomies like global and local, private and public, or physical and virtual, are changing. These concepts are fused to form part of young people's virtual spaces. The language used to represent the activities carried out in physical spaces is extended in a natural way to the activities that they carry out in their virtual spaces. The use of ICTs by young people shows that they take advantage of the possibilities offered by these technologies to develop their social and technical skills. The exploration of new social spaces and new technological tools emerges naturally for young people. Consequently, we suggest that virtual spaces should be viewed as socio-technological spaces. ICTs are a vehicle for testing new facets of identity while simultaneously experimenting with better technical ways of doing so. As we have seen, the activities carried out can be very complex and because of this, they are meaningful and formative practices that should be studied and recognized in schools. In fact, we need more studies on literacy practices and the use of technologies by young people, especially because they can provide valuable information for the development of programs and study plans. As Moje (2002) indicates, these studies can help to avoid the risk of designing educational practices based on an essentialist or idealized vision of young people, instead of designing them based on the knowledge of the cultural practices of students that attend classes.

References

Anolli, L., Villani, D., & Riva, G. (2005). Personality of people using chat: An on-line research, *CyberPsychology & Behavior*, 8(1), 89–95.

Balardini, S. (2004). De deejays y ciberchabones: Subjetividades juveniles y tecnocultura. *Jóvenes: Revista de Estudios Sobre Juventud*, 20, 108–139.

Barton, D., & Hamilton, M. (2000). Literacy practices. In D. Barton, M. Hamilton & R. Ivanic (Eds.), *Situated literacies. Reading and writing in context* (pp. 7–15). London: Routledge.

Beach, R., & Lundell, D. (1998). Early adolescents' use of computer-mediated communication in writing and reading. In D. Reinking, M. McKenna, L. Labbo & R. Kieffer (Eds.), *Handbook of Literacy and Technology* (pp. 93–112). London: Erlbaum.

Black, R. (2005). Access and affiliation: The literacy and composition practices of English-language learners in an online fanfiction community. *Journal of Adolescent & Adult Literacy*, 49(2), 118–128.

Black, R. (2007). Digital design: English language learners and reader reviews in online fiction. In M. Knobel & C. Lankshear (Eds.), *A new literacies sampler* (pp. 115–136). New York: Peter Lang.

Boyd, D. (2006, February). Identity production in a networked culture: Why youth Heart MySpace. Paper presented at the Annual Meeting of the American Association for the Advancement of Science, St. Louis, MO.

Boyd, D. (2007). Why youth (heart) social networked sites: The role of networked publics in teenage social life. In D. Buckingham (Ed.), *Youth, identity, and digital media* (pp. 119–142). Cambridge, MA: The MIT Press.

Buckingham, D. (2008). Introducing identity. In D. Buckingham (Ed.), *Youth, identity, and digital media* (pp. 1–22). Cambridge, MA: The MIT Press.

Cammack, D. (2005). No straight line: Wrinkling binaries in literacy and technology research. *E-Learning*, 2(2), 153–168.

Cassell, J., & Cramer, M. (2008). High tech or high risk: Moral panics about girls online. In T. McPherson (Ed.), *Digital youth, innovation, and the unexpected.* (pp. 53–75). Cambridge, MA: The MIT Press.

Coleman, J. (2008). Ages, stages and theories of adolescence. In *Theorising the benefits of new technologies for youth: Controversies of learning and development* (pp. 11–17). First report in the ESRC (Economic and Social Research Council) Seminar Series: The educational and social impact of new technologies on young people in Britain, Department of Education, University of Oxford & the London School of Economics and Political Science. UK.

DiMaggio, P., & Hargittai, E. (2001). *From the 'Digital Divide' to 'Digital Inequality': Studying Internet use as penetration increases (Working Paper # 15).* Princeton University, NJ: Center for Arts and Cultural Policy Studies.

Dyson, A. (2001). Where are the childhoods in childhood literacy? An exploration in outer (school) space, *Journal of Early Childhood Literacy, 1*(1), 9–39.

Gee. J. P. (1996). *Social linguistics and literacies. Ideology in discourses.* London: Taylor & Francis.

Gee, J. P. (1999). *An introduction to discourse analysis. Theory and method.* London: Routledge.

Gee, J. P. (2000). Identity as an analytic lens for research in education. *Review of Research in Education, 25,* 99–126.

Gee, J. P. (2001). Reading as situated language: A socio-cognitive perspective. *Journal of Adolescent & Adult Literacy, 44*(8), 714–725.

Gee, J.P. (2004). *Situated language and learning: A critique of traditional schooling.* New York: Routledge.

Granjon, F. (2004). Les sociologies de la fracture numérique: Premiers jalons critiques pour une revue de la littérature. *Questions de Communication, 6.* Retrieved August 13, 2008, from http://www.ques2com.fr/index.php?p=accueil&type=details&revue=27&id=27.

Gravett, P. (2004). *Manga: Sixty years of Japanese comics,* London: Laurence King Publishing.

Guichard, J. (2001). La prise en compte des rapports au savoir en médiatique. *Recherches en Communication: Médias, éducation et apprentissages, 15,* 201–217.

Herring, S. (2008). Questioning the generational divide: Technological exoticism and adult constructions of online youth identity. In D. Buckingham (Ed.), *Youth, identity, and digital media* (71-92). Cambridge, MA: The MIT Press.

Jenkins, H. (2004). Why Heather can write. *MIT Technology Review.* Retrieved August 13, 2008, from http://www.technologyreview.com/business/13473/

Kendrick, M. (2005). Playing house: A 'sideways' glance at literacy and identity in early childhood. *Journal of Early Childhood Literacy, 5*(1), 5–28.

Knobel, M., & Lankshear, C. (2007). Online memes, affinities, and cultural production. In M. Knobel & C. Lankshear (Eds.), *A new literacies sampler* (pp. 199–227). New York: Peter Lang.

Lankshear, C., & Knobel, M. (2006). *New literacies: Everyday practices and classroom learning* (Second edition). New York: McGraw-Hill International.

Leander, K. M., & Johnson, K. (2002, April). Tracing the everyday "sitings" of adolescents on the Internet: A strategic adaptation of ethnography across online and offline spaces. Paper presented at the Annual Meeting of the American Educational Research Association, New Orleans, LA.

Levinson, M. (2007). Literacy in English Gypsy communities: Cultural capital manifested as negative assets, *American Educational Research Journal, 44*(1), 5–39.

Livingstone, S. (2008). Internet literacy: Young people's negotiation of new online opportunities. In T. McPherson (Ed.), *Digital youth, innovation, and the unexpected* (pp. 101–122). Cambridge, MA: The MIT Press.

Lubich, D. (1995). Japanimation: The stylish violent Akira made the West sit up. Are we still toonstruck? *The Guardian,* The Guardian Features, London, p. T16.

Martín Barbero, J. (2003). Saberes hoy: Diseminaciones, competencias y transversalidades.

Revista Iberoamericana de Educación, 32, 17–34.

McCarthey, S., & Moje, E. (2002). Identity matters. *Reading Research Quarterly, 37*(2), 228–238.

McGinnis, T., Goodstein-Stolzenberg, A., & Costa Saliani, E. (2007). "indnpride": Online spaces of transnational youth as sites of creative and sophisticated literacy and identity work. *Linguistics and Education, 18*, 283–304.

McKay, T. (2003). Gee's theory of D/discourse and research in teaching English as a second language: Implications for the mainstream. Proceedings of the Symposium "Theory, Culture and Discourse in Education", March 14–15, 2003, University of Manitoba. Retrieved August 13, 2008, from http://www.umanitoba.ca/education/symposium03 /documents/MacKay03.pdf.

McPherson, T. (2008). A rule set for the future. In T. McPherson (Ed.), *Digital youth, innovation, and the unexpected.* (pp. 1–23). Cambridge, MA: The MIT Press.

Moje, E. (2002). But where are the youth: On the value of integrating youth culture into literacy theory. *Educational Theory, 52*(1), 97–120.

Moje, E. (2004). Powerful spaces: Tracing the out-of-school literacy spaces of Latino/a youth. In K. Leander & M. Sheehy (Eds.), *Spatializing literacy research and practice* (pp. 15–38). New York: Peter Lang.

Moje, E. (2007). Youth literacy, culture and identity. In J. Flood, D. Lapp, S. B. Heath, & V. Chou (Eds.), *Handbook of research on teaching literacy through the communicative and visual arts, volume II* (pp. 207–219). Mahwah, NJ: Erlbaum.

Moje, E., Overby, M., Tysvaer, N., & Morris, K. (2008). The complex world of adolescent literacy: Myths, motivations, and mysteries. *Harvard Educational Review, 78*(1). Retrieved August 13, 2008, from http://www.personal.umich.edu/~moje/pdf/Journal/Complex WorldOfAdolescentLiteracy.pdf.

Myers J. (2006). Literacy practices and digital literacies: A commentary on Swenson, Rozema, Young, McGrail, and Whitin. *Contemporary Issues in Technology and Teacher Education, 6*(1), 61–66. Retrieved August 13, 2008, from http://www.citejournal.org/vol6/iss1/ languagearts/article5.cfm

Rowsell, J., & Phal, K. (2007). Introduction. In K. Phal & J. Rowsell (Eds.), *Travel notes from the New Literacy Studies: Instances of practice* (pp. 1–15). Clevedon, UK: Multilingual Matters.

Seiter, E. (2008). Practicing at home: Computers, pianos, and cultural capital. In T. McPherson (Ed.), *Digital young, innovation, and the unexpected* (pp. 27–52). Cambridge, MA: The MIT Press.

Selwyn, N. (2007). Young people and their information needs in context of the information society. Brussels, Belgium. Directorate of Youth and Sport of the Council of Europe/European Agency for Youth Information and Counselling. Date of reviewal 20 june 2008. Available: http://www.coe.int/t/dg4/youth/Source/Partners/Eryica_Selwyn _en.pdf

Stern, S. (2008). Producing sites, exploring identities: Youth online authorship. In D. Bickingham (Ed.), *Youth, identity, and digital media* (95–117). Cambridge, MA: The MIT Press.

Stone, J. (2007). Popular websites in adolescents' out-of-school lives: Critical lessons on literacy. In M. Knobel & C. Lankshear (Eds.), *A new literacies sampler* (pp. 49–65). New York: Peter Lang.

Street, B. (2003). What's 'new' in New Literacy Studies? Critical approaches to literacy in theory and practice. *Current Issues in Comparative Education, 5*(2), 77–91.

Terrero, P. (1997). Ocio, prácticas y consumos culturales: Aproximación a su estudio en la sociedad mediatizada. *Diálogos de la Comunicación*, *49*. Retrieved August 13, 2008, from http://www.dialogosfelafacs.net/dialogos_epoca/pdf/49-07PatriciaTerrero.pdf

Thomas, A. (2007). Blurring and breaking through the boundaries of narrative, literacy, and identity in adolescent fan fiction. In In M .Knobel & C. Lankshear (Eds.), *A new literacies sampler* (pp. 137–165). New York: Peter Lang.

Trier, J. (2006). Reconceptualizing literacy through a discourses perspective by analyzing literacy events represented in films about schools. *Journal of Adolescent & Adult Literacy*, *49*(6), 510–523.

Valkenburg, P., Schouten, A., & Peter, J. (2005). Adolescents' identity experiments on the Internet. *New Media & Society*, *7*, 383–402.

SECTION III

Educational Policies and Professional Identities

CHAPTER SEVEN

Identities in Shifting Educational Policy Contexts: The Consequences of Moving from Two Languages, One Community to English Only

JUDITH GREEN AND ANA INÉS HERAS
With contributions from
MARIA LUCIA CASTANHEIRA, BETH YEAGER, AND CAROL DIXON

Recently, researchers have begun to examine the experience of reform from the point of view of those most directly affected by changes in reform initiatives. McNeil and Coppola (2006), for example, argue that policies are generally developed far from those they are designed to govern and that the organization or people for whom a policy was written are usually not part of the decision-making process. They argue that:

> [r]esearch on policy impact needs to capture the voices of those affected not just because they are recipients of the policy, but because they may have insights unavailable to the formal policy process; the power differential favors the policy makers, while the actual knowledge differential may favor the professionals and families being affected. Framing the research around what the policy is doing to or for children and their education immediately takes the researcher out of the input-output mode and often beyond the assumptions embedded in the policy. (p. 683)

In this chapter, we build on these arguments to explore the impact of changes in policies on the opportunities for learning (Tuyay, Jennings, & Dixon, 1995) and on the potentials for identity constructions (e.g., Holland & Cole, 1995; Holland, Lachoite, Skinner, & Cain, 1998; Castanheira, Green, Dixon, & Yeager, 2007) in fifth grade classes between 1993 and 2000 taught by a teacher (Beth) in two different reform initiatives. The first reform context focuses on the period 1993–1998, where Bilingual Instruction was officially sanctioned; the second period, 1998–2000, focuses on a reform context in which the district-wide and statewide policy actions led to a change to English Only. To explore the impact of these changes on opportunities for learning and potential identities afforded to students, we created a unique data set consisting of class records constructed in a reform period officially supporting Bilingual Instruction (1993, 1996, and 1997), and a changing reform period supporting a move to English Only (1998; 2000). The anchor for this contrastive analysis was a TESOL Newsletter written by the teacher (Yeager, 1999a).

Design of the Case Studies: The Construction of Telling Cases

We present a new analysis of archived records (1993–2000) through a double case-study approach, designed to make visible the impact of changes in reform initiatives and policies (Case Study 1) on conditions shaping the opportunities for learning and for identity formulation inside of the classroom (Case Study 2). By holding the classroom and grade level constant across years (1993–2000), we examined patterns of practice constructed by the teacher with students that constituted the opportunities for learning and for constructing local, situated identities within and across times and events for each year. Then by contrasting each year systematically in a pair-wise contrast across years, we were able to examine the impact of the shifting policy initiatives on teacher and students alike. As the telling cases (Mitchell, 1984) will demonstrate, by using the observed shift in 1998 from Bilingual Instruction to English Only as an anchor, we were able to engage in a process of mapping the inter-play, and histories, of what occurred inside and outside of the classroom.

The Teacher and Her Classes

The selection of Beth's classes for the two case studies was purposeful on multiple levels. First, her classes constitute a multiyear ethnographic archive of life in fifth grade that crosses two major reform initiatives between 1993 and 2000. Second, Beth was a nationally recognized fellow of the Carnegie Foundation's Academy for the Scholarship of Teaching and Learning, a fellow of the South Coast Writing Project, and a published teacher ethnographer (e.g., Yeager, 1999a; 1999b, 2003; Yeager & Green, 2008; Yeager, Green, & Castanheira, 2009). Third, she was, and still is, a partner in ethnography, one who engaged her students in ethnographic work in, and of, their classroom (Yeager, Floriani, & Green, 1998). Furthermore, between 2001 and 2003, she engaged in her own (re)analysis of the 1996 school year for her dissertation in order to explore how students constructed academic identities (Yeager, 2003).

Her work as a teacher-researcher and researcher-teacher (Yeager, 2003) added depth to the analysis of what was present in 1993, 1996, and 1997, and what shifted in 1998 and 2000, as a result of policy changes in multiple areas of the social, school and political systems. Furthermore, her work, and that of her colleagues in a Teacher Research Community funded by The Spencer Foundation (1996–1998) that was part of the archive, was instrumental in uncovering a broad range of shifting policy vectors that converged to limit what she (and they) were able to afford students in 1998 and beyond. These vectors will be presented later in this chapter and draw on an earlier analysis of policy impact published in the Bilingual Research Journal (Dixon, Green, Yeager, Baker, & Franquiz, 2000; Dixon & Green, 2009) as part of a series of reports on the impact of the implementation of the English Only initiative.

The Archive

The ethnographic archive between 1993 and 2000 included a broad range of records for each year: videos, field-notes, student work, teacher plans, documents sent home, documents for teachers, and other artifacts, collected by university-based ethnographers, in collaboration with Beth and her students. In 1998, given the demands on students and Beth for a new way of communicating and writing in classrooms (i.e., the use of English Only in public spaces), the ethnographic team in consultation with Beth decided to withdraw from the classroom, but to continue analysis and support for Beth's work with her students. Beth elected to continue to engage students in work as ethnographers (Yeager, Floriani, & Green, 1998), which included making video records of life in their classroom (Dixon & Green, 2009).

The existence of this extensive data-set enabled us to trace intertextually (Bloome, 1992; Bloome & Egan-Robertson, 1993) and intercontextually (Floriani, 1993; Heras, 1993) related events that members of the class marked in their talk as academically significant. The identification of intertextual and intercontextual ties across particular sequences of events formed the basis for examining how particular content (texts), actions and practices (contextual information, i.e., ways of constructing texts) formed consequential progressions; the intertextually and intercontextually tied events also provided a systematic approach to uncovering historical roots and routes of events.[1] Ties, therefore, were visible in what members socially accomplished in and through what they proposed to each other, recognized and acknowledged in their interactions, and signaled as academically and socially significant for present and

1 For references on this approach, see Durán & Syzmanski, 1995; Putney, Green, Dixon, Durán, & Yeager, 2000; Baker, Green & Skukauskaite, 2008; Castanheira, Green & Yeager, 2009; Dixon, Green & Brandts, 2005.

future work (Bloome & Egan-Robertson, 1993). These cycles of analysis represent the iterative and recursive processes central to ethnography as a non-linear system (Agar, 2004, 2006).

Telling Cases as Analytic Constructions

The approach to case study construction is one grounded in ethnographic research, and differs in scale and focus from other forms of case study (e.g., Borman, Clarke, Cotner, & Lee, 2006; Yin, 2006). Mitchell (1984) contrasts telling cases with illustrative, representative and typical cases, arguing that in ethnographic research:

> [c]ase studies are the detailed presentation of ethnographic data relating to some sequence of events from which the analyst seeks to make some theoretical inference. The events themselves may relate to any level of social organization: a whole society, some section of a community, a family or an individual. What distinguishes case studies from more general ethnographic reportage is the detail and particularity of the account. Each case study is a description of a specific configuration of events in which some distinctive set of actors have been involved in some defined situation at some particular point of time. (p. 222)

Building on Mitchell, we explored two particular configurations of events, each with distinctive sets of actors in particular situations at particular points in time, and traced the changes in policies, the historical roots and routes leading to these policy changes, and the consequences of these policy changes for the teacher and the students. Thus, the telling cases in this chapter make visible relatively unexamined, yet theoretically important, factors that supported and constrained what was possible for the teacher to construct with her linguistically and culturally diverse students in different reform contexts. In this way, we examine what happened to the opportunities for learning and identity construction of teacher and students, when policies changed from support for Bilingual Instruction to support for English Only.

Through these analyses, we also demonstrate why a nonlinear process, that is, an abductive logic of inquiry (Agar, 2004, 2006), was necessary to support a multilayered, multifaceted approach to identifying the dynamic processes across levels of social, school, and political systems and their consequences for teachers and students. As part of the description of the processes, we demonstrate the ways in which triangulating data, theory, method, and/or perspectives (Corsaro, 1981) enabled us to identify unanticipated rich points (Agar, 1994, 2004) that then served as a basis for tracing the historical roots and routes of particular educational reforms and policies. In this way, we present the abductive logic of inquiry central to Interactional Ethnography, the particular approach to ethnography developed by members of the Santa Barbara Classroom Discourse Group in the last four decades.[2]

Constructing Telling Cases of Unanticipated Consequences: Ethnography, Identities, and Opportunities for Learning

We begin this section by presenting the perspective guiding our analysis of the telling cases, grounded in anthropological theories of culture and discourse analysis theories of language-in-use, that frame our study of everyday life in classrooms and of social systems as (re)constructed by participants in and through their moment-by-moment as well as over time interactions in particular social settings. From this perspective, cultural patterns are not a given but a construction by local actors, developed in social fields as they create patterned ways of perceiving, believing, acting, and evaluating everyday life.[3] Central to this argument is the relationship between language and culture. Agar (1994) captures succinctly this relationship when he argues that the concept of "culture," like the concept of "language," has to change:

> The two concepts have to change *together*. Language, in all its varieties, in all the ways it appears in everyday life, builds a world of meanings. When you run into different meanings, when you become aware of your own and work to build a bridge to the others, "culture" is what you're up to. Language fills the spaces between us with sound; culture forges the human connection through them. Culture is in language, and language is loaded with culture. (p.33)

Bakhtin (1986) provides insights into how this language and cultural work become part of the repertoires for action of individuals-within-social-groups and the group itself:

> We assimilate forms of language only in forms of utterances and in conjunction with these forms. The forms of language and the typical forms of utterances, that is speech [written] genres, enter our experience and our consciousness together, and in close connections with another....These genres are so diverse because they differ depending on the situation, social position, and personal interrelations of participants in the communication. These genres have high, strictly official, respectful forms as well as familiar ones. And there are forms with varying degrees of familiarity, as well as intimate forms (which differ from familiar ones). (78–79)

---

2 See Castanheira, Crawford, Green & Dixon, 2001; Dixon, et al., 2000; Green & Bloome, 1997 Green & Dixon, 1993; Green & Wallat, 1981; Rex, 2006; Santa Barbara Classroom Discourse Group, 1992a; b.

3 For references on this approach, see Bloome, Carter, Otto Christian & Shuart-Faris, 2004; Erickson, 1986; Candela, Rockwell & Coll, 2004; Green & Dixon, 1993; Green, Dixon, & Zaharlick, 2003; Santa Barbara Classroom Discourse Group, 1992a; b.

His argument about the diversity of genres and the situated and interpersonal nature of those genres in relationships to particular positions was central to the present analysis. Discourse-in-use (oral or written), viewed in this way, brings with it a range of circumstances that give rise to both the genres and the content of what is being proposed through it, since, following Bahktin once again:

> Any understanding of live speech, a live utterance, is inherently responsive, although the degree of this activity varies extremely. Any understanding is imbued with response and necessarily elicits it in one form or another: the listener becomes the speaker. A passive understanding of the meaning of perceived speech is only an abstract aspect of the actual whole of actively responsive understanding, which is then actualized in a subsequent response that is actually articulated. Of course, an utterance is not always followed immediately by an articulated response. An actively responsive understanding of what is heard (a command, for example) can be directly realized in action (the execution of an order or command that has been understood and accepted for execution), or it can remain for the time being, a silent responsive understanding (certain speech genres are intended for this kind of responsive understanding, for example, lyrical genres), but this is, so to speak, responsive understanding with a delayed reaction. Sooner or later what is heard and actively understood will find its response in the subsequent speech or behavior of the listener. In most cases, genres of complex cultural communication are intended precisely for this kind of actively responsive understanding with delayed action. Everything that we have said here also pertains to written and read speech, with the appropriate adjustments and additions. (p. 68–69)

Drawing on the chain of reasoning created by these theoretical arguments, we constructed an approach to the study of the impact of policies on the opportunities for learning and for identity construction in Beth's classes across the different reform initiatives because it provided a basis for conceptualizing language and culture as dynamic and interdependent processes. It also laid a foundation for our approach to the ways in which policies beyond the classroom door supported in one case (Bilingual Instruction) and limited in a second case (English Only) the material resources (Gee & Green, 1998) available to teacher and students.

We combined this chain of reasoning with Geertz's (1983) argument that people construct local knowledge, and Edwards and Mercer´s (1987) argument that participants construct common knowledge to explore further how the loss of particular language resources constrained what members were able to construct together as academic content and as identities (e.g., Castanheira et al., 2007) in the classroom under the English Only reform initiative. These arguments framed the contrastive analysis of patterns and forms of language use, whether in discourse(s) amongst teacher and students, or inscribed in the documents related to the different policies. This analysis involved examining who used (spoke or wrote) what language, when and where, for what purpose, under what conditions, with whom, in what ways, and with what outcome or consequence. Through this level of analysis we identified missing opportunities and their consequences for learning as well as identity formulation.

To frame this argument further, we drew on work by Lima (1995), who, building on Vygotsky and Brazilian pedagogical thought, argued that:

> We have two dimensions of development [and by implication, learning]: one that resides in the individual and the other in the collectivity. Both are interdependent and create each other. Historically created possibilities of cultural development are themselves transformed by the processes through which individuals acquire the cultural tools that are or become available in their context. (447–448)

From this argument, linguistic and cultural practices, learning and development, and individual and collective are all in a reflexive relationship. Both the individual and the collective are therefore interdependent and the capacity of one depends on, and contributes to, the capacity of the other. This conceptualization of individual–collective relationship lays a foundation for exploring how changes in language use for a particular group of students, for example, English Language Learners (ELL), also resulted in changes in material resources for the group; that is, for all students and the teacher. This chain of reasoning, therefore, led us to examine unanticipated losses for the collective as well as the teacher and individual groups of students.

Theory-Method Relationships: A Conceptual Argument

In this section, we make transparent concepts that grounded our multifaceted study of discourse-in-use (oral and written), and how these concepts led to the need for analyses at multiple levels of scales (time, space, actors). Four conceptual arguments frame this movement across levels of analysis: intertextuality, rich points, frame clashes, and logics at play. Each of these framed a particular level of analysis, and taken together formed a web that enabled us to examine the roots and routes of particular policies or moments of challenge to Beth, students, and community. Although there is a rich body of literature on intertextuality as links between texts, recent arguments by Bloome (1992) and his colleagues (Bloome & Bailey, 1992; Bloome & Egan-Robertson, 1993; Bloome et al., 2004) who propose a dynamic and agentive view of intertextuality as a social accomplishment of people as they engage in events of everyday life were central to our analysis. From this perspective, the construction of intertextual ties between present, past, and future texts (oral, written, and visual) was more than an analytical method; it was part of a dynamic process in which participants propose, recognize, and acknowledge ties between texts that were socially significant to events constructed by particular groups of actors in particular social fields. This view of intertextuality framed our approach to identifying pathways visible in the choices of words and histories inscribed in the oral and written texts of participants. From this perspective, intertextual relationships were visible within a developing event or text and historical times were potentially available to participants and ethnographers alike.

To this argument, we added the concept of frame clashes (Gumperz, 1986; Mehan, 1979; Tannen, 1979) as a basis for identifying anchor points for examining historical circumstances surrounding, and/or leading to, policy shifts at different points in time in the history of a group or system. The combination of these concepts pointed to the need to uncover the actors who contributed to the policy changes. Building on Agar (1994), we viewed such *rich points* as places where *culture happens*. That is, at such points, differences in understanding, interpretation, and/or meanings became marked, or visible to participants (including the ethnographer). By examining patterns of action and meaning construction around such point, we identified the pathways leading to policy changes. From this perspective, moments of frame clash served as anchors for analysis of historical antecedents of the event or the changing circumstances leading to the [present] condition (See Figure 1). By analyzing frame clashes and tracing their historical roots/routes, we were able to identify a range of changing policies that converged to create the challenges Beth inscribed as she planned for students in 1998, the year in which a shift from Bilingual Instruction to English Only occurred in her school (Dixon et al., 2000).

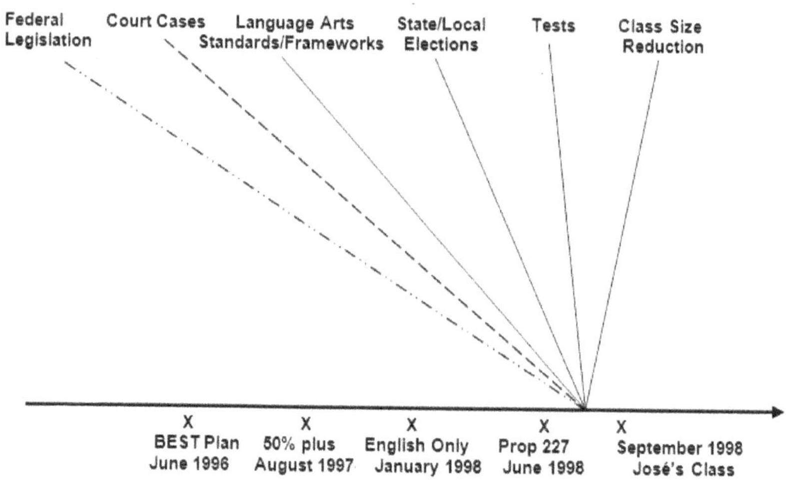

Figure 1. From bilingual education to English Only in less than two years: The converging forces of policy actions.

Although *frame clashes* have not been associated with the study of the impact of policy changes in the past, the importance of considering them is visible in the work of Burin and Heras (2001, 2008; Heras Monner Sans, Burin, & Córdova, 2008). Rather than view them as personal clashes in interpretation, their research focuses on the dynamic interplay between actors at different levels of systems in nonschool contexts. In studying political and economic policies and their impact on community-based organizations, they found that actors in different sets of systems (social fields) were guided by diverse logics and that these logics may or may not be congruent, and that at times, these logics are frankly contradictory. Thus their work points to the need to view actors within their systems of social life and to examine what happens when different *logics are at play*. Their work points to the need to explore how logics across groups in different policy levels are consistent with, or differ from, the logic of others seeking to promote, or take up, the changes (see also Goertz, 2006, and Sutton & Levinson, 2001, on studying policy implementation and policy as practice, respectively).

By adding the concept of the *interplay of logics* for different actors or groups of actors to our orienting framework, we enhanced our ability to examine the factors that supported and constrained how policies proposed by particular actors, or groups of actors, were (or were not) taken up within and across social fields surrounding Beth's classes (see Palmer & García, 2000 for articles that make a visible differential take up of English Only across school districts in California). Through this approach, we identified the complex range of actors within and across particular systems (e.g., school district, state and national governance bodies, law courts, among others). This approach also enabled us to examine closely the positions, and positionings of different actors (Heras, 1993) in the reform process, and through this process, their identities or identity potentials.

The orienting framework of this study (Green, Dixon, & Zaharlick, 2003) did not predict what we would find but rather guided how we approached each analysis, thus enabling us to hold the theory constant, while allowing actors, actions, events, texts, and other social dimensions to vary. By holding the theory constant, we were able to identify intertextually tied records in the ethnographic archive for particular analyses, to identify possible rich points for analysis, and to locate pathways to follow for historical analysis. As will become visible in the discussion of different analyses that follow, when necessary, we added additional theories to our framework that we did not know were needed at the outset of the study (Heap, 1995). In contrast to this orienting framework, explanatory theories were added post analysis to explain the patterns we uncovered through this multifaceted, nonlinear approach.

Schools as Open Systems: Exploring the Historical Roots of Policy Changes

Given our focus on exploring actors within social systems, we added one additional set of conceptual arguments to our orienting framework that of conceptualizing schools as *open systems* (Sagastizábal & Heras, 2005). This conceptualization led us to examine relationships among actors, their actions, the resources and products used, and/or produced, within systems and how changes in policies led to changes in resources that supported or constrained what teachers in the classroom, and therefore students, had available to use. In turn, this chain of reasoning led us to consider how historical changes in a system led to the (re)formulation of what counted as valued or appropriate educational processes within as well as across interconnected systems. The ethnographic studies presented in this section make visible pathways within a system that had an impact on decisions, beliefs, and actions of actors from the classroom outward, across layers of school systems as well as interconnected systems.

The first set of studies focus on work by Barr & Dreeben (1983), who explored *how schools work*. Barr (1987) a literacy educator, and Dreeben, a sociologist of education, combined efforts to examine how policies (e.g., decisions) and other resources were created and used by actors across levels of a school system. By tracing decisions across levels of school systems, they found that at each level of a school system, people, time, and resources were brought together to construct particular products (e.g., decisions, materials), and that the products of one level of a system became resources for other levels. Drawing on this work, Barr (1987) traced the developing curriculum in a high school English class. Her analysis across the year made visible the applicability of this conceptual model to studies of literacy instruction in classrooms. Her analysis examined how the study of intertextual relationships across texts, actors, and events made visible the ways in which each text, read/written at one point in time, served as a resource for the construction and interpretation of subsequent texts. Her analysis demonstrated why an historical analysis across times and events within a classroom was necessary to uncover how small changes had anticipated, and at times, unanticipated outcomes for students in Beth's classrooms (Dixon et al., 2000). Work by Barr (1987) and Barr and Dreeben (1983), therefore, demonstrated that policies are not made by a single actor, or set of actors at one point in a system, and simply implemented by other actors at different points in the system. Rather, their work demonstrated that policies are (re)constructed through dynamic and interconnected processes and practices produced by different actors within and across times, events, and levels of a system or social fields.

The view of schools as dynamic systems is supported by longitudinal ethnographic studies that traced the changing dynamics and history of reform in particular schools. These studies demonstrate how a school can serve as an anchor for uncovering unexpected consequences of particular changes in policies and how these changes are related to changes in actors, which in turn, result in changes in policies.

These studies also make visible how decisions in levels of a system beyond the classroom or school-district levels shape, and are shaped by, texts and actions of actors constructed in other systems (e.g., political and teacher education). The first set of ethnographic studies we discuss are ones undertaken by Smith and colleagues (Smith & Geoffrey, 1968; Smith, Kleine, Prunty & Dwyer, 1986; Smith, Prunty, Dwyer, & Kleine, 1987). These researchers followed the history of an educational innovation in a single school across a 15-year period and four changes in administration. They traced how the orientation and philosophy of the school transformed in relationship to changes in superintendents, who in turn, appointed principals to this school.

By examining the complex social histories of actors within the school and district, and what they as leaders supported as valued instructional approaches, Smith and his colleagues traced the transformation of one school from a student-centered philosophy to a more traditional philosophy across four changes in superintendents.

Their analysis shows how local philosophies were forms of identity for the local school, and how shifts in philosophical identities result from changes in school leaders over long periods of time; thus, demonstrating that changes in a school's approach may be realized without explicit reform movements. By tracing the history/histories of one school, they made visible how transformations in the logics guiding a particular school, at a particular point in time, were related to changes in leadership within the system (see also, Chrispeels, 1997). This series of longitudinal ethnographic studies made visible the necessity of exploring the consequences of transformations in philosophy across times, actors, and leadership at multiple levels of scale.

Converging on this body of work is a 16-year study by Anderson-Levitt (2002) in France. This study made visible how historical analysis from the classroom outward to the larger school systems at the local and national levels provides a basis for examining sources of influence on particular actors (i.e., teachers) within classrooms and schools. Anderson-Levitt traced historical changes within a national context (e.g., the ministry level in France) as well as within local schools to build a grounded explanation of why younger teachers took up a particular strategy (small-group work) that was resisted by older teachers as not being a French way of teaching, a perspective she found was supported by parents. By tracing both historical contexts of policy formulation and local practices and beliefs about practice of an intergenerational group of teachers, she uncovered differences across generations of teachers related to the use of whole class and multigroup instruction. Through her historical analysis of policies and the practices promoted by ministers of education and teacher educators at particular points in time, she located an often unexamined source of influence on teacher actions—changes at macro system levels that defined valued practices that shaped a teacher's professional beliefs and actions.

Anderson-Levitt's work demonstrated the need to go beyond the local school or even city to consider national directions and changes in political movements within a state or national context. What her work also uncovered was the copresence of different logics as well as clashes in the logics at play in particular instances. Thus, this work, combined with work by Burin and Heras, and work by Sagastizábal and Heras, already cited, points to the need to examine convergent and competing logics at play in different social fields across different levels of systems and at points of interconnections of systems (see also, Alexander, 2001; Tobin, Wu, & Davidson, 1991). These studies converge on two interrelated arguments: *policy decisions are the work of particular social actors, in particular social fields, at particular times; and changes, and at times, transformations, in policies related to particular value systems, shape, and their impact is shaped by, actions of particular actors in the ways that they take up (or not) the proposed policy*. These studies also made visible how policies in one social field were interdependent of policies in other systems or social fields across historical periods of time.

In the telling cases that follow we draw on the framework presented in the previous sections to guide analysis of the actions and actors beyond the classroom door (Telling Case 1) that converged in 1998 to (re)formulate the possibilities for Beth and her linguistically and culturally diverse students. After uncovering actions related to the frame clashes inscribed by Beth in her TESOL Newsletter column, we explore how these actions supported and constrained the resources available to Beth and her students in two different reform movements, that is, Bilingual Instruction (1993–1998) and English Only (1998 and 2000) (Telling Case 2).

Telling Case 1: Impact of Policy Changes on Educational Opportunities and Identities

In Telling Case 1, our goal was to uncover the range of actors and policy activity that constituted pathways leading to the observed policy shifts, and to examine who initiated and supported these changes in wider social and political social fields. This telling case is guided by McNeil & Coppola's (2006) call for exploring the voices of those whose lives are the most affected by the policies. By using the TESOL Newsletter column as an anchor for the analyses in this case, we bring forward Beth's voice as a committed professional, and by extension, through her action, the voices of students. By focusing on actors who were part of different policy initiatives, we also bring to the fore a broad range of actors directly involved in policy decisions or in support of the policy changes. This analysis, like ones presented previously, involved a nonlinear chain of reasoning, given the need to uncover historical pathways leading to particular policies and frame clashes that Beth inscribed in her TESOL Newsletter in 1998.

To achieve this goal in a way that provided a coherent text representing this nonlinear process, in Telling Case 1 we adapted a research practice Elliott Mishler (1984) called interruption analysis. Mishler used this approach to interrupt the traditional linear analysis of doctor–patient interactions in order to extract the story of illness that a patient was proposing. By extracting the story from the question and answer form of the dialogue, he was able to hear, transcribe, and read the patient's story of the illness as a whole, leading him to argue that the interpretation of diagnosis arrived at by the doctor did not consider the entire story, and thus led to misdiagnosis. In our analysis of the TESOL column, we adapted Mishler's approach to analyze the pathways leading to the challenges Beth inscribed in her writing. By selecting an identified moment of challenge, a frame clash, we created a point of interruption (a rich point) that served as a beginning point for uncovering pathways and layers of history of reform(s) and policy actions leading to the particular moment of reform action Beth inscribed in her narrative. This process created a sort of *flashback*, a process often used in movies to unfold or fill in (backfill) information and actions of intertextually tied events that were precursors to the rich point.

This analytical process provided a systematic approach to exploring the impact of past actions, historical processes tied to current policies. Once the information was identified through this flashback or tracing process, we returned to the original rich point and removed the pause (Heap, 1992). We then continued analyzing the TESOL text until we identified a new frame clash, which then led to the development of a new rich point, and an iterative process that involved uncovering the pathways leading to, and following from, this rich point. This iterative and recursive process enabled us to identify who contributed to and took part in the political activity leading to changing policies and reform initiatives represented in the challenges and tensions Beth inscribed in her column. By examining the identities of different actors who helped to create, or contributed to, new policies and reform initiatives, we make visible a complex web of policy actors, official and other, who were instrumental in supporting, and in some instances, in constraining the opportunities for learning and identity formulation for Beth and her students in 1998. Through the exploration of histories embedded in her words (cf., Bakhtin, 1986), we bring to the fore historical and current circumstances surrounding the change in reform initiatives visible in 1998, thus creating a telling case within the ongoing ethnographic work in classrooms.

Rich Point 1: Beth's Column for the TESOL Newsletter (1998)

As indicated previously, in 1998 Beth Yeager was invited to write a column on how she was preparing for the new school year in the face of the shift to English Only from more than a decade of Bilingual Instruction. The column was first written in August 1998, prior to the first day of school, and was entitled "First Day." Since publication did not actually appear as intended but was delayed until winter of 1999, the editors asked Beth if she wanted to write a new column or update the column. Rather than rewriting the column, she elected to add a new introductory section that preceded and introduced the original column. Her decision was based on the fact that she felt that her description of the preparation for the first day of school made visible the impact of the shift from Bilingual Instruction to English Only. We begin the analysis of the column with the opening paragraph that Beth added to the introductory section.

Our goal in starting with the opening paragraph was to identify how she inscribed her world (Lakoff & Johnson, 1980), and to locate potential frame clashes that we could turn into rich points to anchor analyses of historical pathways leading to moments of shifting policies:

> When I was asked to write this column, it was August and school in my district hadn't begun. Like teachers in bilingual classrooms all over California, I was going through the painful process of coming to terms with life after Unz (and, in our case in Santa Barbara, of life after the decision to eliminate–destroy?–the bilingual education program in 1998–99 was made by our Board of Education before voters had marked their ballots for Proposition 227). I wasn't being very successful and having to write about what this school year might look like seemed almost impossible. The time I spent sitting in front of a blank computer screen seemed interminable. I didn't have any more of a clue about how to start this article than I had about how I was going to start my school year.

In this statement, Beth made visible a range of changing conditions and challenges (potential rich points) that she was facing personally and professionally related to creating opportunities for students who would be entering her class. In this segment, she inscribed a series of times and actors who made decisions to eliminate Bilingual Instruction: life after Unz and School

Board members' decisions before the vote on a state-level initiative (Proposition 227). In grouping these periods, she proposed an interconnected set of social fields, each with a particular history that shaped actions that we will show were consequential for her and her students.

In following her lead, we viewed these references to two sources of policy (Unz and the School Board) as rich points, and at each point we engaged in a process of backward mapping (Dixon, Green, & Brandts, 2005; Baker & Green, 2007; Baker, Green, & Skukauskaite, 2008) to uncover historical roots (pathways) of the Unz referendum. After uncovering the pathway to Unz, we returned to Beth's column and continued analysis until we came to the point in her text in which she argued that the Board of Education in her district sought *to eliminate–destroy?–the bilingual education program in 1998–before voters had marked their ballots for Proposition 227*. At this point, we then interrupted the analysis of her TESOL Newsletter once again, and engaged in a new process of backward mapping the pathways leading to and following from the actions of the Board of Education between 1996 and 1998. Through these analyses, each of which involved a chain of abductive reasoning as we will demonstrate, we were able to identify a complex web of actors, positions available to actors, and layers of actions (agency) that were historically significant to the chain of policy actions that made possible Proposition 227 and the move to English Only.

Interruption Analysis 1: Uncovering the Pathways to Unz

As indicated above, Beth inscribed in the first paragraph a period of time she calls by the phrase *life after Unz*. In referring to her present condition for teaching as *life after Unz*, Beth constructed an identity to a particular social field as well as for the person who initiated the construction of this field, Ron Unz (an identifiable political figure). This phrase enabled us to identify the boundaries of the periods of time that were shifting for Beth. The period of "Unz" was bound on one end by a political process in which Unz and his supporters (an official identity) created a political movement leading to Proposition 227, and on the other end by the statewide vote and subsequent law enacted by the State Legislature (an official identity of an elected policy group). Within this time frame, Unz and his supporters were required by state policies to locate sufficient registered voters (an official identity), who could be convinced to sign the petition for Proposition 227 (an identity for a referendum) that was known as English for the Children (identity of recipients of the policy action).

This referendum was designed to shift California's education approach from one supporting Bilingual Instruction to one mandating English Only in the schools (Palmer & Garcia, 2000). Thus, the phrase *life after Unz* is a period of time; Unz is an *identity* for a political movement and an identity for an individual actor within a particular political world, the state of California. Identity as used in this analysis is situated in particular roles and relationships available to, constructed by, and/or taken up by people in interconnecting systems. Identities viewed in this way also resulted from the agency of particular actors. From this perspective, identities were not attributed to individuals in fixed ways and identities can be attributed to organizations, initiatives, and to groups of actors within particular social systems. Therefore, in tracing the roots of Unz's initiative, we began by asking what made this initiative possible.

Having identified the boundaries of the Unz period, we then proceeded to examine the roots of the initiative process as well as the routes leading to this particular initiative, Proposition 227. The exploration of identities related to *life after Unz* led us to question how it was possible for a citizen of California to initiate a potential revision to the state constitution or to state law. Therefore, the rich point, created by Beth in framing this period of challenge for her planning of the first day, led to an exploration of the history of Propositions in California and the identities for actors participating in the construction of this state-level policy. Questions guiding this analysis included: *What gives a citizen of California the right to initiate a law through the proposition process, and what does this process require?* This analysis made visible multiple identities, embedded in a series of roles and relationships, framed by a developing set of norms and expectations associated with, or resulting from, particular actions that constitute the *rights of citizens*. Analysis of identities, viewed in this way, involved exploration, not only of the actions and events inscribed in Beth's column but also of those inscribed in intertextually tied records of the past, and of conceptualizations of actors and possible actions inscribed in legal texts. From this perspective, we add to work on identities as multiple, as being constructed in each event or social field, and as historical (Holland & Cole, 1995; Holland et al., 1998) as well as to studies of personhood as inscribed in texts, including legal texts (Egan-Robertson, 1998; Merchant & Willis, 2000).

Pathway 1: Roots of the Proposition Process Uncovered

Analysis of the California government website (http://www.CA.gov) took us to a description of the history of the proposition process that led to passing of a constitutional amendment that insured the right of voters (an official identity) to initiate propositions:

> In a special election held on October 10, 1911, California became the 10th state to adopt the initiative process. That year, Governor Hiram Johnson began his term by promising to give citizens a tool they could use to adopt laws and constitutional amendments without the support of the Governor or the Legislature. The new Legislature put a package of constitutional amendments on the ballot that placed

> more control of California politics directly into the hands of the people. This package included the ability to recall elected officials, the right to repeal laws by referendum, and the ability to enact state laws by initiative. The initiative is the power of the people of California to propose statutes and amendments to the California Constitution. (Cal. Const., art. II, Section 8(a))

What is important to note in this inscription of the history of propositions is that the action by Governor Johnson and the legislature involved constitutional changes, not just the passing of laws. These changes were approved by more than two-third of the legislature and initiated a series of rights for citizens of California (an official identity).

In tracing the roots of what Beth called *Unz*, we located the onset of historical roots that served to create a pathway for citizens to take action in shaping the way the state created particular types of policies. Given the history of use of these pathways, the existence of 226 other propositions prior to the Unz initiative, we viewed this history as creating an *environmental or policy press* that Beth, and other educators and people in the state, experienced in September 1998 (Dixon et al., 2000). The initiative for English Only, or rather English for the Children (the public relations identity for Proposition 227), therefore, was part of an historical process where individual citizens were able to initiate and qualify an initiative for a referendum process that registered voters (an official identity) in California (and 10 other states) could then vote to accept or reject. This right afforded California citizens with a potential identity, that is, policymakers.

Pathway 2: Who Counts as a Voter and Who Voted to Support Proposition 227

To understand more fully the extent of the press that this process created for change in 1998, we interrupted the analysis of the roots of the referendum process to initiate a new pathway, one that took us forward from 1911 to 1998 and the time of the vote on the referendum. This analysis examined the numbers and types of actors who were required to participate in the election, or had the right to participate in the election as well as the time requirements for qualifying a proposition. This information was found in the handbook for creating initiatives that is on the California government website (http://www.sos.ca.gov/elections/elections_htm). The period designated is *131 days before the next statewide election*. Thus, in examining the time required for propositions, we were able to identify the potential boundaries of a local social field, that is, the time frame within which the discourse about English Only was officially discussed in public venues surrounding the school within the state. Given that the qualifying date is 131 days prior to the election in June,

1998, we found that the initial boundary had to be expanded to include the period of recruiting signatures on the petition that would insure placement of the referendum on the ballot. Thus, the time frame surrounding the discourse about English Only, prior to the vote, was greater than the 131 days required and included the period during which Unz and his supporters obtained the required signatures. To explore how this qualifying process worked, and who participated, we examined the handbook on propositions further. This analysis located another source of environmental or policy press–the number of registered California voters (another identity) who were required to sign a petition to endorse the proposition. The handbook states that:

> Petitions proposing initiative statutes must be signed by registered voters. The number of signatures must be equal to at least 5% of the total votes cast for Governor at the last gubernatorial election (Cal. Const., art. II, Section 8(b); Section 9035). The total number of signatures required for initiative statutes is 433,971 [for the 1998 election].

Given the number of voters required to sign as designated in the state's constitution, we saw this petition as representing more than Unz and his supporters' perspectives and goals; it also potentially represented the beliefs and values of those California voters who signed the petition. Viewed in this way, the role of signer of the petition was an official identity and a locally constructed identity based on the agency of individual voters.

Having located the criteria for qualifying a proposition, we then interrupted that analysis to explore who participated in the election as well as who had the right to participate but did not. Given the requirement of 5 percent of those voting for governor in the last election as the number required, we had to examine the data on the CA government website on the number of people voting in the previous election. This analysis led us to uncover not only the number required by a series of issues related to this process and a range of possible identities for people who were citizens (a political identity) of California (potentially more than 6,000,000 eligible voters). When we examined the number of people who voted for the proposition by identity, a telling case within the larger interruption analysis was constructed.

The initiative was passed by 67 percent of those voting in the election, but this figure, as indicated previously, was not 67 percent of all eligible voters (a political identity). When we examined the numbers of those registered, and those eligible to vote, we gained new insights into who constituted the "majority" (a collective political identity) passing this initiative. Only 42.49 percent of registered voters chose to participate in the election (another identity and an act of agency). This state of affairs meant that only 20.05 percent of all eligible voters supported Unz. Thus these figures showed that although two-third of those voting supported English Only, this vote does not represent the *will of "the" people*, a phrase often used in politics. People in this instance referred to only those voting, a small segment of the 6 million people eligible to vote.

This line of analysis led us to ask a range of questions: *Who takes up what rights? Who cannot take up these sets of rights, given that they are not afforded, or do not seek, the citizen identity? What are the consequences of these actions? For whom, where? And, what is the relative weight that a proportion of voters assume, even if it cannot be said that it represents the will of the people?* In this section, therefore, we uncovered a range of actors and identities associated with the referendum process. We also uncovered an often invisible role afforded to citizens, the role of policymaker (an identity) in relation to Unz (an inscribed political position). Thus, although one person initiated this movement (a collective identity) and financed it (a political identity), the passage of this initiative was the result of a broad range of actors both in the face-to-face spaces of 1998 and the historical contexts copresent in the referendum process as a constitutional right. These discourses and actions around this process can be seen as creating, what Gee (1990) calls, Big D Discourses. The constitutional nature of the right to referendums meant that this law had the press of a large segment of the voting populations, not just the legislature, who had to ratify this referendum. Thus, the reform press created by this referendum brought multiple actors' beliefs and actions as well as multiple histories to bear on Beth and her decisions for action in 1998.

Pathway 3: From the Local to National Policies

At this point in examining historical processes at the state level, we once again saw a need to interrupt the analysis of the state-level policies in order to examine legal actions at the federal level that were copresent with this state sanctioned process. We used Beth's name for students as bilingual and her concern for silent students of the past as anchors (rich points) to trace a process that predated the Unz initiative. Given that Beth was a bilingual teacher (an identity she inscribed for herself and others), we decided to trace actions by the Supreme Court (a political identity for a group that is the judicial arm of the federal government in the US and is in charge of making decisions that acquire the level of jurisprudence). The legal decisions of this body affirmed students' rights to language support in schools and led to the creation of the Bilingual Instruction program, the initiative that was being challenged by Unz. Federal legislation, and court rulings along a national pathway, became a new rich point within the initial point of interruption. Therefore, to examine the federal support for the Bilingual Instruction program offered by Beth's district, we traced the roots to a series of policy initiatives at the federal level that constituted a policy press for the schools in California prior to the Unz initiative.

Although there are other areas of federal legislation involved in civil rights legislation (e.g., *Oliver L. Brown et al. v. the Board of Education of Topeka, Kansas*, 1954), in this chapter we focus on the Supreme Court case, *Lau v. Nichols* (1974) that set in motion legal rights for US citizen (an identity) to language support in educational settings at the national level. We include this policy initiative for two reasons. First, like Unz, this initiative was rooted in actions taken by citizens of California, members of the Chinese-American community (a linguistic, binational political and social identity). Second, as stated above, this initiative afforded students in California (an official identity) with the right to language support for learning in the public schools accepting federal monies.

In a landmark Supreme Court case, citizens of California within the Chinese-American community began a process that involved these citizens, represented by Lau, in a series of legal processes at different levels of the legal system in the federal courts (a legal identity). Through a series of appeals (an identity attributed to a legal process) of decisions of lower courts (an identity for particular part of the legal system), the supporters of this case were able to have their case (a legal identity) presented in an oral argument by lawyers who have the right to present cases before the Supreme Court (particular legal identities). The education.gov website provides a full text of the Supreme Court decision and inscribes a range of actors who contributed to the decision.[4] The *Syllabus* of *Lau et al. v. Nichols et al.* states:

> The failure of the San Francisco school system to provide English language instruction to approximately 1,800 students of Chinese ancestry who do not speak English, or to provide them with other adequate instructional procedures, denies them a meaningful opportunity to participate in the public educational program and thus violates 601 of the Civil Rights Act of 1964, which bans discrimination based "on the ground of race, color, or national origin," in "any program or activity receiving Federal financial assistance," and the implementing regulations of the Department of Health, Education, and Welfare.[5] (pp. 565–569)

By including *Lau et al. v. Nichols et al.* in the analysis of the history of initiatives in California, we made visible multiple histories and intersecting and interconnecting systems that constitute the circumstances surrounding the Unz referendum. Additionally, this historical analysis uncovered a broad

---

4 (http://www.ed.gov/about/offices/list/ocr/ell/lau.html) (No. 72-6520, Supreme Court of the United States, 414 U.S. 563, December 10, 1973, Argued, January 21, 1974, Decided.)

5 Douglas, J., delivered the opinion of the Court, in which Brennan, Marshall, Powell, and Rehnquist, J. J. joined. Stewart, J., filed an opinion concurring in the result, in which Burger, C. J., and Blackmun, J., joined, post, p. 569. White, J., concurred in the result. Blackmun, J., filed an opinion concurring in the result, in which Burger, C. J., joined, post, p. 571.

range of actors, in particular social fields that participated in the processes constituting key vectors of policy action. Through this analysis, we also identified multiple potential identities for actors associated with actions in particular social fields and how these identities were often constructed by people who took up the opportunities to participate by law.

This all-too-brief set of analyses of complex historical actions, and the changes that they supported, made visible why it was not possible to focus solely on the Unz initiative to understand the impact of the transformation to English Only on Beth and her students. As inscribed by Beth, this shift was embedded in historical movements that included the history of civil and human right issues (related to immigration, citizenship, forms of education, and rights to education (See e.g., VanSledright, 2008). Her tensions, therefore, were historical and her use of the term *destroy* in her column inscribed a larger grounding, as we uncovered in this section. Although a discussion of these movements is beyond the scope of this paper, what is important to note is Beth's awareness of the competing systems and the tensions that she faced given her position as a teacher as well as a professional committed to providing access to all of her students. In her TESOL column, Beth presented this tension to the reader as a challenge of how to address competing logics and political actions while meeting her commitments to her students and her legal requirements as a teacher.

Rich Point 2: The Decisions of the Local School Board

Once we identified the series of state and federal legal actions that converged to create a policy press on Beth as a bilingual teacher, in what was becoming a monolingual district, we returned to Beth's column to explore the next rich point identified previously in the Newsletter column—the decisions made by the *local Board of Education* (an elected body and a political identity) that Beth argued occurred *before a vote was taken*. This rich point led to a new pathway for analysis and a new question: What changes were made by the school board and who initiated these changes? This question led to a (re)analysis of the records related to the local Board of Education's actions beginning in 1998. This analysis showed that the five elected members of the school board voted unanimously to eliminate Bilingual Education six months prior to the statewide vote on Proposition 227. In describing these actions, Beth used two different terms to represent the impact of these decisions, *eliminate–destroy?* These terms suggested a new pathway, one that examined what was in place at the district level and what changed, in what ways, initiated by whom for what purposes, under what conditions, with what outcome or consequence for Beth and her students.

In this section, we use this new rich point to explore the local social fields, their actors, and the ways in which their decisions not only raised a challenge for Beth but also challenged her identity as a bilingual teacher, who had, over an extended period of time (29 years), created a particular kind of world in, and identity for, her classes (e.g., Castanheira, 2004; Castanheira et al., 2007; Castanheira, et al., 2009; Yeager, 2003; Yeager, et al., 2009). Given the need to understand these sources of change in terms of their contributions to the impact on Beth's identity and the identity of her class, we elected to interrupt our analysis of what she inscribed in her column in order to examine a chain of actions in the school district that led to the closure of Bilingual Instruction in her district and that removed particular resources that were previously available for Beth to use with her students. This analysis is important, given that some districts within California took up this law differentially, and continued to afford students language support (Palmer & García, 2000). Through this analysis, we make visible how local constraints were put in place between 1996 and 1998, prior to the referendum on English for the Children.

Interruption Analysis 2: School Board Actions, Multiple Years, Multiple Policy Changes

We begin the analysis of the changes between 1996 and 1998 by focusing on the change in policymakers at the district level. This analysis uses the composition of the school board resulting from elections between 1996 and 1998 and actions related to these changes. Analysis of the ethnographic records related to the school board actions showed that in 1998, the five elected members of the school board (a political identity), voted unanimously to eliminate bilingual instruction, even in the face of opposition by teachers, parents, community members, and other community activists. The analysis is represented in Figure 2, which provides a map of changes at the district level related to the move to English Only over a four-year period, 1996–2000. This figure was constructed from records and information in our archive. In constructing the text of Board actions between 1998–1996, we examined the relationship between official resources afforded to Beth through the school district policymakers and how students in the district were officially and unofficially named—a form of *inscribed personhood* as indicated previously.

As indicated in Figure 1, through mapping the decisions of the board from 1998 backward to the period of board elections when Bilingual Instruction was sanctioned as the approach (1996), we identified changes across a four-year period. Using this period as an anchor, we identified decisions made in each school year by different configurations of actors in particular social fields: at the community level with the election of school board members, and within the school board in different areas of work. This analysis led to the identification of two periods of shifting decisions, one from 1996–1997 with the change in composition of the elected members of the school board, and a second period of such changes in 1999, with election of new members of the school board. What is significant is that these elections shifted the political configuration of the five-member school board, which created the possibility for changes in policy, resources, supported activity, and educational approach.

Policies Actions Identified	1996-1997	1997-1998	1998-1999	1999-2000
School Board Election	3 new members elected	→	Re-elected 1 (of 2) school board members and elected 2 new members	→
School Board Decisions				
Bilingual Education & Language of Instruction				
Revised Bilingual Education Plan (BEST)	June 1996			
English Learner Plan		August 1997		
English Only		January 1998	→	→
Textbook adoption		Recommendations by Committee		
K-2 English		Open Court	→	→
K-2 Spanish		Macmillan	*No Spanish readers*	
Grade 3		Macmillan	→	Open Court chosen
Grades 4-6		Macmillan	→	→
Packard Foundation Grant for Open Court Coaches			→	→
Test selection	Iowa Test of Basic Skills/SABE	STAR 9 English Only	→	→
Class size reduction (tied to selection of Phonics-based readers)	K-2	K-3	→	→
Decisions at José's School				
Textbooks adopted				
K-2 English		Open Court	→	→
K-2 Spanish		Macmillan	*No Spanish readers*	
Grade 3		Macmillan	Open Court	→
Grades 4-5		Macmillan	Open Court	→
Open Court Coaches (Funded by Private Foundation)			K-5	→

Figure 2. Policy actions at the local district an school level.

The change between 1996 and 1997 shifted the composition from one supporting a Bilingual Instructional approach to one supporting English Only approach. Analysis of data to construct Figure 2 made visible the range of decisions taken by different actors across a variety of social fields, each with a particular responsibility for action and decision making. The areas of action identified included, but were not limited to, elections, curriculum decisions, statewide assessments (tests), and personnel (e.g., the use of non-district personnel–the Packard Foundation). Through this analysis, we identified a range of actions and actors, not a single policy or group of actors, who were instrumental in eliminating the official and public identities of bilingual speakers (a public as well as classroom identity) by the local board. As we will demonstrate the school board's actions also eliminated the possibilities of the public display of being multilingual beings in the local schools for all students, not just those who were officially identified as bilingual speakers (Heras, 1998; Santa Barbara Classroom Discourse Group, 1995; Yeager et al., 2009).

Analysis of the School Board's actions made visible the presence of multiple policy presses that converged to narrow the opportunities for teaching and for resource use for Beth and other teachers in bilingual schools in her district (Dixon et al., 2000). The first area, or what we called policy vector, in which we identified changes was the vector of elections and the intersection with areas of oversight by the school board. As indicated in the area of Bilingual Instruction in Figure 2, in 1996 the existing five members of the School Board, including three new members had appointed committees to work on revising the Bilingual Instruction Program in the district. In 1997, they added a committee to develop an English Learner Plan. In 1997, they also had a committee that recommended textbooks for adoption, a process that had been in place in the district and California for several decades. These recommendations included Spanish-language versions of the Macmillan reading textbooks.

However, when we examined what remained in place and what changed following the election in 1998 of two new board members, we identified a shift in the policy logic by the (re)constituted board. An analysis of the bilingual education committees showed that these committees were disbanded. So were the committee to review textbooks that included parents, teachers, and administrators. In 1998, after the Board election, the Board removed the Spanish textbooks that had been officially approved, thus eliminating a resource that had been available for teacher use with ELL. In 1999, the Board also replaced the Macmillan reading series at all grade levels with *Open Court*, a more phonics oriented and scripted reading program. Given that the advisory committee on textbooks and curriculum had been disbanded, there were no internal committees, or cross-group committees to object.

These changes were accompanied by a mandate at the beginning of the school year in 1998 to remove all Spanish from public spaces, making the use of Spanish books, even as supplementary texts, difficult for teachers and students alike, given the local interpretation of the statewide referendum. Thus, local actions, which preceded the vote on Proposition 227 converged on Beth in fall 1998, creating a web of (re)formulations of what counted as education in the local schools and district. The actions of the School Board represented in Figure 2, make visible changing beliefs, values, logics, and resources tied to changing Board composition. These actions, therefore, (re)formulated what counted as reading as well as what language students and teacher could use to read or teach reading. One impact of this aspect of the policy changes was that these changes (re)formulated who could be viewed as a competent reader in the face of the elimination of the Spanish readers. In this change, those who were competent readers of Spanish (performance-based identities) became viewed as *beginning readers* of English, a consequence identified previously by Moll and Diaz (1987) in an earlier study.

The shift in values is further supported by the School Board's decision to bring in coaches (an identity assumed by local teachers) to insure that the teachers were following the script in the textbooks as prescribed and were using English as the language of instruction. What is significant about the use of coaches is that they were funded by a private foundation (a political identity) that sought to make certain that phonics and basic skills in English, as inscribed in the textbook series, were implemented. The changing values in this district is further confirmed when the question of whether other districts in California accepted the offer of the coaches tied to the changing textbooks. As with the take up of Proposition 227, these policies (the use of coaches) potentials were not taken up by other districts, including neighboring ones.

Although this picture is a partial representation of the range of changes and actions beyond the classroom door at the local level, the analysis of the chains of action represented in Figure 2 demonstrated that the movement to English Only was not a simple mandate but was one supported by the elimination of resources and levels of participation in the decision-making process at the district as well as state levels. These changes, in turn, led to a change in what counted as the teaching of reading, as the public display of reading knowledge, and in the instructional program available to teacher, and in turn, students. One unanticipated consequence of the School Board's actions was the elimination of the designation of bilingual reader for all students (e.g., identities as Spanish Readers for English-dominant students), not just second language learners (e.g., English Readers for Spanish-dominant students).

The significance of this policy change was also visible at the school level. In Beth's school, prior to 1998, all students learned a second language, and were able to learn their heritage language, while also acquiring a new language. The school had developed programs in English as a Second Language (ESL), Spanish as a Second Language (SSL), and Spanish for Native Spanish Speakers (SNS). In this way, the school supported the acquisition, development, and identities of native language and second (or third) language learners (Castanheira et al., 2007). With the changes to English Only, these identities as language learners and readers were eliminated for English-dominant and bilingual students (whose native as well as nonnative language(s) were being developed previously). Furthermore, at no time did the policymakers at the district and school board level take into consideration what actually occurred in Beth's, and by implication others', classrooms, or what was lost for all students. In the next section, we explore how these policies and resources decided beyond the classroom door had an impact on what was possible inside of Beth's classroom, as a telling case.

Telling Case 2: The Impact of Policy Changes on Opportunities for Learning

We return to an analysis of the TESOL column to explore additional areas of tension Beth inscribed in her column: *what will this first day be like and how will I address both the legal requirements and what I know, as a bilingual teacher, is necessary to do on the first day?* In stating this, she captures a dual challenge, her commitment to being, and education as, a bilingual teacher, and her legal responsibilities as a teacher and a public employee. These tensions are ones that address the external supports and constraints and how she saw these entering her classroom. In framing this, she identified multiple sources of influence on the opportunities she is able to develop with students. As the following excerpt makes visible, the shift from bilingual instruction to English only has led to a series of uncertainties that faced her in August of 1998 in preparing for the first day:

> This is the day we begin to construct together the community of learners we'll have for the rest of the year, the day I begin to frame and build with the students what life in this classroom is going to look and *sound* like, what will "count" as learning, whose voices will count, what will be important, what we will value. So I sit and re-read Evelyn's and Joaquin's words, hoping they'll somehow give me a clue as to how I'm going to do this framing, because I know that this first day, this year, will be different. Actually, I've been avoiding thoughts about the nitty-gritty of what I'm going to do without bilingual instruction this year, it's been too demoralizing, but now I think that if I can figure out that first day, I'll be able to get to the next day and the week after that, because, no matter what, my kids are coming through the door.

She framed her concern for *what life in her classroom will look and sound like, what will "count" as learning, and whose voices will count.* She then asked three questions: *what will be important, how will we begin building our community on the first day, given the elimination of a language resource, and what will we value?* In inscribing "we" she inscribed others in this decision. She also inscribed a loss she and her students were facing, *what I'm going to do without bilingual instruction this year.* In talking about the loss in this way, she made visible that the loss of instructional opportunities for her is also a loss for her students. In this way, she made visible her understanding of the relationship between teaching and learning as a collective construction, initiated by her but then constructed collectively—thus "we" in the phrase, *what we will value in the community of learners that they will begin to construct together.* In framing the challenge in this way, she made visible another rich point, the beginning of community building on the first day. Thus Beth framed a pathway that we used in our analysis of the history of community building between 1991 and 1998 (e.g., Floriani, 1993; Castanheira et al., 2007; Yeager et al., 2009). In this analysis we contrast what she called the *nitty-gritty* work she did with students in periods with *bilingual instruction* with what was possible in English Only.

Pathway 1: On Community Building and the First Day of School

Having identified the need to examine the *nitty-gritty of community building,* we decided to interrupt the narrative analysis once again to review past work on the first day across years and to construct a contrastive analysis of the *nitty-gritty* of community building in 1993, the first day that Beth taught fifth grade, and 1998, the first day of teaching without bilingual instruction as a resource. These two first days, we argue are comparable, in that they are first moments of a changing instructional group. Through the contrastive analysis of instructional and community building practices in these two time periods, we identified areas of common practices and areas of difference that we will demonstrate had an impact on the opportunities for learning that Beth was able to construct with her students and thus on the construction of potential identities.

Table 1 provides a map of the first day of school in 1993 and the contrast with 1998.[6] In this table, we (re)presented the literate practices, the language used and the organizational patterns constructed on the two first days of school in 1993 and 1998. Analysis of the similarities and differences in the two first days showed that in 1993, the teacher, using multiple languages, was able to construct a series of actions that became literate practices on the first day as the students worked with her to actively develop the events and discourse of that day. On the first day in 1998, the topics remained the same but the ways in which they were initiated differed.

As indicated in Table 1, in 1993 Beth used both languages in a fluid way to create a view of what counts as the *language of the classroom* (Lin, 1993). On the first day of school in 1993, given the composition of her class, she used three languages, one her native language (English), one that she spoke as a second- language learner who was able to read write and speak in this language

---

6 The map is a (re)presentation of activity on the first morning, using present continuous verbs. This form of mapping (Green & Meyer, 1991; Green & Wallat, 1981) is designed to capture the moment-by-moment actions that teacher and students construct as they work together to develop the events of classroom life. Viewed in this way, the ebb and flow of activity forms a basis for identifying the events constructed. By using present continuous verbs and the objects of these verbs, we were able to identify the literate actions and the practices that members constructed and used with each other within and across the events of the first day of school.

Table 1. Events and practices of the first day of school by language available 1993-1998

Phases/Sub-phases in Classroom Activity	1993–PATTERNS Literate and Social Practices	Language(s) 1993	Language(s) 1998	1998–PATTERNS POST 227 Literate and Social Practices	Patterns of Organization & Interaction 1993 and 1998
Developing Collective					
Beginning of collective	* selecting name cards	E/S	E	* selecting name cards	* individual
* forming table groups	* choosing where to sit in table groups	E/S		* choosing where to sit in table groups	* individual
	* drawing on name cards				
	* talking with table group members	S/E		• drawing on name cards	* individual in whole group
	* introducing chime as signal	S/E	E	• talking with table group members	
	* explaining active listening				* individual in table group
* establishing roles and relationships, norms and expectations	* introducing adults in community	E/S	E	* introducing chime as signal	
	• student teacher BCLAD	S/E			* whole group
	• teacher aide SSL	E/S	E	* roles of adults	* whole group
	• university ethnographers Bilingual				* whole group
				* talking about studying own class	
	* introducing ethnography as community practice	E/S		* defining prior self	* whole group
	* discussing life in prior communities	S/E	E/S	* defining Tower member	* individual in whole group
* Name Game activity	* defining ways of living in Tower		E	* defining school member	
	community	E/S	E		
	* explaining insider knowledge as				* whole group
	member of McKinley community	E/S	E		* whole group
	* defining self	S/E/V			

Continued on next page.

Table 1 *(Continued)*

	* introducing self to table group	S/E	E	* providing description of self	
	* introducing self to whole group	E/V/S		* introducing descriptive	* individual in table
			E	self	group
					* individual in table
Developing Inquiry as Re-	* defining mathematicians	S/E			group
source	* introducing how to use Learning Logs	E/S		* defining student	* individual in
Watermelon Project	* explaining tradition of watermelons		E	* Mathematicians	whole group
* utilizing Learning Logs	* formulating questions as part of in-	S/E		* introducing Learning	
	vestigating		E/S	Logs	* whole group
	* asking particular question to be ans-	E/S		* listening to teacher na-	* whole group
	wered		E	rrative	* whole group
	* making a guess	S/E		* writing question in	* individual in
* transitioning to	* making an estimate, collecting data		E	Learning Logs	whole group
problem	* revising the estimate from data collec-	E/S	E/S	* defining question as	* whole group
	tion	S/E	E	problem to be solved	
	* explicating the process used so far	E/S	E	* making entry in Learning	* individual in
		S/E	E/S	Logs	whole group
			E	* making entry in Learning	* individual in table
				Logs	group
				* making entry in Learning	* individual in table
				Logs	group
				* copying chart on white	* individual in
				board	whole group

(Spanish), and one she had learned phrases in (Vietnamese). The use of the three languages signaled to students that language(s) of all members, not just specific groups, would be a resource for this developing community. In attempting Vietnamese on the first day, within this event in which languages were introduced, she demonstrated a new identity, risk taker who tried a new language to include the other in the developing community.

Analysis of actions required of and available to all students in this class made visible a common set of demands or expectations in 1993—all students (and the teacher, teacher-aide, student-teacher, and university-based ethnographers) were expected to learn the languages of the others to work and participate in the community across languages. The interweaving of multiple languages provided opportunities for learning of English and Spanish as well as awareness of Vietnamese. In this way, Beth created a form of language immersion for all students. She also used code-switching, providing bilingual students with a model of a discourse practice that they could use to help others at their table group. Additionally, after observing students working together for three days, Beth (re)configured table groups to include bilingual, English-dominant, Spanish-dominant speakers, native bilingual speakers, and bilingual speakers of different levels Finally, given the presence of a Vietnamese-speaking student, she created ways of including her in the class, even though Beth did not speak Vietnamese. To provide help for this student, Beth gave the student's aunt, who spoke English, an overview of the day so that the student had a map in her mind of what was happening. She also obtained a tutor for the student from the local community college who spoke and read Vietnamese and located books in English and Vietnamese as well as Spanish and English to support students in reading a common text in their own language, thus creating a common opportunity for learning across the languages. The model of language use in 1993, therefore, was one of second (or third) language learning for all students, and one in which multiple languages were a resource for learning and for identity construction (Santa Barbara Classroom Discourse Group, 1995).

Further analysis of the patterns of language used on the first day in 1993 and 1998 represented in Table 1 made visible a range of differences in what could be proposed to students in and through the languages used in 1998. A contrastive analysis of the phases and subphases of activity made visible a common set and sequence of events and subevents constructed by the teacher and the class members. However, when the patterns of social and literate practices constructed were examined, a pattern of difference was identified. Although the topics were similar, the fact that the teacher could use English and Spanish in 1993 permitted students to respond in the language of their choice. Students were also given permission to record their thoughts and ideas in the language of their choice. However, in 1998, this pattern was no longer possible.

While the teacher introduced a few key words in Spanish across the events (e.g., *comunidad, investigar, un diario de aprendizaje*), the dominant language of the first morning was English and the teacher used what is referred to as *sheltered English* instructional practices to help students gain access to the academic content she was introducing and engaging them in. This process enabled her to present common topics across years but not to present them in common ways. One notable exception to the common practices, given the shift to English Only, was the fact that students were required to write in English to record their estimates and to copy what was on the board into their learning logs. The latter strategy was not used in 1993, given that students were able to record information in the language of their choice. We will explore the impact of this state of affairs further in the next section.

Pathway 2: Triangulation, Contrastive Analysis, and Impact of Practices across Five Years

As indicated in Table 1, there were common activities/events but not common discourse processes or practices. There were common organizational patterns, but who could speak with whom about what in what ways differed. However, in Table 1, we only contrasted two years. To examine further the stability of these actions and their consequences for student learning, we undertook one additional contrastive analysis, an analysis focusing on the practices and actions constructed in and through the moment-by-moment interactions in the classroom for the first three weeks of school. This contrastive analysis of practices identified across five years, three during the Bilingual Instruction reform initiative (1993, 1996, 1997) and two for English Only (1998, 2000), is presented in Table 2.

As represented in Table 2, with three exceptions, the practices constructed and used in the first three weeks of school were similar across the five years. That is, each year the teacher introduced to, and constructed with, students a common range of literate and social practices, with three notable exceptions.

The three notable exceptions to this pattern were associated with language and were: the choice of language to talk and to write in, and the use of writing to record student thinking about the processes in which they had engaged. These differences raised questions about how changes in policies also had an impact on the identities of participants as members of a multilingual community and on their potential identities as speakers of one or more languages. These latter issues are rarely raised in the dialogues on the achievement gap or on how to support opportunities for learning academic content for one group of students. As the analysis in Table 1 made visible, all students in 1993 had access to learning other languages, to use languages for learning, and to a common set of social and academic opportunities for learning.

Table 2. Actions and Practices Observed on the First Day of School 1993, 1996, 1997, 1998 and 2000

Actions	9-9 1993	9-11 1996	9-4 1997	9-9 1998	9-8 2000
Observing	x	x	x	x	x
Using two languages	x	x	x		x
Writing in language of choice	x	x	x		
Introducing & defining roles	x	x	x	x	x
Collecting data	x	x	x	x	x
Interpreting data	x	x	x	x	x
Comparing data	x	x	x	x	x
Working in pairs	x	x	x	x	x
Working in groups	x	x	x	x	x
Explaining/practicing new processes	x	x	x	x	x
Defining terms	x	x	x	x	x
Asking questions	x	x	x	x	x
Reporting to class	x	x	x	x	x
Participating as member of audience	x	x	x	x	x
"Writing to think"	x	x	x		
Learning logs	x	x	x	x	x
Revising thinking	x	x	x	x	x
Defining what things mean		x	x	x	x
Negotiating group answer	x	x	x	x	x
Supporting ideas with evidence	x	x	x	x	x
Sharing opinions & ideas	x	x	x	x	x

The contrast between what was possible in the Bilingual Language period (1993–1997) and what was possible in 1998, made visible lost opportunities for all members of the class, given that English-dominant students no longer had the opportunities for language learning, for particular types of social relationships, and for constructing a multilingual community. The removal of languages other than English in instructional events, therefore, meant that English speakers and bilingual students as well as Spanish-dominant speakers no longer had the opportunity to see themselves as becoming multilingual; nor were they able to experience what a multilingual society was like and how in such a society they could use the differences in language as a resource for community building as well as academic access. Thus, what was lost in the shift were the opportunities for all students to see themselves as potential speakers of another language, as a learner of a second (or third) language, and as a competent speaker of one or more languages. Additionally, the limited use of Spanish in 1998, in contrast to the more balanced and fluid use in instruction in 1993, signaled markedly different values for language at the community level, creating a privileged position for one language over the other in a school context.

Without the contrast across years, the differences in opportunities for all students would not have been visible. Additionally, by holding the actions and practices constant across the five years, we were also able to identify which practices were lost for particular groups of individuals across the two reform initiatives. The contrastive analysis across years showed that, while oral language choice returned in 2000, the choice of language(s) in which to write did not. The removal of the ability to write to think eliminated one key dimension of the inquiry oriented curriculum in Beth's class–the idea that your own thinking, written in your language of choice, when documented from the first-to-last day of the school year, becomes a textbook of your thinking and a way of seeing your own growth. The consequences of this loss for Spanish-dominant students can be seen in the final project for this class. In this project, students were asked to construct Showcase portfolios that provided evidence of their thinking, creativity, ability to work collaboratively in groups, to use evidence, among other dimensions of the inquiry process (Castanheira et al., 2009).

The move to English Only instruction, and the requirement that students write in English, therefore, ignored the type of curriculum that had been in place and the ways in which inquiry oriented curriculum involved the public use of multiple languages to support the content learning of all students. The loss of the practice of writing in the language of choice meant that some students had an incomplete record of the work they had done (e.g., Castanheira et al., 2007; Yeager, 1999a, 1999b; Yeager & Green, 2008), raising the question–how is it possible to write complex ideas in a language that you have just begun to learn? The consequences of this for the individual is captured in the following statement by a student in 1998, "I used to know that," which referred to the fact that he knew the concept in Spanish but did not know it in English (Dixon et al., 2000).

The contrastive analysis presented in this section, therefore, demonstrated that the loss of opportunities for learning and for identity construction were ones faced by all students, by the teacher, and by the community that was being constructed. While the debate continues today about bilingual language instruction and its consequence for one group of students, the analysis in this section identified a missing element in this debate, the loss of opportunities for learning and for identity construction for all students. We argue that the shifting policies had an impact on all members of the community, not just those targeted by the English Only policy change.

The Need for an Abductive Logic of Reasoning: Ethnography as a Nonlinear System

One final outcome of this (re)analysis was made visible in this chapter, the need for a nonlinear ethnographic approach not only to data collection and analysis but also to presentation of the analyses. Agar (2006) argued that "[a]ny trajectory in the ethnographic space will run on the fuel of abduction" (para. 66). In this chapter, a process of abductive reasoning provided a foundation for exploring the interplay of policy decisions in systems beyond the classroom door that converged to transform and (re)formulate the educational approach in California, from one that officially sanctioned Bilingual Instruction to one that sanctioned English Only. By anchoring each analysis in a common rich point, the classes for a fifth-grade bilingual-teacher with whom we have engaged in a longitudinal ethnography, and by using her TESOL Newsletter column as an overall anchor for further analysis, we demonstrated the need for a multifaceted, multilayered, and multilevel system for uncovering the histories of actors and the consequences of differences in opportunities for learning.

By using abductive reasoning and a nonlinear process guided by this reasoning, contrastive analysis, and interruption analysis, we uncovered a series of unanticipated losses in opportunities for learning as well as identity construction of actors both inside and outside of the classroom. We also made visible a broad range of actors, who contributed a series of copresent and historically related policy changes that supported in one reform initiative particular instruction practices and languages, and constrained their use in a subsequent reform initiative. In this way, we explored, and developed grounded warrants about the consequences of anticipated and unanticipated actions on the opportunities for learning and identity construction of all students.

Still unexamined, and thus invisible are questions about how these shifts in opportunities shaped beyond the classroom door had impact on the academic knowledge base that these students needed for success across their careers in education. Before closing, however, one irony at the level of the larger community in the city, state, and nation needs to be acknowledged. At the local level of the city, all official documents related to the legal system and to schooling remained in English and Spanish (or other language) to provide access to the political, business, and social worlds. Therefore, in addition to exploring the impact on student careers, future work needs to examine the impact on access to other institutional contexts as well as to resources in the social world.

References

Agar, M. (1994). *Language shock: Understanding the culture of conversation.* New York: William Morrow and Company, Inc.

Agar, M. (2004). We have met the other and we're all nonlinear: Ethnography as a nonlinear dynamic system. *Complexity,10*(2), 16–24.

Agar, M. (2006). An ethnography by any other name. *Forum: Qualitative Social Research,* 7(4). Retrieved from http://www.qualitative-research.net/index.php/fqs/article/view/177.

Alexander, R. (2001). *Culture and pedagogy: International comparisons in primary education.* Oxford, UK: Wiley-Blackwell

Anderson-Levitt, K. (2002). *Teaching cultures: Knowledge for teaching first grade in France and the United States.* Cresskill, NJ: Hampton Press.

Baker, W.D., & Green, J. (2007). Limits to certainty in interpreting video data: Interactional ethnography and disciplinary knowledge. *Pedagogies* 2(3), 191–204.

Baker, W.D., Green, J., & Skukauskaite, A. (2008). Video-enabled ethnographic research: A micro ethnographic perspective. In G.Walford (Ed.), *Ethnography in Education.* London: Tufnell Press.

Bakhtin, M.M. (1986). The problem of speech genres. In C. Emerson & M. Holmquist (Eds.), *Speech genres and other late essays* (pp. 60–102). (Translated by Vern McGee). Austin: University of Texas Press. (Original work published in 1953).

Barr, R. (1987). Classroom interaction and curricular content. In D. Bloome (Ed.), *Literacy and schooling.* Norwood, NJ: Ablex.

Barr, R., & Dreeben, R. (1983). *How schools work.* Chicago, IL: University of Chicago Press.

Bloome, D. (1992). Interacción e intertextualidad en el estudio de la lectoescritura en las aulas: el microanalisis como tarea teorica. (Interaction and intertextuality in the study of classroom reading and writing events: Microanalysis as a theoretical enterprise.) *Investigación etnográfica en educación.* Mexico City: Universidad Nacional Autonoma de Mexico, pp. 123–180.

Bloome, D., & Bailey, F. (1992). Studying language and literacy through events, particularity and intertextuality. In J.L. Green, R. Beach, M. Kamil & T. Shanrahan (Eds.), *Multidisciplinary perspectives on literacy research* (pp. 181–209). Urbana, IL: NCTE.

Bloome, D., Carter, S. P., Christian, B. M., Otto, S., & Shuart-Faris, N. (2004). *Discourse analysis and the study of classroom language and literacy event: A microethnographic perspective.* Mahwah, NJ: Erlbaum.

Bloome, D., & Egan-Roberston, A. (1993). The social construction of intertextuality in classroom reading and writing lessons. *Reading Research Quarterly, 28*(4), 305–333.

Borman, K., Clarke, C., Cotner, B., & Lee, R. (2006). Cross-case analysis. In J. Green, G. Camilli, and P. Elmore (Eds.), *Handbook of Complementary Methods in Education Research* (pp.123–140). Mahwah, NJ: Erlbaum.

Burin, D., & Heras, A.I. (2001). Enfoque de sistemas y análisis comunicacional aplicados a procesos de desarrollo local. In D. Burin & A. I. Heras (comp.) *Desarrollo local: una respuesta a escala humana a la globalización* (pp. 53–85). Argentina: Editorial CICCUS.

Burin, D., & Heras Monner Sans, A. I. (2008). Política pública de empleo y modelos de desarrollo en localidades rurales del noroeste argentino. In A. I. Heras Monner Sans, Ana Inés & D. Burin (Coord.), *Trabajo, desarrollo, diversidad* (pp. 263–291). Buenos Aires, Argentina: Editorial CICCUS.

Candela, A., Rockwell, E., & Coll, C. (2004). What in the world happens in classrooms?

Qualitative classroom research. *European Educational Research Journal*, *3*(3): 692–713.

Castanheira, M. L. (2004). *Aprendizagem contextualizada: discurso e inclusão na sala de aula.* Ceale; Autêntica: Belo Horizonte.

Castanheira, M. L., Crawford, T., Green, J., & Dixon, C. (2001). Interactional ethnography: An approach to studying the social construction of literate practices. *Linguistics and Education*, *11*(4), 353–400.

Castanheira, M. L., Green, J., Dixon, C., & Yeager, B. (2007). (Re)Formulating identities in the face of fluid modernity: An interactional ethnographic approach. *International Journal of Education Research*, *46*(3–4), 172–189.

Castanheira, M., Green, J., & Yeager, B. (2009). Investigating inclusive practices: An interactional ethnographic approach. In K. Kumpulainen, C. Hmelo-Silver & M. Cesar (Eds.), *Investigating classroom interaction: Methodologies in action.* Sense Publishers.

Chrispeels, J. H. (1997). Educational policy implementation in a shifting political climate: The California experience. *The American Educational Research Journal*, *34*(3), 453–481.

Corsaro, W. (1981). Entering the child's world: Research strategies for studying peer culture. In J. Green & C. Wallat (Eds.), *Ethnography & Language in Educational Settings* (pp.117–146). Norwood, NJ: Ablex.

Dixon, C., & Green, J. (2009). How a community of inquiry shapes and is shaped by policies: The Santa Barbara Classroom discourse group experience as a telling case. *Language Arts*, *86*(4), 280–289.

Dixon, C., Green, J., & Brandts, L. (2005). Studying the discursive construction of texts in classrooms through interactional ethnography. In R. Beach, J. Green, M. Kamil & T. Shanahan (Eds.), *Multidisciplinary perspectives on literacy research.* Cresskill, NJ: Hampton Press/National Conference for Research in Language and Literacy.

Dixon, C., Green, J., Yeager, B., Baker, D., & Franquiz, M. (2000). "I used to know that": What happens when reform gets through the classroom door. *Bilingual Education Research Journal*, *24*(1 & 2), 113–126.

Edwards, D., & Mercer, N. (1987). *Common knowledge.* New York: Methuen.

Egan-Robertson, A. (1998). Learning about culture, language and power: Understanding relationships among personhood, literacy practices, and intertextuality. *Journal of Literacy Research*, *30*(4), 449–487.

Erickson, F. (1986). Qualitative methods of research on teaching. In: M. Wittrock (Ed.), *The handbook of research on teaching* (pp. 119–161). New York: Macmillan.

Floriani, A. (1993). Negotiating what counts: Roles and relationships, texts and contexts, content and meaning. *Linguistics and Education*, *5*(3–4), 241–274.

Gee, J. P. (1990). *Social linguistics and literacies: Ideology in discourse.* London: Falmer Press.

Gee, J. P., & Green, J. (1998). Discourse analysis, learning and social practice: A methodological study. *Review of Research in Education*, *23*, 119–169.

Geertz, C. (1983). *Local knowledge: Further essays in interpretive anthropology.* New York: Basic Books.

Goertz, M. (2006). Policy analysis: Studying policy implementation. In J. L. Green, G. Camilli & P.B. Elmore (Eds.), *Handbook of complementary methods in education research* (pp. 681–700). Washington, D.C.: Erlbaum.

Green, J., & Bloome, D. (1997). Ethnography and ethnographers of and in education: A situated perspective. In J. Flood, S.B. Heath & D. Lapp (Eds.), *Handbook for literacy educators: Research in the communicative and visual arts* (pp. 181–202). New York: MacMillan.

Green, J., & Dixon, C. (1993). Talking knowledge into being: Discursive and social practices in classrooms. *Linguistics and Education, 5*(3-4), 231-239.

Green, J. L., Dixon, C., & Zaharlick, A. (2003). Ethnography as a logic of inquiry. In J. Flood, S. B. Heath, & D. Lapp (Eds.), *The Handbook for Research in the English Language Arts* (pp. 201-204). Mahwah, NJ: Erlbaum.

Green, J., & Meyer, L. (1991). The embeddedness of reading in classroom life: Reading as a situated process. In C. Baker, & A. Luke (Eds.), *Towards a critical sociology of reading pedagogy*. Philadelphia, PA: John Benjamins.

Green, J., & Wallat, C. (1981). Mapping instructional conversations: A sociolinguistic ethnography. In J.L. Green & C. Wallat (Eds.), *Ethnography and language in educational settings* (pp.161-205). Norwood, NJ: Ablex.

Gumperz, J. (1986). Interactive sociolinguistics on the study of schooling. In J. Cook-Gumperz (Ed.), *The social construction of literacy* (pp. 45-68). New York: Cambridge University Press.

Heap, J. (1992). Seeing snubs: An introduction to sequential analysis of classroom interaction. *Journal of Classroom Interaction, 27*(2), 23-28.

Heap, J. (1995). The status of claims in "qualitative" educational research. *Curriculum Inquiry, 25* (3), 271-292

Heras, A. I. (1993). The construction of understanding in a sixth-grade bilingual classroom. *Linguistics and Education, 5*(3-4), 275-300.

Heras, A. I. (1998). The post-propositions era and the role of university scholars. Newsletter-Noticiero, Chicano Studies Department and Center for Chicano Studies, Universidad de California, Santa Bárbara.

Heras Monner Sans, A. I., Burin, D., & Córdova, L. (2008). Política de empleo activa: Análisis del Plan Manos a la Obra y su puesta en marcha en una comarca patagónica. In A. I. Heras & D. Burin (Eds.), *Trabajo, desarrollo, diversidad* (pp. 223-262). Buenos Aires, Argentia: Editorial CICCUS.

Holland, D., & Cole, M. (1995). Between discourse and schema: Reformulating a cultural-historical approach to culture and mind. *Anthropology and Education Quarterly, 26*(4): 478-489.

Holland, D., Lachoite, W., Skinner, D., & Cain, C. (1998). *Identity and agency in cultural worlds.* New York: Cambridge University Press.

Lakoff, G., & Johnson, M. (1980). *Metaphors we live by*. Chicago, IL: University of Chicago.

Lau et al. v. Nichols et al. (1974). Supreme Court decision. US Department of Education, Office of Civil Rights site, Retrieved from http://www.ed.gov/about/offices/list/ocr/ell/lau.html.

Lima, E. (1995). Culture revisited: Vygotsky's ideas in Brazil. *Anthropology & Education Quarterly,* 26(4): 443-457.

Lin, L. (1993). Language of and in the classroom: Constructing the patterns of social life. *Linguistics and Education, 5*(3-4), 367-409.

McNeil, L. M., & Coppola, E. (2006). Official and unofficial stories: Getting at the impact of policy on educational practice. In J.L. Green, G. Camilli & P.B. Elmore (Eds.), *Handbook of complementary methods in education research* (pp. 681-700). Washington, DC: Lawrence Erlbaum.

Mehan, H. (1979). *Learning lessons*. Cambridge, MA: Harvard University Press.

Merchant, B., & Willis, A. (2000). *Multiple and intersecting identities in qualitative research.* Mahwah, NJ: Erlbaum.

Mishler, E. G. (1984). *The discourse of medicine: Dialectics of medical interviews*. Norwood, NJ: Ablex.

Mitchell, C. J. (1984). Typicality and the case study. In R. F. Ellens (Ed.), *Ethnographic research: A guide to general conduct* (pp. 238–241). New York: Academic Press.

Moll, L., & Diaz, E., (1987). Ethnographic pedagogy: Promoting effective bilingual instruction. In E. García & R. V. Padilla (Eds.), *Advances in bilingual education research.* (pp. 127–149). Tucson: University of Arizona Press.

National Commisssion on Excellence in Education (1983). A nation at risk: The imperative for educational reform. Available at: http://datacenter.spps.org/sites/2259653e-ffb3-45ba-8fd6-04a024ecf7a4/uploads/SOTW_A_Nation_at_Risk_1983.pdf

Palmer, D., & García, E. (2000). Voices from the field: Bilingual educators speak candidly about Proposition 227. *Bilingual Research Journal, 24*(1–2).

Putney, L., Green, J., Dixon, C., Durán, R., & Yeager, B. (2000). Consequential progressions: Exploring collective-individual development in a bilingual classroom. In C.D. Lee & P. Smagorinsky (Eds.), *Vygotskian perspectives on literacy research: Constructing meaning through collaborative inquiry* (pp. 86–126). New York: Cambridge University Press.

Rex, L.A. (2006). *Discourse of opportunity: How talk in learning situations creates and constrains.* Cresskill, NJ: Hampton Press.

Sagastizábal, M. Á., & Heras Monner Sans, A. I. (2005). *Incidencia de las representaciones sociales acerca de los alumnos en el trabajo docente: consideraciones para su estudio. Krinein N1, Revista de Educación* (pp. 107–139). Santa Fe, Argentina: Facultad de Humanidades, Universidad Católica de Santa Fe.

Santa Barbara Classroom Discourse Group (1992a). Constructing literacy in classrooms: Literate action as social accomplishment. In H. Marshall (Ed.), *Redefining student learning: Roots of educational restructuring* (pp. 119–150). Norwood, NJ: Ablex.

Santa Barbara Classroom Discourse Group (1992b). Do you see what we see? The referential and intertextual nature of classroom life. *Journal of Classroom Interaction, 27* (2), 29–36.

Santa Barbara Classroom Discourse Group (1995). Two languages, one community: An examination of educational opportunities. In R. Macias & R. Garcia (Eds.), *Changing schools for changing students: An anthology of research on language minorities, schools and society* (pp. 63–106). Santa Barbara, CA: Linguistic Minority Research Institute.

Smith, L. M., & Geoffrey, W. (1968). *The complexities of an urban classroom.* New York: Holt, Rinehart & Winston.

Smith, L., Kleine, P., Prunty, J., & Dwyer, D., (Eds.), (1986). *Educational innovators: Then and now.* London: Falmer Press.

Smith, L., Prunty, J., Dwyer, D., & Kleine, P. (1987). *The fate of an innovative school: The history and present status of the Kensington School.* London: Falmer Press.

Statewide Ballot Initiative Handbook, State of California, Available at: http://www.sos.ca.gov/elections/elections_h.htm.

Sutton, M., & Levinson, B., (Eds.), (2001). *Policy as practice: A sociocultural approach to the study of educational policy.* Westport, CT: Ablex Press.

Tannen, D. (1979). What's in a frame? Surface evidence for underlying expectations. In R. Freedle (Ed.), *New directions in discourse processing* (pp. 137–181). Norwood, NJ: Ablex.

Tobin, J., Wu, D., & Davidson, D., (1991). *Preschools in three cultures. Japan, China, and the United States.* New Haven, CT: Yale University Press.

Tuyay, S., Jennings, L., & Dixon, C., (2005). Classroom discourse and opportunities to learn: An ethnographic study of knowledge construction in a bilingual third-grade classroom. *Discourse Processes, 19*, 75–110.

VanSledright, B. (2008). Narratives of nation-state, historical knowledge, and school history education. *Review of Research in Education, 32*(1), 109–146.

Yeager, B. (1999a). Reflections on the community. *Matters*. TESOL.

Yeager, B. (1999b). Constructing a community of inquirers. Primary Voices. Champaign Urbana, IL: National Council of Teachers of English. 7(3), 37–52.

Yeager, E. [B]. (2003). 'I am a Historian': Examining the discursive construction of locally situated academic identities in linguistically diverse settings. Doctoral dissertation. University of California, Santa Barbara.

Yeager, B., Floriani, A., & Green, J. (1998). Learning to see learning in the classroom: Developing an ethnographic perspective. In A. Egan-Robertson & D. Bloome (Eds.), *Students as researchers of culture and language in their own communities* (pp.115–139). Cresskill, NJ: Hampton Press.

Yeager, B., & Green, J. (2008). 'We have our own language as well as the languages webring': Constructing opportunities for learning through a language of the classroom. In J. Scott, D. Straker & L. Katz (Eds.), *Affirming students' right to their own language: Bridging language policies and pedagogical practices* (pp. 153–175). New York: Routledge with National Council of Teachers of English.

Yeager, E., Green, J. L., & Castanheira, M. L. (2009). Two languages, one community: On the discursive construction of community in bilingual classrooms. In M. César & K. Kumpulainen (Eds.), *Social interactions in multicultural settings*. Rotterdam, Netherlands: Sense Publishers.

Yin, R. (2006). Case study methods. In J.L. Green, G. Camilli & P.B. Elmore (Eds.), *Handbook of complementary methods in education research* (pp. 95–110). Washington, DC: Erlbaum.

CHAPTER EIGHT

Power, Identity and Discourse in the Institutionalization of Basic Education in Mexico

"Invisible power can be exercised only with the complicity of those who do not want to know that they are subject to it or even that they themselves exercise it."
-Pierre Bourdieu

ALMA CARRASCO AND ROLLIN KENT

This chapter explores expressions of union identity construction in Mexico's K-9 teachers within a framework of discourse as a representation system, following Gee (2005, p. 10), as he points out that identities are "always and everywhere social and products of social histories." Conventional wisdom and academic research has for many years recognized that the national teachers' union in Mexico has a powerful effect on the workings of the educational system and on teachers' identity (Arnaut, 1992, 1996; Loyo, 1997, 1999; Raphael, 2007). These themes have also been extensively covered in the press, especially since the union leadership expanded its power through the creation of a political party, thus surpassing the sphere of labor and contractual negotiations (Raphael, 2007). It is frequently assumed, especially in media accounts, that the politicization of the union as an organization and the hierarchical and corrupt practices known to prevail in it have a deleterious effect on teaching and learning. However, there has been surprisingly meager discussion of the effects of this institutional environment on teachers' ordinary discourse and pedagogical practice. This chapter explores the relationships between the identity of teachers as union members and their discursive constructions as educators. To this end, it brings together various theoretical strands from the sociology of Pierre Bourdieu, the work of J. P.

Gee, and the work of institutionalist sociologists such as John Meyer, Richard Scott, and Johan Olsen.

The national teachers' union in Mexico—Sindicato Nacional de Trabajadores de la Educación (hereafter referred to as "SNTE")—affiliates all K-9 teachers and educational staff in the public sector, with a membership of over a million workers. It must be stressed that SNTE is the largest teachers' union in Latin America. In the mid-1950s, it became an important electoral tool for the Partido Revolucionario Institucional (Institutional Revolutionary Party: PRI), the political party that dominated the Mexican political system for more than half a century. In the 1960s, SNTE emerged as a major power center linked to the PRI (Arnaut, 1996) and has since then functioned as a major instrument of electoral mobilization for the PRI. In addition, SNTE's role cannot be fully understood without recognizing its dealings with the ministry of education, (Secretaría de Educación Pública: SEP). The intricate connections between the union and the ministry are broad and deep, reaching all levels of management of the educational system. Therefore, we will refer to what is commonly termed "the SEP-SNTE system.[1]" To this end, we will use the framework of neoinstitutionalism in sociology (Scott, Meyer & Associates, 1994; Olsen, 2007).

> The core idea that organizations are deeply embedded in social and political environments suggests that organizational practices and structures are often either reflections of or responses to rules, beliefs, and conventions built into the wider environment....The signature of the new institutionalism has been a focus at the field level, based on the insight that organizations operate amidst both competitive and cooperative exchanges with other organizations. This attention to the structure of relations and the formulation of logics within a field has opened the door to studying the emergence of competing mind-sets and logics, as well as an understanding of how contention develops within a field. (Powell & Colyvas, 2007)

Our argument assumes that the SEP-SNTE system constitutes three important dimensions: a set of political relationships between the state and the national union; a complex hierarchy of interconnections between them at the level of educational administration; and an "institutional environment" made up of norms, symbols, forms of expression and modes of interaction that are widely accepted as legitimate "rules of the game" within the Mexican educational system that constitute teachers' identity. Additionally, we will find it useful to utilize several concepts developed by Pierre Bourdieu, particularly his notion of field and habitus. For this purpose, we will refer to selections of Bourdieu's work edited by García (1984) and by Hanks (2005). García addresses one of the main questions that underlie Bourdieu's work: How do the economic and the symbolic spheres connect to the processes of power

---

[1] The very existence of this term in common usage is a relevant fact in and of itself.

reproduction, differentiation, and construction? With Hanks, we will examine the idea that "language, ideology, style and interaction respond to multiple effects of the relationship between habitus and field" (Hanks, 2005, p. 78). We present an exploratory argument that builds on our experiences, conversations, and interactions with diverse actors of the Mexican educational system, as well as on publicly available information on K-9 education. Two concerns stand out in this argument: the high tolerance to cognitive dissonance between formal discourse and common practice in the daily work of teachers, and the practical difficulties of any attempt to change the curriculum. We pose some questions for further investigation, trying to combine ideas stemming from various theories.

Contextualizing the SEP-SNTE System

The following quote from Muñoz (2008) sets the stage for our argument. "Although the right-wing Partido de Acción Nacional (National Action Party: PAN) won the presidential election in 2000, the National Teachers' Union still maintains its hierarchical structure and continues to count on the acquiescence of political authorities for managing crucial aspects of the educational system and for its use of public funds for electoral campaigns. The [persistence of the SEP-SNTE system under a new government] is a result of this organization's strategic role in preserving the governance of the education sector—i.e., control over workers—and of its leaders' pragmatic attitude toward the executive branch: educational policies proposed by the president obtain union approval in return for allowing the union leadership's discretionary use of public funds and its control over numerous positions within the public education system" (Muñoz, 2008, p. 377).

The SNTE affiliates 1.2 million educational workers in the public sector, including teachers, principals, supervisors, and administrative staff in K-9 education, as well as teachers in some higher education sectors, such as normal schools [teacher education colleges] and some public technical institutes of higher education. This enormous mass of education workers in the public sector is stabilized and institutionalized under a single union organization. The union is characterized by a clear political hierarchy and an extraordinary degree of political and administrative autonomy vis-à-vis governmental authorities. SNTE is a national organization comprised of 56 sections, which are in turn composed of a total of 7,000 local units. According to Muñoz (2008, p. 400), the union's National Executive Committee has the sole authority to convene local, sectional, and national conferences where union delegates are elected.

Table 1. Schools and Teachers in the Mexican Educational System

	Schools in the Public & Private Sectors		Teachers	
Levels of the educational system	Public	Private	Public: SNTE union members	Private: no union affiliation
Pre-school	77,547	15,206	179,787	44,954
Elementary	90,694	7,638	514,352	52,457
Middle school	30,020	4,013	314,182	52,549
High school (a)	8,229	4,144	123,611	84,033
Higher Education	1,158	3,009	39,703 (b)	114,567
Total by sector	207,648	34,010	1,171,635	348,560

(a) Not included are the high schools managed by public universities, thus not under SNTE affiliation; it does include some public technical schools.

(b) Includes only normal schools and some technical institutes but excludes public and private universities. The total number of professors of higher education is 252,247.

Source: Statistical Annex, 2nd Annual Presidential Address, Felipe Calderón, 2008

It may even fail to convene an electoral conference when one is due, thus effectively extending the mandate of an incumbent union committee for four more years. Thus control over workers is assured from the top. Labor legislation in the Mexican public sector establishes that only one union may legitimately exist (and thus negotiate labor contracts) within the Ministry of Education, thereby securing monopoly status for SNTE over teachers in the public sector.[2] Since the union has traditionally controlled promotions and access to public housing (an important contractually negotiated benefit), it is in the interest of the teacher to maintain cordial relationships with union officials (Muñoz, 2008, p. 410).

The union's operations receive financing from two sources: fees paid by affiliated members (deducted from their paychecks) and funds allocated by the government through contractual negotiations. Members' dues flow to the National Executive Committee. Union funds are managed at the discretion of the national leadership.

Union leadership has been extraordinarily stable. Since 1972 there have been only two national leaders, both of whom were designated by the president of the republic in consultation with the National Executive Committee. Elba Esther Gordillo was designated secretary general of the union in 1989, and in 2007 a specially convened national conference elected her

2 Nonetheless, in the context of the push for decentralization of K-9 education since the early 1990s, teachers in some states (Baja California) and in certain institutions (the National Polytechnic Institute) have mobilized to create independent unions. Opposition movements within SNTE are alive in various other states (Hernández, 2009).

to the new post of union President until 2012 (Raphael, 2007). The hierarchical structure that has historically characterized SNTE thus has a tendency to elaborate new posts in the political ladder.[3]

In 2006, President Calderón appointed Gordillo's son-in-law, Fernando González, as under-secretary for basic education of the federal Ministry of Education. This degree of union control over national policy is actually a recent phenomenon, although the SEP-SNTE system has elaborated extensive interlocking influences at all levels of educational administration. But it is not a surprising outcome given the fact that the legitimacy of the union leadership rests not only on the votes of the rank and file but on the relationships between SNTE's national leadership and the highest level of the political system (Muñoz, 2008, p. 399). It also demonstrates the importance of SNTE's recent evolution as an electoral machine: in 2005 the union created an electoral spin-off, a political party of its own, which provided Felipe Calderón the small number of votes he needed to win the hotly contested presidential election of 2006 (Raphael, 2007).

It must be noted that being an active member in the SNTE may be the first step toward a political career or it may provide access to positions in the education bureaucracy at the federal or state levels. Throughout the history of the SEP-SNTE system, numerous union leaders have later thrived within the PRI and various levels of government. Union militancy and loyalty are well-known prerequisites for gaining positions as school principal, inspector, or as head of a government agency. Union activists interested in a political career will strive to gain positions as local or national union officials. From there one might aspire to be a state or national legislator. SNTE offers important and attractive opportunities to escape from teaching drudgery and to circulate for years in the many positions of the complex and extensive union structure. Such "union commissions" are publicly funded and are a very important issue for negotiation between the union's leaders and the national and local governments. Funds allocated by the government for such commissions are quite significant and their amount has been made public only recently (Del Valle, 2009).

The SEP-SNTE's Rules of the Game from the Neoinstitutionalist Perspective

The union structure described above is a highly institutionalized sector in that it is extensively constituted by both formal and informal "rules of the game"

---

3 The changing nature of SNTE as a political organization and its varied interactions with educational institutions and government agencies are extensively documented by a growing number of teachers' blogs. See References.

that are widely accepted as legitimate by its members. Teachers' conventional wisdom accepts that the union organization comprises an institutional environment whose importance is equal to that of the formal educational system. Being a member of SNTE implies that one accepts its importance as a political actor within the educational system. The conventional wisdom accepts as normal practice that political considerations may often supersede educational issues.

Thus, it is useful to distinguish between the organizational and the institutional dimensions. Organizationally, the Mexican public education system can be functionally defined as an agency established according to the Constitution, with its own goals, functions, resources, staff, and formal structure. The teachers' union is another organization with its own formal structure. Formally, both organizations coexist but are separate. But we are also interested in examining these enormous organizations and their interaction as an "institution." Following Olsen (2007), the institutional dimension is that which creates elements of order, predictability, and identity. From this perspective, an institution can be described as an often informal set of rules, practices, values, and ways of thinking that are reproduced within a formal organization. Institutionalization is the process by which social entities are "infused with motivational or affective value beyond the technical requirements of the task at hand" (Selznick, 1957, p. 17). In their classic statement, Berger and Luckmann (1967) define institutions as socially constructed realities that result from interaction and adaptation, becoming receptacles of commitment and shared values. Institutionalists take the symbolic world seriously. Organizations and their members operate within institutional environments, where cultural rules define social entities and legitimate types of action. "Institutional environments are in organizations and inside individuals" (Scott et al., 1994, p. 97). Institutionalized rules do not only regulate social activity through exchanges of demands, resources, and sanctions. These rules are also "constitutive" in that they define and legitimate forms of behavior: "Actors enact as much as they act: what they do is inherent in the social definition of the actor itself. Consequently, rules constituting actors legitimate types of action, and legitimated action constitutes and shapes the social actors" (Meyer, Boli, & Thomas, 1994, p. 20).

Any teacher in the Mexican public school system could explain the distinction between the organization and the institution: he/she knows that formal rules and structures are in practice subject to negotiation and reinterpretation, and that this practice responds to informal rules that are assumed by all actors as legitimate modes of interaction, which are subordinated to political goals and values. What goals and values are these? Fundamentally, they revolve around the need to preserve the union's hierarchical structure and the interests it represents. The union's capacity to confront and negotiate with the government is another important goal. Internally, the national leadership is particularly sensitive to challenges from opposition in the rank and file, whose political action has been consistently defeated over the course of many decades. In turn, educational authorities recognize SNTE's political power and must negotiate with the union on many specifically educational issues and not only wages and benefits. What is specific to the experience of the Mexican public school teacher is the institutional amalgamation of the educational system and the union structure, which we call the "SEP-SNTE system."

Hence, the values and discourses of education cannot be disassociated from those of power and control, following Bourdieu, who interpreted symbolic structures as more than a particular form of power: "a dimension of all power, another name for legitimacy, a product of the acknowledgement (or the lack of knowledge), the belief that bestows prestige upon the people who exercise authority."

How Teachers are Inducted into the SEP-SNTE System

Gee (2005) defines identity as the expression of those groups to which an actor belongs: "What we say, think, feel and do is always indebted to the *social groups to which we have been apprenticed* [our emphasis]" (Gee, 2005, p. 12). Teachers are apprenticed to the values and authority structures (rules) described above since their early formative stages upon entering a normal school [teacher education college]. These rules impregnate most of the important decisions they will be making (or be affected by) throughout their professional career. Institutional identity is enacted by individuals as they make their way through a persistent set of authority structures, rules, and practices for which they construct meanings and a sense of belonging.

A post as a full-time K-9 teacher in Mexico is a coveted position. The relative modesty of teacher's wages is overly compensated by a wide range of benefits, a significant margin of individual freedom (relative, say, to industrial workers), life-long stability, and membership in a politically powerful union organization with an entrenched identity. The standards set by entrance exams to a normal school are relatively low, for it is known that these schools are not academically demanding. Since normal schools are a closely guarded bastion of union power, the practices and relationships that a newly inducted student experiences during the four years of study prepare him/her for the institutional environment that will permeate the future teaching career. A main attraction of studying at a normal school has been that graduates were assured access to a teaching position. Competitiveness and academic standing have not been typically characteristic of induction to the teaching profession. In recent years, however, as changing demographics have led to declining demand for elementary schooling, access to teaching posts has become less automatic but not more meritocratic. Today, in the face of growing scarcity of teaching positions, a normal school graduate faces the following choices: to leverage political influence, to inherit a teaching position from a relative on the verge of retirement, or to buy a position. However bizarre these choices may seem from the perspective of other educational systems, they are actually a longstanding tradition in Mexico. The notion of the worker as "owner" of his/her post was enshrined in labor legislation in the early 1960s for workers in the public sector and is a result of the strong bargaining positions gained by unions at that time. Successive contractual negotiations between SEP and SNTE established the possibility of inheriting and selling positions that "belong" to teachers, thus generating a widespread secondary market for positions. This *de facto* privatization of part of the educational labor market evidently could not function without cóllaboration between the education authorities (the hiring employer) and the union representatives (the intermediaries who negotiate positions and receive a fee from the interested teacher).

Once a position as a part-time teacher is secured, it will be necessary to curry favor with union leaders in order to obtain a full-time contract, to advance to a higher pay grade or to transfer to a different school. If a teacher is interested in becoming a principal or a supervisor, he/she must have built political alliances within the union, whose opinion is taken into account by educational authorities in such designations. On the contrary, teachers who engage in opposition activism will surely find it difficult to advance professionally or to obtain a leave of absence to carry out postgraduate studies.

This brief description of the transactions that characterize the teaching career exemplifies the types of rules that have become institutionalized in the SEP-SNTE system.

These transactions have many implications. They demonstrate the degree of autonomy achieved by SNTE regarding one of the core functions of the education system: the regulation of the professional career, which is only marginally based on academic merit or on teaching performance, thus impinging crucially on a teacher's self-image: reputation as a good teacher is less important for teachers' identity than loyalty to the SEP-SNTE system. Important consequences are also derived for the implementation of educational policy, since demands made by policy on teachers are necessarily mediated by the SEP-SNTE system. Other implications are sociological and cultural: there is no doubt that the mechanisms previously described have given rise to whole "teaching families" (or "tribes") that inherit positions as well as the accompanying value patterns from one generation to another. Economically speaking, it is clear that the stability, benefits, and marketability of teaching positions make this a choice profession, especially in economically disadvantaged regions, where a teaching position represents an important source of income stability. All of these implications are undoubtedly important, but the most significant one for our argument is that throughout a teacher's induction into the profession and his/her future career, the individual develops a *habitus* and an identity that places political allegiance above pedagogical effectiveness.

Ramifications for the Identity of Educators

As a whole, membership in the SEP-SNTE system implies an identity forged around a deeply institutionalized set of cultural, political, and practical rules. Is it reasonable to imagine that the discourse, norms, and practices of teachers *as educators* can be separated from this deeply ingrained system of favors and clienteles? We do not believe so, although our aim is not to repudiate the work of large numbers of committed teachers. Nevertheless, given the assumptions we have established, we cannot avoid inquiring about the cognitive, discursive, and practical strategies deployed by teachers vis-a-vis the *de facto* rules of the game set by the SEP-SNTE system. How do teachers negotiate their vocation as educators, as well as the formal goals of educational policy, and their identity as members of the SEP-SNTE system?

Since the early 1990s the content of educational policy in Mexico has developed a clear focus on themes such as quality, student-centered pedagogy, and higher levels of teacher training. The primary school curriculum has been reformed and new textbooks have been developed. Major policy initiatives have emerged around student assessment and school-centered management. The secretary of education developed a system of merit-based incentives for teachers. To judge from the formal policy discourse, the Mexican educational system has experienced significant reforms that align it with the current international policy trends.

At the same time, however, we suggest that the power, influence, and autonomy of the national union as a political entity have increased, and traditional union practices and values have only become more entrenched. The distance between traditionalism and modernization has actually increased, posing dire problems for policy makers, who do not seem capable of surpassing the "capture" of the educational system by the union.[4]

There is a clear and growing gap between the content and the goals of educational policy and the values of the deeply institutionalized system

---

[4] A notable example is the capture by SNTE of the rules and procedures for allocating teacher bonuses through the "Carrera Magisterial," an incentive system established by the Ministry in the early 1990s with the intention of rewarding effective teachers on an individual basis.

described earlier. It would seem that teachers must navigate between two dissonant discourses.

How does this policy impasse play out at various levels? At the national level, judging from the positions of national policy makers, this impasse does not exist. On the contrary, the federal education ministry now asserts that policy is elaborated in direct collaboration with the union leadership.[5] This is justified in terms of acceding to the age-old union demand of "inclusion of teachers" in policy and in terms of more effective implementation. In actual fact, the rank and file was not consulted over the decisions made by the national union leadership with the federal government.

At the local level, we have observed a variety of responses. In several states opposition movements within the union have sprung up over these policy decisions. These are typically political reactions by organized groups of educators who mobilize against local union leaders. But at the level of individual educators, our extensive contact with teachers indicates that, as obvious as the dissonance between formal policy discourse and the prevailing practices may seem to an external observer, such dissonance is either not perceived as important or it has been accepted as normal (*appropriate*). It is surprising to us that the issue of dissonance does not raise many questions among many educators. When pressed on this issue, however, teachers express various positions. One explanation offered by some teachers is that they try to separate their activities as union members–for instance, in union meetings, demonstrations, and electoral activities–from their pedagogical concerns. This response, of course, does not address the concerns posed in this chapter over the deep practices and values that have become institutionalized in the SEP-SNTE system.

Another explanation consists in stating that the actions of the national leadership have always been and the actions are increasingly distant from the teachers' local concerns. But little can be done about this, given the hierarchical structure of the union and the fact that educational authorities are allied with union leadership. This fatalistic response is actually quite widespread and would seem to be an expression of the success of the SEP-SNTE system.

A third type of response that we have observed is the trivialization of policy reforms. "This is old wine in new bottles, but we must pay lip service to it." Teachers attend policy workshops and training sessions where they assimilate the new policy language (and get to spend a few days away from classroom drudgery). When pressed on the implications of policy reforms for pedagogical practice, a common response is the rote repetition of the new

---

5 The policy document, called the "Alliance for Educational Quality," was signed in public by the president, the secretary of education, and the president of the union in 2007. As of that moment, the President of the union consistently made public statements about the implementation of policy.

terminology with little reference to actual problems experienced in the classroom. The discourse of policy innovation seems to supersede perceptions of dissonance with pedagogical practice. Far from having an instrumental function in conceptualizing and reflecting on practice, the new terminology is assimilated and used as a means of covering up and legitimating current pedagogical experience. In a way, then, this is also a trivialization of language itself.

Power and Discourse in the SEP-SNTE System

We turn now to issues of language, discourse, and power. It must be evident that institutionalized systems produce certain kinds of discourse. If the rules—formal and informal—of an institutionalized environment are to be assimilated as *appropriate* or legitimate, they must have a means of expression, a means of discursive exchange among members. But it is not only a question of a specific terminology or jargon, that may or may not be specialized regarding the technical tasks that individuals carry out in that environment. It is also a question of *how language itself* is used. Institutional discourse, then, expresses these rules but is also a manifestation of the ideology that originates and maintains them. "Language is deeply linked to ideology and cannot be understood or analyzed without it" Gee (2005, p. 11). This is where our analysis must depart from institutionalist sociology, which only rarely concerns itself with issues of power, conflict, and dissonance.[6]

Bourdieu points out that "one of the ways to define a field[7] is to identify what is at stake and the specific interests" (quoted in Garcia, 1984, p. 36). What is at stake in the institutional environment of the SEP-SNTE system? We have insisted that it is preserving power. Bourdieu (1985, quoted in Hanks 2005, p. 73) lists three explicit features of a field, namely: (a) language games that follow certain objectives and use certain specific discursive resources towards a definite end, (b) a series of beliefs and the assumption that such beliefs underlie the game, and (c) what is specifically at stake (what can be won or lost, how and by whom)." Thus, "participants in a field share a set of interests, a common language, an 'objective complicity that underlies all antagonism. ' That is the reason why participating in the struggle contributes to the reproduction of the game, by believing in the game's worth. Those who dominate the accumulated capital, the basis for power or authority, tend to adopt strategies of conservation or orthodoxy, whereas those with the less capital or the newcomers prefer strategies of subversion, heresy" (García, 1984,

6 The relative deafness of institutionalist sociology to issues of power and conflict is one of the important critiques leveled at this perspective (Powell & Colyvas, 2007).

7 Which for our purposes may be equivalent to an institutional environment.

p. 19). We might add that this dichotomous view of orthodoxy versus heresy should be complemented by a third position, that of fatalism.

We have argued that the SEP-SNTE system is a complex environment, rich in positions and strategies in which actors constantly maneuver in order to access or defend positions, as well as to impede access to available positions to other players (Street, 1992). Our experience in working with teachers suggests that, in terms of habitus, the dynamics of the SEP-SNTE system institutionally envelops and hegemonizes the educational system. In the words commonly used by teachers, "education is subordinated to politics." Values, linguistic codes, accepted hierarchies, and identities are created and reproduced within the SEP-SNTE environment. Referring again to the example of how new teachers are recruited, we suggest that the values implicit in this trajectory start shaping the self-perception of a teacher as a professional whose "technical" identity, that is, his/her certificated proficiency in teaching contents and methods, is enveloped and subordinated to his/her identity as a participant in the SEP-SNTE system. Interaction with other teachers, principals, inspectors, and education officials is usually mediated by their common participation in that environment. This environment is characterized by dynamics of production and reproduction of power, which are in turn paradoxically legitimized by an education discourse about quality and the "knowledge society."

Stating that union organizations and educational systems are fields of power struggle is old news. There is no novelty in pointing out that educational discourse may be used as a political instrument. What is specific to the phenomenon at hand is the *invisibility of the evident dissonance* between proclaimed educational values and actual practice in the SEP-SNTE system. Our contention is that this paradoxical situation not only trivializes educational discourse and tends to generate fatalism among teachers but it most crucially devalues the use of language itself. Educational discourse is *language rich*: it is full of complex arguments about teaching, learning, content, and pedagogical technique. Teachers master and assimilate this discourse, but at the same time they acknowledge implicitly that this complex language is not expected to translate into action. The legitimation function of language becomes paramount, thus diminishing its cognitive and instrumental value.

What consequences may derive for teaching? We are not suggesting a determinist linkage between institutionalized discourse and educational practice and thought. Rather, we are highlighting the contradictions that teachers face. A starting point for further investigation could be the construction of a typology of cognitive, normative, and discursive strategies developed by teachers faced with the aforementioned dilemma. Such a typology could serve as a working hypothesis for exploring teachers' responses to innovations or policy changes. The first issue to investigate would of course be whether dissonance is actually perceived, an important theme in and of itself. If dissonance is perceived, how is it resolved? The various strategies for resolving this contradiction should, we suggest, have important implications for classroom practice (investigated through language practices) as well as for how individuals construct their vocation[8] as educators.

References

Arnaut, A. (1992). La evolución de los grupos hegemónicos en el SNTE. México: CIDE.

Arnaut, A. (1996). *Historia de una profesión: Los maestros de educación primaria en México, 1887–1994*. México: CIDE.

Berger, P. L., & Luckmann, T. (1967). *The social construction of reality*. New York: Doubleday.

Berger, P. L., & Kellner, H. (1981). *Sociology reinterpreted: An essay on method and vocation*. Garden City, NY: Anchor Books.

Del Valle, S. (2009). Esconden SEP y SNTE fideicomiso millonario. *Reforma Newspaper*, México, 23 de marzo.

García, N. (1984) Introducción: la sociología de la cultura de Pierre Bourdieu. In P. Bourdieu, *Sociología y cultura* (pp. 9–53). México: Grijalbo-CONACULTA.

Gee, J. P. (2005). *La ideología de los discursos*. España: Ediciones Morata, S.L. (1st English edition: 1990)

Hanks, W.F. (2005). Pierre Bourdieu and the practices of language. *The Annual Review of Anthropology*, *34*, 67–83.

Hernández, M. L., (2009). ¿Qué sindicalismo para los profesores poblanos?, daily online newspaper *e-consulta.com.mx*, January 18. Retrieved from http://www.e-consulta.com/index.php?option=com_content&task=view&id=22214&Itemid=177.

Loyo, A. (1997). *Los actores sociales y la educación: Los sentidos del cambio (1988–1994)*. México: UNAM-Plaza y Valdés.

Loyo, A. (1999). El sindicalismo magisterial en México, Boletín. *Proyecto Sindicalismo Docente y Reforma Educativa en América Latina*. Buenos Aires: PREAL-FLACSO, N 3.

Meyer, J., Boli, J., & Thomas, G. M. (1994). Ontology and rationalization in the Western cultural account. In W. R. Scott & J. W. Meyer (Eds.), *Institutional environments and organizations: Structural complexity and individualism* (pp. 9–31).Thousand Oaks, CA: Sage Publications.

Muñoz, A. (2008) Escenarios e identidades del SNTE entre el sistema educativo y el sistema político. *Revista mexicana de investigación educativa*, *13*(37), 377–417.

Olsen, J. P. (2007). Understanding Institutions and the Logics of Appropriateness: Introductory Essay. Center for European Studies (ARENA), University of Oslo, Working Paper N 13. Retrieved December 13, 2008, from http://www.arena.no.

Powell, W. W., & Colyvas, J. A. (2007). New institutionalism. *International encyclopedia of organization studies*. Thousand Oaks, CA: SAGE. Retrieved from http://sage-ereference.com/organization/Article_n336.html

Raphael, R. (2007). *Los socios de Elba Esther*, México: Planeta.

---

8 We understand "vocation" to be "an ethically self-conscious reflection on one's work" (Berger & Kellner, 1981, p. vii).

Scott. W. R., Meyer J., & Associates (1994). *Institutional environments and organizations: Structural complexity and individualism*. Thousand Oaks, CA: Sage Publications.

Selznick, P. (1957). *Leadership in administration*. New York: Harper & Row.

Street, S. (1992). El SNTE y la política educativa, 1970–1990. *Revista Mexicana de Sociología, 54*(2), 45–72.

Blogs on SNTE, education and teachers:

http://educacioncafe.blogspot.com

http://setebc.wordpress.com

http://www.wenceslao.com.mx

http://www.normalistas.com

http://md-nuevosindicalismo.blogspot.com

CHAPTER NINE

The Globalized World of English Scientific Publishing: An Analytical Proposal That Situates a Multilingual Scholar

KAREN ENGLANDER

Introduction

The phenomenon of publishing scientific work in English, particularly on the part of nonnative English speakers, ought to be seen as a manifestation of the globalization occurring in the world today. Applied linguistics have paid in-creasing attention to the phenomenon in recent years of scientific texts written by nonnative speakers of English (e.g., Li, 2006; Burgess, 2002; Flowerdew, 1999a, 1999b) and the process of international publishing (Salager-Meyer, 2008; Lillis and Curry, 2006; Burrough-Boenisch, 2003) (see Uzuner, 2008 for a literature review of empirical studies). My aim is to better understand the social construction of publishing on the part of scientists situated outside the English-dominant countries. Thus an analytical framework is needed that integrates political entities, publishing policies, and the individual scientist-author.

In this study, I bring together several theoretical lenses to focus on a telling case of one scholar's publishing experience. I call upon social geography, sociolinguistics, and discourse and identity studies. This work builds on Blommaert's (2006a) presentation of sociolingustic scales. Centrally, the metaphor of scales exposes power and inequality in social semiotic processes, and this metaphor will form the basis of the subsequent discussion. This exercise can lead to a comprehensive framework for theorizing the relationship among publishing, discourse, and identity as it affects multilingual[1] scientists in a globalized world.

Global–Local Continuum

Studies of globalization within the fields of history and social geography use the metaphor of scale. To capture the phenomenon, a continuum is used with the micro and local phenomenon at one extreme while the macro and global is at the other extreme (Fig. 1) (Lefebvre 2000, cited in Blommaert 2006a).

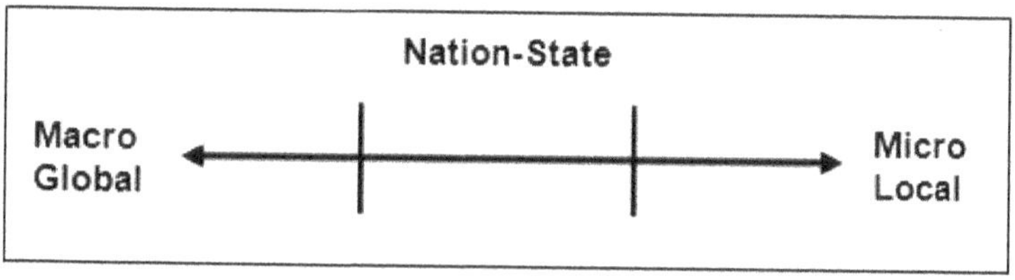

Figure 1. Continuum of Global-Local, based on Lefebvre, 2000.

However, Blommaert (2006a) contributes the notion that the scale is layered vertically, not horizontally. The events and processes of globalization occur at different scale-levels where the micro/local can be seen at the bottom of the scale, the macro/global at the top layer, and intermediary levels occur in between, such as the nation state, for example. Such a vertical scale makes explicit the power relationship among the actors in this social phenomenon. I add that using vertical scales as a metaphor makes explicit the notion that weight is distributed unevenly and that the larger bears down upon the smaller (Fig. 2).

While it might be argued that the micro/local was always dominated by a more powerful entity—the nation state—globalization has rendered the nation state to a mere mid-level status (Burbules & Torres, 2000). Thus the processes that affect the local and the individual have multiplied with the normalization of globalization.

For Blommaert, scale should be understood not only as a spatial metaphor, but one of time as well. Time situates events, including linguistic events, and delimits those events. In any literacy event, there is a history of the materials, the so-called "apparatus of literacy" (Brandt & Clinton, 2002). These books, ledgers, files, documents, computers and so on build and sustain larger and longer pieces of the world "across time and space." Literacy events

[1] Consistent with Uzuner (2008) the term *multilingual* will be used to refer to academics from outside the Anglo-speaking countries who use English as an additional language for international publication.

can be delimited with a beginning and end, whether it is a conversation, a classroom lesson, an informational brochure, or a scientific research article. Therefore, to understand literacy events, it is necessary to collapse the two phenomena of time and space into the single notion of TimeSpace (Wallerstein, 1997). Every socially situated event occurs in this TimeSpace.

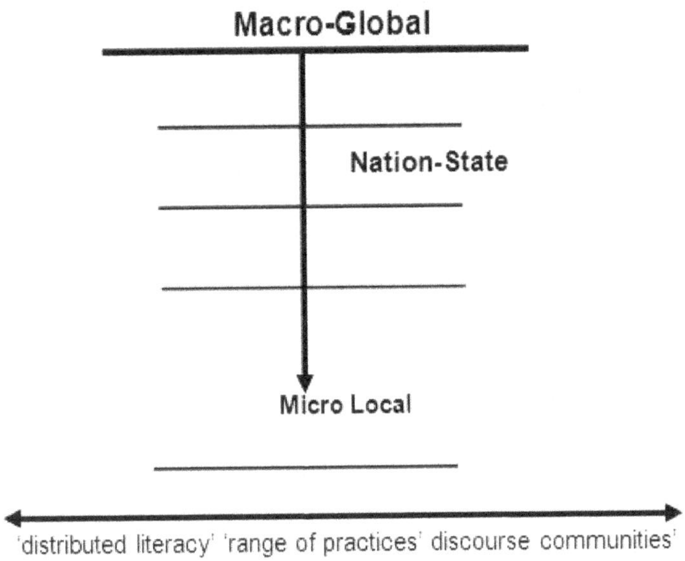

Figure 2. Reconceptualized vertical and horizontal scales of the global and local.

Global and local phenomenon can be layered in scales that are differentiated by TimeSpace (Table 1). Globalization occurs at the higher scale, where the neoliberal discourse identifies the phenomenon as the inevitable march of progress– "timeless" –and as a supranational reality–spatially broad.

Globalization, presented as "modern, reasonable, realistic and pragmatic" (Kennedy, 1994, cited in Silbey, 2001, p. 260), entered the discourse in the 1970s and has become the ideological "common sense" of the times (see Bordieu & Wacquant, 2001). Progress is a manifestation of eternal TimeSpace in which there is eternal change (Wallerstein, 1997). In contrast, the lower scale positions the individual, the event, and the particular. At this level, phenomena are momentary or time-bound and situated locally. [2]

---

[2] This notion of collapsing of time and space where neither is privileged is also consistent with Bakhtin's term *chronotype*, in which worldviews and genre features of a language are represented (Bakhtin, 1981).

Table 1. Sociolinguistics and globalized/localized phenomenon as analyzed through scales

Scale	Phenomenon	TimeSpace
Higher Scale	Globalization and socio-linguistic phenomena of powerfulness.	Continually reenacted. 'Timeless.' Translocal. Widespread.
Lower Scale	Localization and socio-linguistic phenomena of powerlessness.	Momentary. Time-bound. Local. Situated and Particular.

Globalization is the process of transforming the world through a combination of economic, technological, sociocultural and political forces (Burbules & Torres, 2000). Thus exploring the link between globalizing processes and sociolinguistic ones permits a new analysis of the transformations occurring in the production of scientific texts by multilingual authors today.

Sociolinguistics and Contextualizing Scales

Sociolinguists and critical discourse analysts seek to understand the effect that society has on the way language is used and conversely how language use affects society (van Dijk, 1998; Fairclough, 2001). Literacy practice, as a concept, links "activities of reading and writing and the social structures in which they are embedded and which they help to shape" (Barton & Hamilton, 1998, p. 6). In fact, "There is no way in which language can be 'context-less'" (Blommaert, 2006b, p. 4). However, as pointed out by Lillis (2008), most studies of academic literacy which attempt to understand the relation between text and context take their focus "outward," from text to context (p. 374). Few academic literacy studies move from context to text. The vertical scale metaphor is applicable to sociolinguistics and critical discourse, which explore who and what has power over others through language and literacy (Fairclough, 2001). By adopting scales, we can expose the context which shapes the literacy history and language use; this is illustrated by the case study presented later in this chapter.

Blommaert (2006a) uses the metaphor of scales in his approach to sociolinguistics to indicate the layering of society and the way that discourse is used to position people within it. Some people may have access to the local or lower scale, and their language is reflective of that social position. Others may access the higher scale, and use that position to either bolster their own position or (and perhaps simultaneously) distinguish themselves from the one of lesser position.

Blommaert (2006a) offers the example of an interaction between a professor and a doctoral student: The student remarks, "**I'll** start **my** dissertation with a chapter reporting on my fieldwork." The professor responds saying, "**We start our** dissertations with a literature review chapter **here**." The words put in bold emphasize the contrast. The student's discourse positions him at the lower level because his use of the individual personal and possessive pronouns and future tense; this makes the student's comment centered on his personal work and plans. In contrast, the professor uses "we" and "our" and the timeless present tense, thereby invoking larger academic and institutional communities. The professor makes a vertical move to invoke those more powerful norms and rules of the institution and community and creates a position that is aligned with the higher scale levels. Bureaucrats too, he argues, have access to the higher scale levels by using the language and procedures which create systems and cases from the individual and personal experiences of those interacting with the bureaucracy. To the individual, she or he has a particular situation at a particular time, the TimeSpace of the lower level, but to the bureaucrat, that situation is transformed into a procedurally shaped discourse of the institution. This higher scale jump is manifested by removing the individual and immediacy of the petitioner's situation and invoking a set of prescripted procedures that effectively silence the individual (and his or her experience) at the lower layer. As my discussion here continues, I am adapting Blommaert's (2006a) configuration of layered scales that are differentiated by TimeSpace. This metaphor is then used to discuss and connect the theories within the disciplinary fields I am calling upon.

In addition to the vertical layering of scales, Blommaert (2006a) points out that scale as a spatial metaphor continues to have a horizontal dimension. Horizontal metaphors, particularly in sociolinguistics, lay important theoretical foundations and terms such as "distributed" literacy, "spread," "community of practice," "discourse community," and "range" of literacy practices permeate the literature. Therefore, "'scale' does not reject the horizontal images of space; it complements them with a vertical dimension of hierarchical ordering and power differentiation" (Blommaert, 2006a, p. 4).

Globalization and Scientific Publishing

"English is the universal language of science at this time in history," states Thomson Scientific Publishing, arguably the most important database for academic work (Testa, n.d.). It has come to be commonplace that English is termed *the* language of science. Whether from a critical perspective (Phillipson, 2001; Canagarajah, 2002) or a neoliberal one (Kuznetsov & Dahlman, 2008), participation in the international world of scientific knowledge requires English. It wasn't always this way (Ammon, 2001). French, German, and

Russian each have their own longstanding traditions of communicating science across national borders. However, since the Second World War, English has taken on an increasingly prominent position. With the advent of databases and the internet, English is inescapable. English is clearly positioned in the TimeScale at the level of globalization. This is evidenced in many facts:

- 89% of the 5,000 articles published every day are published in English (Martel, 2001).
- The vast majority of articles indexed in international databases are written in English (Gibbs, 1995).
- The Web of Science/International Science Index, which indexes 9500 journals world-wide has a distinct preference for journals which publish in English, stating that they focus "on journals that publish full text in English or at very least, their bibliographic information in English....However, going forward, it is clear that the journals most important to the international research community will publish full text in English" (Testa, n.d.).

The dominance of English is captured in Medgyes and Kaplan's (1992) statement: "The English-speaking nations control an information cartel that makes OPEC's energy control seem trivial" (p. 68). In addition, "theoretical and methodological perspectives provided in the core theories of [a] discipline [are] delineated mostly by theorists and researchers in the Anglo-European centers (e.g., US, UK)" (Lin, 2005, cited in Oda, 2007, p. 125).

Academics, whether they are within or beyond the English-language centers, apply these "global theories" (emphasis in Oda, 2007, p. 125) to local issues and places. Epistemologically as well as geographically, English language journals have a boundless reach. Further, the impacts of their being indexed in databases and their citation trajectories have a timeless permanence.

As alluded to above, there is a world of publishing which does not occur in English, nor emanates from English-speaking countries. In fact, even the vast Web of Science covers less than one-quarter of the peer-reviewed journals worldwide (Salager-Meyer, 2008). This non-English international realm is typically referred to as "peripheral publishing" (Canagarajah, 1996, 2002; Braine, 2005). The difficulties that these journals face are many, as explained by Salager-Meyer:

> Being written in local (i.e., not widely read) languages, [the journals] are seldom seen or commented on in the mainstream publishing community....Their readership is very small: it hardly ever transcends national boundaries....Financial restrictions affect their publication and distribution. (Salager-Meyer, 2008, p. 123)

For individual researchers, there is social capital (Gee, 2005) and monetary reward that emanates from publishing in international English language journals. In Mexico for example, scientists can apply to join the Mexican National Organization of Researchers (*Sistema Nacional de Investigadores*, SNI), which measures scientific productivity through a point system. Points are awarded if an article appears in an internationally indexed, referred journal. Publishing in peripheral, national or local journals have little value particularly in the sciences. Also, the SNI provides direct income to scientists based on their membership in the organization, and public universities maintain a merit pay system that favors scholars who publish in international English journals over national and/or Spanish-language journals. Similar systems of merit that privilege English journals exist in other Latin American countries as well (Salager-Meyer, personal communication).

Publishing in Spanish-language journals, despite their potential reach throughout Latin America and Spain, cannot be positioned as global nor on par with English-language journals. Further, their content, by being marginalized, loses its timeless quality and becomes situated locally and momentarily. In this analysis, peripheral journals are set on the lower scale (Table 2).

Table 2. Publishing as Analyzed through Scales

Scale	Phenomenon	TimeSpace
Higher Scale	International (English) Journals	Continually reenacted. 'Timeless.' Translocal. Widespread.
Lower Scale	Peripheral (non-English, non-Anglo-situated) journals	Momentary. Time-bound. Local. Situated and Particular.

Multilingual Publishing and Scales of Discourse

Publishing itself moves situated and particular knowledge into the realm of the timeless and geographically broad reach of a printed and disseminated text. Thus, a scientist's desire to publish, to some extent, is always an indexical jump from the lower scale to a higher one. For scholars in non-English dominant countries, publishing in international journals constitutes a distinct jump from lower to higher. However, to explore these phenomena, the framework of Gee (2005) is useful.

Gee describes two discourses, one with a capital D, and the other with lower case. The convention of capitalizing one brings it to a higher level than the other, thus we can position the two discourses in Table 3. Big D discourses are of the higher scale. In time, they "existed before each of us came on the scene and most of them will exist long after" (Gee, 2005, p. 27). In space, they occur as indicating a group or social network (Gee, 2005, p. 26). In fact,

Gee describes the TimeSpace phenomenon of big D Discourse saying, that it constitutes the "ways of using language, of thinking, valuing, acting, and interacting, in the 'right' *places* and at the 'right' *times* with the 'right' objects" (my emphasis, Gee, 2005, p. 26). The ways in which we enact the TimeSpace of Discourse not only allows us to understand our world, but it shapes our world: it comprises our world.

Table 3. Discourse as Analyzed through Scales

Scale	Phenomenon	TimeSpace
Higher Scale	Discourse	Continually reenacted. 'Timeless.' Translocal. Widespread.
Lower Scale	discourse	Momentary. Time-bound. Local. Situated and Particular.

The level of big D Discourse is indexically higher than small d discourse. The latter means "language-in-use or stretches of language" (Gee, 2005, p. 26). The discourse is limited in TimeSpace to particular utterances in particular places and situations. Utterances have meaning when they communicate a socially situated identity in a socially situated activity. They are localized in a time and place. Thus the TimeSpace dimension of discourse is indexically low, such that the time is momentary and the space is local and situated.

A discourse does not necessarily allow direct access to a Discourse. These two phenomena occur at different levels on the scale. The insufficiency of discourse at the local level to allow one access to the Discourse is manifested in Gee's notion of recognition work. It is not enough for one to position him/herself as particle physicist or a gangbanger. The individual must be recognized by others who comprise that Discourse as also being a member, and thus entitled. By being recognized, the individual is able to continue that Discourse "through history" (Gee, 2005, p. 27). Thus a Discourse occurs at a TimeSpace level that has more timelessness, and more translocality, in Blommaert's terminology, than a discourse.[3] Discourse/discourse too enters into the scales

[3] It is important to note that Discourses are not immutable. They change. New ones are created and old ones die out. Discourses can merge and transform. Further, the individual is not wholly subject to the Discourse. If a person enacts a Discourse in such a way that it is "different enough from what has gone before, but still recognizable" that new performance can change and transform the Discourse. However, if the performance is not recognized, then the person simply isn't "in" the Discourse. Thus there is the possibility of the local level affecting the global. But generally, we can assume that the weight of the TimeSpace is from the higher bearing down on the lower.

as shown in Table 4. Again, the inequities of power and weight give precedence to the higher level, not the lower.

Table 4. Synthesis: Sociolinguistics and Globalized/Localized Phenomenon as Analyzed through Scales

Scale	Phenomenon	TimeSpace
Higher Scale	Globalization and sociolinguistic phenomena of powerfulness International (English) journals Discourse	Continually reenacted. 'Timeless'. Translocal. Widespread.
Lower Scale	Localization and sociolinguistic phenomena of powerlessness Peripheral (non-English, non-Anglo-situated) journals discourse	Momentary. Timebound. Local. Situated and Particular.

Scales and Identity

As my particular interest is in the act of publishing one's written work, there is one more dimension to the scale that needs to be discussed: identity. This is explored through autobiographical and discoursal identity (Ivanič, 1998).

> Autobiographical identity is the identity which people bring with them to any act of writing....This identity they bring with them to writing is itself socially constructed and **constantly changing** as a consequence of their developing life-history....[It] constitutes their **current** way of being. (Ivanič, 1998, p. 24, my emphasis)

Additionally, the writer creates an identity through the discourse, i.e., a discoursal identity. It is identifiable through variations in the sentence-level arrangement of the text. This discoursal identity is not the same as the person. The person is understood through the autobiographical self: the lifetime of experience and knowledge that goes into the writing task. In contrast, the discoursal self is the way the writer is portrayed in the text. This portrayal may be deliberately created or unconsciously so.

For the multilingual scholar who desires to publish in the international English-speaking world, the autobiographical self is further complicated by the need to produce the manuscript in English. These scholars already bear the "higher investment in language learning and additional costs of producing linguistically adequate texts" (Ammon, 2001, p. vii) from which native English-language scientists are exempt[4]. At the discoursal level, the multilingual scholar may have less deliberate control of the self who is presented in the text due to his (possibly lesser) ability to manipulate and control the language.

The distinction between the autobiographical self and the discoursal self can also be understood in TimeSpace levels. Autobiographical self is momentary, situated, constantly changing. These are the characteristics of the lower level. In contrast, the discoursal identity is that which is portrayed in a text, and a text, particularly a written one, has permanence. It is accessible throughout time as unchanging, although how it is understood by any particular reader at any particular time of course is situated. However, the self that is presented in the text is immutable, placing the discoursal self on the higher level. Thus we have an intersection of time, space, writer, and text that can be seen on multiple levels (Table 5).

Table 5. Incorporating Identity into Sociolinguistics and Globalized/ Localized Phenomenon as Analyzed through Scales

Scale	Phenomenon	TimeSpace
Higher Scale	Globalization and sociolinguistic phenomena of powerfulness; International (English) journals; Discourse; Discoursal identity in text	Continually reenacted. 'Timeless.' Translocal. Widespread.
Lower Scale	Localization and sociolinguistic phenomena of powerlessness; Peripheral (non-English, non-Anglo-situated) journals; discourse; Autobiographical identity	Momentary. Time-bound. Local. Situated and Particular.

Case Study of a Multilingual Scholar Publishing

How then do these forces impact an individual researcher in a local context? A case study was conducted with a scientist, which is reported here. Victor is a well established marine biologist at a major public university in Mexico. All his formal education was completed in Mexico, and he obtained his doctorate at the country's most prestigious National Autonomous University of Mexico.

4 Man, Weinkauf, Tsang, & Sin (2004) report that the importance of English ability is crucial to scientific productivity. Proficiency in English as measured by national scores on the Test of English as a Foreign Language (TOEFL) actually has a greater correlation with scientific productivity than does a nation's spending on research, measured as a percentage of gross domestic product.

He has been involved with more than a dozen externally funded research projects, and published 18 English-language articles in refereed journals. He is a long-standing member of the Mexican National Organization of Researchers (*Sistema Nacional de Investigadores*, SNI.).

In this particular instance he is leading a research group concerning the detection of a virus –the yellowhead virus (YHV)– in shrimp in Mexico. He submitted his manuscript to the *Journal of Fish Diseases*: it has an impact factor of 1.587 and is ranked as 6th among the 40 journals in the field of Fisheries. He is attempting to access the higher level globalized journal with its attendant Discourse.

When Victor submitted his manuscript he received two reviewer responses. One of the reviewers wrote: "The finding of natural YHV infection in shrimp farmed in Mexico is of significant importance and has significant ramifications." The repeated use of the word "significant" and the collocation of "significant ramifications" indicates that the reviewer views the manuscript as worthy of the Discourse of the globalized journal. The manuscript is addressing a situation that is greater than local and contains ramifications that take the finding beyond the momentary. The TimeSpace indicates a higher level phenomenon. However, the reviewer also writes:

> As English is not the author's native language, there are also many grammatical errors and other textual deficiencies. These inadequacies should have been addressed prior to submission of the manuscript for review. Significant rewriting to address textual and technical deficiencies identified below is needed before I would endorse publication.

The reviewer is addressing the discourse, a lower level phenomenon. He makes clear that the discourse is not sufficient to allow Victor into the Discourse. According to the reviewer, not only is the discourse that was presented in the manuscript inadequate, but more importantly, the inadequacies "should have been addressed prior to submission." The reviewer is chastising Victor for performing an identity that is insufficient to the Discourse of internationally published scientists. The reviewer situates Victor with an identity as a non-native English speaker and a careless author. He is not recognizing Victor as a member of the Discourse. He is not yet welcome to the higher level.

Victor revised his manuscript, resubmitted it to the journal, and it was accepted. At the discourse level, important changes were made to his manuscript. A detailed study of the textual changes from the originally rejected version to the revised and accepted version is presented in Englander (2006a) and Englander (2006b). For example, Victor's initial manuscript had many sentences of complex syntactic structure. In his initial manuscript, the opening sentence states:

> The yellow head virus (YHV) is an ssRNA (+) strand virus of the Order Nidovirales which has provoked severe damage to the shrimp culture industry in the South Asian and Indo Pacific countries since its description in Thailand in 1991 ([three references]).

Syntactically, this is a principal clause plus a subordinating clause plus a group followed by a citation. In the revised manuscript, he writes:

> The yellow head virus (YHV) is an ssRNA (+) strand virus ([two references]).

Syntactically, this is a principal sole clause with a citation. Another of the same syntactic structure follows this sentence, which defines the genetic class and order of the virus. A new paragraph then introduces the content of what had been a subordinated clause in the original. Also 65% of the sentences in the original version of his Introduction section have a marked theme, i.e., they begin with a word or phrase that is not the grammatical subject of the clause. This is seen in: *Subsequently, Durand, Tang & Lightner (2000) confirmed*...and, *By means of transmission electronic microscope, they detected a pleomorfic virus*....In both cases, the markedness is removed in the accepted version of the manuscript. The first sentence is rewritten as: *Durand, Tang & Lightner (2000) confirmed and extended Nunan et al.'s results*. The second is rewritten as: *These authors analyzed frozen shrimp imported from Asia on sale in markets in Arizona, USA, by means of PCR*. Victor's propensity for longer, more syntactically complex sentences is consistent with the qualities of good academic writing in Spanish (Montaño-Harmon, 1991).

Lexicogrammatical features that invite reader interaction with the text are also present. *Then, there is no doubt that*, allows the reader to challenge the content by asserting that there is a doubt. Victor emphasizes his ideas with adjectives and emphatic verb forms. For example, in his original Victor wrote that another author's findings induced *these authors* to advance the hypothesis *that given the huge amount of shrimp entering the USA from Asia and given the strong epizooties of viral origin the shrimp farms have been suffering in the south east of Asia*...(under-lining is my emphasis to indicate the decorous and emphatic language). In the revised manuscript the equivalent passage reads, *These authors hypothesized that given the devastating epizooties generated during that time in South-east Asia and the huge amount of shrimp imported to the USA from that world region*,...This emphatic and interactive style of writing is also consistent with good academic writing in Spanish; yet many of those features are minimized or eliminated in the final manuscript which was accepted for publication.

There seems to be a discrepancy between the reviewers and Victor in the social language (Gee, 2005) or register (Gee, 2004) that is expected in a scientific article. The reviewers required a social language that is an English-language notion of a scientific text, yet the social language Victor is enacting is not quite that. Instead, he had been using the social language of a Spanish-language author. As he says, it was a product of his Spanish thinking. Through his language, Victor had been attempting to take on the identity of, and be recognized as a scientist credible to write for an English-language international journal. But instead, his social language positioned him differently in the eyes of the reviewers. His desire to be emphatic was not accepted by those who confer entry into the big D Discourse.

Additional evidence of his softening his discourse is seen in the Discussion section where he hedged the strength of his claim. The first sentence of the Discussion in his rejected manuscript reads, *This study presents evidences of YHV presence in shrimp farms along the Pacific Coast of North America, for the first time.* In the accepted version, before he arrives at the equivalent statement, he includes two paragraphs in which he reviews the presence of the virus in Asia, and then postulates reasons why massive mortalities at Mexican shrimp farms were not attributed to the YHV virus. His third paragraph begins with a statement similar to the previous one: *This study presents the first presumptive evidence of the presence of YVH in shrimp farms on the Mexican Pacific coast.* He was less "firm," and used more hedging in the final version through the addition of *presumptive*, substituting the *Mexican Pacific coast* for the coast of the entire continent, and by moving the adjective *first* into a less prominent position in the sentence. This reduction in strength of claim is urged by the reviewer who points out that the title of the manuscript ought to be changed. His original title read, *Detection of YHV in shrimp farms from the Northwestern Coast of Mexico.* The reviewer recommends that the means of detection be identified in the title, so that it would read, *Detection of yellow head virus by PCR in ...* Ultimately, the published title is even more hedged by adding the word *presumptive*: *Presumptive detection of yellow head virus by [two methods]...* He succeeded in convincing his editor that his findings were credible, in part, by being more circumspect.

It is not unusual for a scientist to limit the strength of his or her claim in response to reviewer comments (Berkenkotter & Huckin, 1995; Knorr-Cetina, 1981; Myers, 1990). However, Victor believes that it was because of his status as a Mexican scientist, being not of the Discourse and not a native-English-speaker that caused him to be judged harshly. Victor feels that the reviewers' caution about his manuscript was not justified. In explaining the reviewers' comments, he talked about their prestige within the scientific community. Although the reviewers' comments were not signed, Victor knew their identities.

> These reviewers are the most important researchers in the field....These reviewers are used to being the people who publish the newest and the most important things. When suddenly someone from Mexico, unknown, wanted to throw in something that is important, they say, "No, that has to be said by me.'

This view that important findings are generated only by those within the Discourse has been reported by other researchers (Guardiano, Favilla &

Calaresu, 2007; Flowerdew, 2004; Gordon, 1980). Despite claims of reviewer objectivity, "a higher frequency of favourable evaluations" (Gordon 1980, p. 274) was found when the reviewers were judging papers from institutions similar to their own or from the same country, either the U.S. or the U.K. It seems that scientists who are members of English-dominant communities of practice perform the role of maintaining their hegemony as the creators of scientific knowledge. A hierarchy of status is perceived and perpetuated by their practices.

Victor said that his findings challenged a previously published article authored by one of the reviewers who had written that the virus was not present in North American stocks. Victor said, "It is not pleasant that I am confirming that now it has occurred in Mexico." Victor's confrontation with the scientific hierarchy was manifested in two ways: first by being situated outside the English-dominant countries and by claiming that an earlier finding was no longer sufficient. These challenges to the scientific hierarchy led Victor to believe that his manuscript was scrutinized with particular vigor.

This brief study of Victor's experience in revising his manuscript for publication illustrates the phenomenon of levels quite distinctly (Table 6).

Table 6. Victor's Positioning through Scientific Texts

Scale	Phenomenon	TimeSpace
Higher	• English Globalization • English scientific Discourse • English scientific discoursal identity	Continually reenacted. 'Timeless.' Translocal. Widespread throughout the English and English-globalized world.
Mid	• Spanish Globalization • Spanish/English academic Discourse • Spanish/English discoursal identity	Continually reenacted, 'Timeless,' **But not English**. Translocal across the Spanish-speaking world
Lower	• Localization • Spanish discourse • Autobiographical identity	Momentary. Time-bound. Local. Situated and Particular.

At the lower and local level, Victor has been a university professor for 26 years in two different institutions, including serving as head of his department. He even participated in five local radio broadcasts about his field. At the higher level, Victor has had a successful history of publishing in English-language journals. However, in moving to the highest level of global publishing, to a journal with a high impact, he encountered a Discourse that did not recognize him as a member, despite his history as a published biologist in both English and Spanish. To enter the TimeSpace of the higher level, he needed to change his discourse such that it was acceptable to those in the position to grant him access. The journal reviewers demonstrated their ability to grant him recognition, and thus access, as evidenced in their comments instructing him in imperatives and privileging their first person singular status.

The phenomenon that complicates this analysis is that Victor is an accomplished biologist in Mexico. He is a published scientist in both Spanish and English and his articles have more than 140 citations. He is not a novice in the field. But he still encountered great difficulty in publishing this particular article. Thus the dichotomy of lower level and higher level scales requires an intermediate level(s) to account for Victor's experience. I suggest that just as the local/global scales ought to include an intermediate level of the nation; there is a need for an intermediate level between discourse and Discourse. That would have to be non-English discourse-Discourse (Table 6).

Victor's initial manuscript exemplifies the qualities of good academic writing that is consistent with Spanish writing. The Spanish propensity for introductory phrases that become marked themes, and multiple subordinating phrases and groups (Montaño-Harmon 1991; Santos Garcia 2001) bears strong similarity to Victor's construction of the original submission. His emphatic adjectives are consistent with the description of Spanish writing which values "flowery, poetic language" (Montaño-Harmon, 1991, p. 421). His high degree of interaction with the reader is consistent with Martín-Martín and Burgess (2004) and where interpersonal connection between reader and writer is permitted to be explicit in the text.

Victor altered his discoursal identity to fulfill the expectations of the English scientific Discourse. Importantly, not only was the discourse –the language– different, but he presents himself and his work differently. He is less passionate, less emphatic, less urgent. Looking back at the two manuscripts, Victor said that in the original "I seem very emotional" and in the revision, "I seem a little more, um, reasoned." He knows that the structure of English writing is "more rigid, more simple" and that he should "communicate the idea directly without so many adjectives." Interestingly, though, he also said,

> *I like [the original] better*; it is a product of my Spanish thinking. Perhaps the emotion that I was trying to communicate in English came literally from what was in my mind in Spanish. I wanted to be very firm, but it did not work. They told me, "you exaggerated; you were excessive." I wanted to strengthen some of the results, but I overdid it.

His desire to be emphatic was not accepted by those who confer entry into the big D Discourse of international English publishing. For Victor and other nonnative English speaking scientists like him, resistance to any great degree is largely futile. Despite calls for a greater critical response on the part of multilingual scholars (Benesch, 1993; Pennycook, 1994) the writer must comply with the reviewers' demands. To reach his desired audience, there is no equi-valent publication in Spanish, neither in readership nor impact even though Spanish is a transnational language of 21 countries. But Spanish does not carry the geopolitical weight of English, nor even French or German (Mignolo, 2004, cited in Godenzzi, 2006). It behooves us to recognize, then, that global is actually English.

Further, Victor's autobiographical identity also changed, i.e., the identity one brings to an act of writing (Ivanič, 1998). Victor thought that he was well established in his international disciplinary community and in a position to bring an important finding to an international (English language) prestigious journal. This experience challenged his identity in this regard. Upon receiving the reviewers' comments he said, "I felt very depressed because this was not the first article I wrote in English, it is the twenty-second! Am I going crazy or what is happening?" The change in his autobiographical identity can be seen in his giving to me reprints of three of his articles published within the past five years. He told me that they had been published with no criticism at all of his language and that the editors had hardly changed a single word. He was deeply shaken by the recent experience. Victor returned to the local university's language school to enroll in conversation classes to rebuild his confidence.

Victor reconceptualized the scientific publishing community as one that is more hierarchical and more distrustful of scientists outside Anglo countries than he had previously recognized. Victor said previously his work had been published in journals of "moderate impact." In contrast, "This is a journal of greater impact: it has more readers and it is often cited." His topic is much more controversial as well. Previously he wrote about genetics of populations in "simple articles that did not affect anybody." This article has an effect because it means there was a failure in the control of shrimp stocks. The confluence of reviewer prestige, high impact English journal and the importance of his findings helps him to explain the treatment he received. In short, he was jumping to a higher scale level.

At the same time, too, he was strengthened in his ability to interact in this global publishing world. Victor did convince the editor of the worth of his work, and he got a commitment to publish two additional articles on the subject. For him, this vindicated his research. We must recall, however, that Victor liked his original version of the manuscript better than the final, published version. He acknowledged that "my emotions were being communicated right into the English" even though he knows that the structure of English writing is "more rigid, more simple" and that he should "communicate the idea directly without so many adjectives." In his revised and published manuscript, he created an alternative discoursal identity that was acceptable at the higher level of the scale, and in doing so, his autobiographical identity has been altered. This new autobiographical identity, at the local level, will embark on the next writing project, in which he will decide whether to situate his work on the international Spanish-speaking level or the English globalized level, with all its attendant consequences.

Conclusion

What I have argued here is that the pressure to publish internationally occurs both as an institutional reality but also as a manifestation of the Discourse of participating in the international scientific community. As Ammon (2001) points out, "the prevalence and dominance of English in science is a global fact, but it varies...to its effects between language communities and countries" (p. ix). For multilingual scholars, this global fact carries additional difficulties because the scholar may well be distinguished at a national level, but dismissed at the international. Shohamy (2007) argues that focussing on language rather than content leads to serious injustices for multilingual speakers, because "content can be delivered in any language with appropriate infrastructure such as translations" (Shohamy, 2007, p. 130). However, a social language was required in Victor's case that differed from a mere translation from Spanish to English. The recognition work of Discourse in the English-language scientific community required this scientist to adjust his discourse in ways that were contrary to the norms of his national discourse. This raises precisely the conflicts of identities that Gee identifies, where "different social identities...may seriously conflict with one another" (Gee, 2005, p. 25). Victor was able to demonstrate some resistance to the demands of the reviewers, but this was done by negotiating with the editor for additional articles that allow him to articulate his evidentiary data in greater detail.

Layers of scales are presented in this chapter to expose the interrelated contexts which shape the language, community affiliations and identities available to Victor. These layers also constrain and comprise the context in which the scientific journals function. Additionally, the layers expose the power that journal reviewers (or literacy brokers to use another term, see Lillis & Curry, 2006) hold to position authors as worthy or not of participation in the Discourse. This study thus links the context to the text by examining the economic-social structures in which publishing activity occurs. It occurs within the layers of higher and lower scales.

The relationship between the local and the global is sometimes characterized as a "break" where the global is something that bears down on the local context from "larger social structures [that] sit out somewhere in space bearing down on us" (see Brandt & Clinton, 2002). I hope that I have demonstrated that the high levels on the scale are not "out somewhere in space." Rather, the scales of the local, the mid, and the high have identifiable consequences at the local and individual level, and these are evident as confluences of TimeSpace in scientific publishing, discourse and identity.

References

Ammon, U. (2001) Editor's preface, in U. Ammon (Ed.), *The dominance of English as a language of science: Effects on other languages and language communities* (pp. v–x). Berlin: Mouton de Gruyter.

Benesch, S. (1993) ESL, ideology, and the politics of pragmatism, *TESOL Quarterly 27*, 705-717.

Berkenkotter, C., & Huckin, T. (1995). *Genre knowledge in disciplinary communication: Cognition, culture, power*. Hillsdale, NJ: Erlbaum.

Blommaert, J. (2006a). Sociolinguistic scales. *Working Papers in Urban Language and Literacies, 37*. London: Institute of Education.

Blommaert, J. (2006b). Ethnography as counter-hegemony: Remarks on epistemology and method. *Working Papers in Urban Language and Literacies, 34*. London: Institute of Education.

Bourdieu, P., & Wacquant, L. (2001). NewLiberalSpeak: *Notes on the new planetary vulgate. Radical Philosophy, 105*, 2–5.

Braine, G. (2005). The challenge of academic publishing: A Hong Kong perspective. *TESOL Quarterly, 39*, 707–716.

Brandt, D., & Clinton, K. (2002) The limits of the local: Expanding perspectives of literacy as a social practice. *Journal of Literacy Research, 34*, 337–356.

Burbules, N. C., & Torres, C.A. (2000). Globalization and education: An introduction. In N.C. Burbules & C.A. Torres (Eds.), *Globalization and education: Critical perspectives* (pp. 1–26). New York: Routledge.

Burgess, S. (2002). Packed houses and intimate gatherings: Audience and rhetorical structure. In J. Flowerdew (Ed.), *Academic discourse* (pp. 196–215). London: Longman.

Burrough-Boenisch, J. (2003. Shapers of published NNS research articles. *Journal of Second Language Writing, 12*, 223–243.

Canagarajah, A. S. (1996). Non discursive requirements in academic publishing, material resources of periphery scholars, and the politics of knowledge production. *Written Communication, 13*, 435–472.

Canagarajah, A. S. (2002). *Critical academic writing and multilingual students*. Ann Arbor: University of Michigan Press.

Englander, K. (2006a). Non-native English-speaking scientists' successful revision for English-language publication: A discourse analytic and social constructivist study. Unpublished Ph.D. dissertation. Indiana University of Pennsylvania.

Englander, K. (2006b). Revision of scientific manuscripts by nonnative-English-speaking scientists in response to journal editors' criticism of the language. *Journal of Applied Linguistics*, 3, 129–161.

Fairclough, N. (2001). *Language and power*. Boston, MA: Pearson.

Flowerdew, J. (1999a). Writing for scholarly publication in English: The case of Hong Kong. *Journal of Second Language Writing, 8*, 123–145.

Flowerdew, J. (1999b). Problems in writing for scholarly publication in English: The case of Hong Kong. *Journal of Second Language Writing* 8, 243–264.

Flowerdew, J. (2004). Problems of writing for scholarly publication in English: The case of Hong. In G.M. Saracino (Ed.), *Writing for scholarly publication in English* (pp. 81–113). Lecce: Mani.

Gee, J. P. (2004). Discourse analysis: What makes it critical? In R. Rogers (Ed.), *An introduction to critical discourse analysis in education* (pp. 19–50). Mahway, NJ: Erlbaum.

Gee, J. P. (2005). An introduction to discourse analysis: *Theory and method.* (2nd edn). New York: Routledge.

Gibbs, W. (1995). Trends in scientific communication: Lost science in the third world. *Scientific American, August,* 76–83.

Godenzzi, J. C. (2006). Spanish as a lingua franca. *Annual Review of Applied Linguistics, 26,* 100–122.

Gordon, M. D. (1980). The role of referees in scientific communication. In J. Hartley (Ed.), *The psychology of written communication: Selected readings* (pp. 263–275). London: Kogan Page.

Guardiano, C., Favilla, M.E., & Calaresu, E. (2007). Stereotypes about English as the language of science. *AILA Review 20,* 28–52.

Ivanič, R. (1998). *Writing and identity: The discoursal construction of identity in academic writing.* Amsterdam: Benjamins.

Knorr-Cetina, K. (1981). *The manufacture of knowledge: An essay on the constructivist and contextual nature of science.* Oxford: Pergamon.

Kuznetsov, Y., & Dahlman, C. (2008). *Mexico's transition to a knowledge-based economy.* Washington, DC: The World Bank.

Li, Y. (2006). A doctoral student of physics writing for publication: A socio-politically oriented case study. *English for Specific Purposes. 25,* 456–478.

Lillis, T. (2008). Ethnography as method, methodology and "deep theorizing": Closing the gap between text and context in academic writing research. *Written Communication, 25,* 353–388.

Lillis, T., & Curry, J.M. (2006). Professional academic writing by multilingual scholars: Interactions with literacy brokers in the production of English medium texts. *Written Communication, 23,* 3–35.

Man, J. P., Weinkauf, J. G., Tsang, M., &Sin, D. D. (2004). Why do some countries publish more than others? *European Journal of Epidemiology, 19,* 811–817.

Martel, A. (2001). When does knowledge have a national language? Language policy-making for science and technology. In U. Ammon (Ed.), *The dominance of English as a language of science: Effects on other languages and language communities* (pp. 27–58). Berlin: Mouton de Gruyter.

Martín-Martín, P., & Burgess, S. (2004). The rhetorical management of academic criticism in research article abstracts. *Text 24,* 171–195.

Medgyes, P., & Kaplan, R. B. (1992). Discourse in a foreign language: An empirical survey of the foreign language competence of leading Hungarian scholars. *International Journal of the Sociology of Language, 98,* 67–100.

Montaño-Harmon, M. R. (1991). Discourse features of written Mexican Spanish: Current research in contrastive rhetoric and its implications. *Hispania, 74,* 417–425.

Myers, G. (1990). *Writing biology: Texts in the social construction of scientific knowledge.* Madison, WI: University of Wisconsin Press.

Oda, M. (2007). Globalization or the world in English: Is Japan ready to face the waves? *International Multilingual Research Journal, 1,* 119–126.

Pennycook, A. (1994). *The cultural politics of English as an international language.* London: Longman.

Phillipson, R. (2001). English for globalization or for the world's people? *International Review of Education, 47,* 185–200.

Salager-Meyer, F. (2008). Scientific publishing in developing countries: Challenges for the future. *Journal of English for Academic Purposes, 7*, 121–132.

Santos García, S. (2001). Diferencia en las convenciones retóricas del inglés y del español y su influencia en la escritura en inglés como idioma extranjero por hispanohablantes Mexicanos. [Difference in the rhetorical conventions of English and Spanish and their influence in writing in English as a foreign language by Mexican Spanish-speakers]. *Mextesol Journal, 24*(3), 35–49.

Shohamy, E. (2007). Reinterpreting globalization in multilingual contexts. *International Multilingual Research Journal, 1*, 127–133.

Silbey, S. S. (2001) "Let them eat cake": Globalization, postmodern colonialism, and the possibilities of Justice. In N. Blomley, D. Delaney & R. T. Ford (Eds.), *The legal geographies reader: Law, power and space* (pp. 256–275). London: Blackwell.

Testa, J. (n.d.). The Thompson scientific journal selection process. Retrieved March 5, 2008, from http://scientific.thomson.com/free/essays/selectionofmaterial/journalselection/

Uzuner, S (2008). Multilingual scholars' participation in core/global academic communities: A literature review. *Journal of English for Academic Purposes, 7*, 250–263.

Van Dijk, T. A. (1998). *Ideology: A multidisciplinary approach.* Thousand Oaks: CA: Sage.

Wallerstein, I. (1997). The time of space and the space of time: The future of social science. Retrieved March 6, 2008, from http://fbc.binghamton.edu/iwtynesi.htm

CHAPTER TEN

Bicultural or Intercultural? Official Discourse and Its Appropriation by Indigenous Teachers in Mexico

GUADALUPE TINAJERO-VILLAVICENCIO

Introduction

Bicultural/bilingual and intercultural/bilingual policies are two of the most significant proposals for indigenous education in Mexico. Although considered as top-down public policies, they are also the result of the claims of indigenous communities and organizations, which have struggled for decades for their right to education and right to gain respect for their culture. Although the conceptual bases, as well as the political and educational contexts in which these policies were formulated are quite different, they both target a similar reality: the indigenous school with its history of castellanización,[1] assimilation, precarious functioning, and poor training of its teachers. Following Moya's (1998) ideas, conceptual, technical, and legal considerations do not always have an exact correspondence with the reality in which they will be operating.

During the last two decades, Mexican education programs—which reflect the education discourse for the population at large and, particularly, for ethnic groups—have insisted on equity, social justice, indigenous participation, and respect for linguistic and cultural diversity (Secretaría de Educación Pública [SEP], 1988, 1995, 2001, 2007). However, education figures show that such

---

1 Within this text, *castellanización* can be understood as an attempt for cultural assimilation targeted at native Mexican communities, based on the propagation of Spanish as both language and culture.

policies have increased the gap between the indigenous and the non-indigenous population.

Available data shows important contrasts between indigenous and non-indigenous populations: illiteracy among the former is triple the national average (22.1 percent vs. 7.63 percent) (Instituto Nacional de Evaluación Educativa [INEE], 2006), and their school dropout and failure rates are twice the national average (3 percent vs. 1.5 percent, and 8.4 percent vs. 4.2 percent, respectively). Also, completion rates among indigenous students are below the national rate (82.2 percent vs. 91.7 percent) (SEP/Dirección General de Educación Indígena, 2008). As to the results of standardized evaluations to assess advances in mathematics and Spanish, INEE reported that in 2007 the indigenous elementary schools' students obtained the lowest grades: 42.4 percent of them were below the basic proficiency level in Spanish versus 10.6 percent of urban schools' students (Martínez Rizo, 2008).

Such statistics are available because in Mexico there is a separate school system for indigenous children through the end of elementary school. This subsystem of indigenous education within the national Department of Education was created to serve the rural and ethnic areas where indigenous populations are located. It continues to have its own administrative body, the General Office of Indigenous Education (or DGEI for its Spanish initials) and develops its own educational policies, which are the focus of this paper.

The poor educational results relate to the organization of indigenous schools: Unlike the regular education system, where most schools have a complete organization—that is, every grade has a homeroom teacher—only 22 percent of all 9,881 schools in the indigenous subsystem are arranged in this way, whereas most are run by five, four, three, and even one teacher.

Despite the discouraging figures, the last few years have witnessed a growth in the indigenous education system: enrollment for elementary school went from 781,460 children in 2000 to 838,683 in 2007. In those same years, the teacher staff grew by 11.2 percent and 1,192 schools were built, reaching a total of 9,881. (SEP/Dirección General de Educación Indígena, 2008)

Evidently, growth has not solved the enduring problems of the indigenous subsystem, particularly those related to service quality. The greater coverage was probably supposed to address educational backwardness, but given the rates of completion, failure and dropouts —which, as shown above, are higher in the indigenous system—we see that school failure persists for some children at indigenous schools. Education authorities attribute poor quality to the lack of training of indigenous teachers (Rebolledo, 2001; Schmelkes, 2006).

Indeed, professionalization of teachers is not a minor issue. When indigenous education programs began there were no indigenous educators, so the government promoted the inclusion of individuals who had only basic education, as long as they spoke the required indigenous language. This access procedure has prevailed for a long time. As figures show, 14.75 percent of active teachers attended Teachers College (Escuela Normal), another 15 percent concluded undergraduate and graduate studies, whereas the rest range from unfinished elementary to high school studies (SEP/Dirección General de Educación Indígena, 2008).

This chapter aims at exploring the teachers' appropriation of the values, beliefs, and social identities derived from the official discourse of indigenous education. The results shown here belong to two independent studies undertaken at different points in time. The first one took place in 1994, when the bicultural/bilingual proposal was in effect. I interviewed 24 teachers from la Mixteca, most of whom were founders of the first indigenous elementary schools in San Quintín Valley in Baja California. This particular study sought to locate the pedagogical perspectives of indigenous teachers as well as their opinion on the bicultural/bilingual proposal (Tinajero, 2007). The second study took place in 2008, when I interviewed those teachers from the initial sample that were still in the region, to explore their vision on the newest proposal: intercultural/bilingual education. Inductive analysis (Lofland, 1971, quoted in Martínez, 1994) of the interviews allowed for a categorization of the teachers' opinions on the pedagogical proposals they have worked with, as well as for the recognition of the concepts and elements they have incorporated from the discursive texts developed in various workspaces, such as the indigenous education subsystem and indigenous government agencies.

Discourse and Identities

Gee makes an important distinction between discourse and Discourse: the former relates to language chains that make sense, such as reports, arguments, essays, etcetera. The latter refers to that which goes beyond language. Hence, discourse is part of Discourse. A broader definition of Discourse is:

> A socially accepted association among ways of using language, other symbolic expressions and "artifacts," of thinking, feeling, believing, valuing and acting that can be used to identify oneself as member of a socially meaningful group or "social network," or to signal (that one is playing) a socially meaningful "role." (Gee, 2002, p. 144)

Gee also makes a series of observations that allow us to situate the importance of this concept and its value for analytical purposes. According to Gee (2002), Discourse is intrinsically ideological; it resists external critique, and defines what acceptable critique is. Also, Discourse defines positions in relation to other Discourses and marginalizes their points of view and fundamental values. Finally, Gee considers Discourses to be "deeply linked to social power distribution and to hierarchical structure in society" (p. 145).

Discourses not only define positions: they also allow for identity recognition. Anthropology has defined an ethnic group as a stable set of individuals that determine social identity links among them, based on the assumption that they are a political unit (real or virtual, past or present) with exclusive control rights over a universe of cultural elements considered as their own (Bonfil, 1987). In this sense, identity cannot be explained per se: it is rather the result of the preexisting relationship between the group and its own culture, which acts as a core of autonomous culture, or a cultural matrix, that gives sense to all cultural elements, allowing for the existence of the group as an ethnically differentiated entity (Pérez Ruiz, 1990).

Hence, identity develops within a given culture, and thus must be understood as "the space for shared values, recognition, common interests and the affinity of collective knowledges" (Paquet Sévigny, 1991, quoted in Gómez Mont, 2005, p. 102). Also, identity cannot be considered as something static. On the contrary, it is formed and reinvented according to changes in society and several other factors such as migration.

Identity implies that an individual can be recognized as a certain type of person in a given context (Gee, 2002); thus, one single individual may assume multiple identities according to his/her roles in society. Gee establishes four categories to analyze identity: natural identity, institutional identity, discursive identity, and identity by affinity. The first type refers to the natural characteristics of people, such as ethnic group; the second type is given by power institutions and is mainly a position, such as being a teacher. The third type refers to an individual feature that interacts or enters into dialogue with other individuals. Finally, identity by affinity takes place when social relations are built upon specific interests based on experience.

Thus, it can be said that the indigenous Discourse—developed by the governments that followed the Mexican Revolution—created, produced, and reproduced a "certain type of individual" (Gee, 2002): the indigenous teacher. Conceived as a public-sphere Discourse, indigenous Discourse maintained for a long time a series of beliefs regarding Mexican indigenous population and the educational needs of indigenous children. It has also imposed a hierarchical vision of integration, at the expense of diversity. On the other hand, the indigenous Discourse has been appropriated in various ways by listeners and adapted to their own social and political contexts, responding at all times to their own values.

Therefore, we consider that workspaces such as the indigenous education system "produce a series of related social practices that configure a Discourse" (Gee, 2002, p. 147). It is worth asking if teachers share the Discourse's perspective on indigenous instruction, how they have fulfilled their role as indigenous teachers, and what changes they observe in the indigenous education system since the new pedagogical proposal.

Indigenous Discourse: Between Exclusive Integration and Inclusive Participation

For many decades, policies derived from the Discourse of post-Revolution governments sought to integrate ethnic groups under a single indigenous identity. School had a major role in integrationist efforts. Although since the 1930s the Discourse incorporated certain concepts related to the respect and dignity of indigenous culture and recognized the importance of autochthonous languages in the early teaching stages, policy actions were oriented toward "the linguistic unification of the country, in order to build a single, homogeneous language and cultural identity" (SEP/Dirección General de Educación Indígena, 1986, p. 28). Broadly:

> ...*castellanization* campaigns that took place during the first decades of the [20th] Century in many of the [Latin American] region's countries had the goal of contributing to the linguistic and cultural homogenization, as a mechanism that supported the conformation and/or consolidation of Latin American nation-states. Such a project considered diversity as a problem to be overcome or eradicated. (López, 2001, p. 4–5)

Although respect to ethnic diversity was proclaimed and various languages were recognized, they were considered an obstacle that had to be overcome through schooling. Therefore, as an institution, school was conceived of and used as a tool for integrating the indigenous people into the national society (Greaves, 1999). Indigenous–integrationist Discourse was mainly nourished by the anthropological conceptions that sought national unity and limited pluralism (Díaz Polanco, 1992).

According to Díaz Polanco (1992): "Integrationism can be characterized as a pragmatic eclectism that embraces bits and pieces of the most diverse theories as it finds convenient, without digging deeper on the specificity of such approaches" (p. 96).

In the 1970s, scholars started questioning the theory and practices set by the indigenous Discourse. Using internal colonialism, González Casanova (1971) offered a different explanation for the persistence of the indigenous' problems. First, he rejected it as a regional problem, recognizing its national scale, and its political nature. From his point of view, internal colonialism was not an international phenomenon; it rather occurred within an ethnically heterogeneous nation where some groups allied with the dominant classes whereas others became dominated. Hence, the indigenous issue was a matter of internal colonialism. González Casanova conceived the indigenous community as a colony within the Mexican nation, sharing the characteristics of a colonized society (González Casanova, 1971). He argued that the ethnical question was a national matter and as such, other actors of the national culture had to be involved. This new approach was polemic since it contradicted the thesis and practices promoted by the government in the previous decades.

González's argument questioned the official Discourse and caused changes in policies aimed at indigenous populations, particularly in those related to education. Although several indigenous teacher training projects had been promoted since the late 1920s—with varying results (Dietz, 2000; Loyo, 1999) and a National System of Cultural Promoters and Bilingual Teachers had been created in 1965—it was not until 1978 that an institutional space that included indigenous professionals was organized under the DGEI. This office responded to a series of mobilizations of indigenous teachers that took place during the 1970s and culminated in the formation of the National Alliance of Bilingual Professionals, A.C. (ANPIBAC), a non-governmental organization that was pivotal to the development of the bilingual proposal (Dietz, 2000) that the government appropriated as its own.

There is no doubt that upon the DGEI's creation, the official Discourse defined a new position toward the integrationist policies implemented thus far: it shifted to a participatory approach where those "affected" could be formally included. It also incorporated concepts such as participation, social inequity, bilingualism, and biculturalism, which became the axes of many other actions implemented during most of the 1980s and the early 1990s.

The official Discourse defined a new position when it stated that: "Indigenous populations are not the subject of an externally-defined development scheme but rather the actors of their own development. Public action must provide technical and economic resources in order to support the guidelines set by development subjects" (Instituto Nacional Indigena [INI], 1992, p. 50–51). This renewed Discourse opposes and criticizes the five-decade-old integrationist trend and proposes, at least in theory, an action aimed toward social justice that rejected the state's paternalism.

The Shift: New Arrangements for Diversity

Parallel to the conceptual renovation, national authorities promoted a series of modifications to legal and constitutional norms that materialized in 1992: Article 4 of the Constitution was rephrased, recognizing the multiethnic composition of the Mexican society. Nevertheless, the recognition of the linguistic and cultural rights of nearly 12 percent of the population (Comisión Nacional de los Pueblos Indígenas, 2001) was questioned by the emergence of the Ejército Zapatista de Liberación Nacional (EZLN, or Zapatistas) in 1994. This uprising in the state of Chiapas made visible the social injustices and the exclusion that indigenous groups had endured for years.

At this time--which coincides with the 1994–2000 presidential terms—not only indigenous populations' rights were discussed in various forums, but the

Acuerdos de San Andrés [Agreements], signed between the EZLN and the government forced the latter to rethink some of the policies that had been implemented in the education field. Among other things, the Acuerdos and the law on indigenous culture and rights seek to guarantee that indigenous people receive an education that respects and leverages their knowledge and traditions (Rebolledo, 2001). Indeed, the Zapatista movement and the civil society's rejection of the government's management of the Chiapas conflict were two factors that enriched the discussion and allowed for a consideration of the approach—and hence the Discourse—that had given rise to the policies for indigenous communities. Although in writing there was an acceptance of society's diversity and the possibility for native groups to preserve their culture and identity, in practice indigenous people had been invisibilized (López, 2001) in every way.

The Zapatista position was incorporated into the official discursive texts, which now stated that policies for indigenous populations should respond to their needs, demands, culture, and language. However, the most outstanding shift in the official Discourse was to invoke society at large, arguing that it was necessary to "combat the manifest and non-manifest forms of racism and to promote a fair valuation of the indigenous people's contribution to the construction of the Mexican Nation" (SEP, 1995, p. 47).

The official Discourse was moving to establishing intercultural relationships in the national context. This new vision was to be revised when a new political party gained the 2000 election, although not immediately.[2] The indigenous problem was again linked to poverty, not to diversity, and the proposed solution was to increase governmental support in order to address the economic problems that most of the indigenous population faced, although no political rights were granted (Rebolledo, 2001). The new dimension of the inequity issue, construed in the interaction between the indigenous population and the Mexican state and questioned by the EZLN, as well as the political program that linked political and ethnic demands to a democratic society free from exclusions (Torres, 2008), was approached in a reductionist fashion and, like in the past, offered solutions solely from an indigenous standpoint.

The proposal to address the indigenous question was limited to the creation of the National Commission for the Development of Indigenous Peoples, which included a General Office for Bilingual Intercultural Education, a public office in charge of:

Advising on the formulation, implementation and evaluation of innovative programs of bilingual intercultural education regarding curricular models

2 In 2000, Partido Acción Nacional (PAN) won the presidential election, ending more than seven decades of Partido Revolucionario Institucional (PRI) hegemony.

that take diversity into account; training of teachers, principals and technical staff; indigenous languages development and diffusion; regional-level production of didactic material in indigenous languages and conducting research on education (Hernández, 2003, quoted in Aguilar Nery, 2004, p. 46).

As a matter of fact, this office has developed and implemented the bilingual intercultural approach to education. Mexican authorities have insisted on the fact that this approach must prevail in the education system. Due, at least, to globalization and ethnic diversity, multiculturality has been recognized (Tinajero & Englander, in press). Nevertheless, it is argued that the bilingual intercultural approach is mostly a descriptive concept, since it only refers to "groups with different cultures coexisting in the same territory" (Schmelkes, 2005, p. 5) and does not take into account the relationship between cultures, thus avoiding recognition of exploitation, discrimination, and racism. It is therefore argued that interculturality is a much more relevant term, since it implies a relationship between culturally different groups on an equal basis. This term, however, is still aspirational: "Interculturality does not have room for asymmetries, i.e., power-mediated inequities between cultures that benefit one group at the expense of other(s). As an aspiration, interculturality is part of a nation project" (Schmelkes, 2005, p. 5).

The political and pedagogical Discourse emerging from the inclusion of interculturality as a concept has been institutionalized through a series of norms (laws, ordainments, agreements, and declarations). Since 1992, a Constitutional amendment recognized Mexico as a pluricultural nation, sustained on its indigenous peoples. Additional modifications in 2001 re-affirmed such conviction. For the particular case of education, it was stated that in order to "combat the scarcity and backwardness that affect indigenous populations, authorities must guarantee and spread intercultural bilingual education" (Article No. 2, United States of Mexico's Constitution, 2001).

Bicultural/Bilingual Education: A Proposal for Emancipation

In 1985, indigenous public teachers from the DGEI and a group of professionals created a series of working papers that proposed a new model for indigenous education. Some of the objectives defined included offering education services to the whole of the indigenous population, a greater coverage of the existing services for bilingual preschool instruction, bilingual/bicultural elementary education, boarding schools, bilingual radio broadcasts, research and development of didactic materials, development of a grammar system for indigenous languages, and the reinforcement of undergraduate programs in ethnolinguistics and pedagogy, aimed at indigenous students.

Due to an extensive diagnostic of the indigenous children's instruction, this proposal was profound and extremely critical. The scarce training of indigenous teachers and their identity and loyalty conflicts were acknowledged, as well as the insufficient quality and cultural irrelevance of didactic material, the high failure and dropout rates, the low completion rates, and the linguistic and cultural conflicts, sharpened by an education system that was oftentimes inconsistent with the community's reality (Varese, 1987; SEP/ Dirección General de Educación Indígena, 1986).

What were the main goals of the bicultural/bilingual proposal? Briefly, it aimed at the full development of reading and writing competencies and the grammar structure of both the languages, Spanish and native. Also, it sought the integration of the bicultural aspect (mother culture, i.e., indigenous philosophy, values, and objectives) to pedagogical contents and methods. One of the main assumptions was that "if the mother tongue served as a 'bridge' to the majority's language, the native culture could also allow for [such] transit" (Moya, 1998, p. 5). Specific materials in indigenous languages were developed in order to attain such goals. There is no doubt that bilingualism and castellanización have been both the central theme and the problem of indigenous education.

Although the bicultural/bilingual proposal tried to move beyond castellanización, according to Hernández (1997, quoted in García, 2004), it was trapped in contradictions and reproductions. According to Gigante (2004), the main obstacles were related to the construction of the curriculum and the working proposals for teachers. Particularly, schools in this subsystem had to respond to enormous demands, such as using two languages, including the local culture's values, contents, and cosmovisión to their program and catering to multiple socioeconomic needs, all from an emancipation perspective. Another major obstacle was that teachers had to assume their ethnic identity and pass it on to their students. A third referred to incorporating the concepts of language, culture, and ethics into the proposal, since they are all divergent in nature and are very complex to approach with pedagogy. Moreover, Gigante (2004) considers that although indigenous education was attributed to a strong political and ideological significance, there was insufficient conceptual work on its explicit, medullar notions such as culture, bilingual education, bicultural, and ethnic identity on the part of the teachers. Finally, Gigante (2004) believes there was not a pedagogical perspective capable of supporting such an ambitious project.

Although this proposal was legitimate, since it represented many of the stakeholders' aspirations and constituted a long-term project (Muñoz, 2002), no measures were taken to make it operational. A radical shift was intended after years of projects that sought to integrate the indigenous peoples at the expense of their ethnic identities. Nevertheless, consistent with Gigante, the intended changes were excessive and impossible to translate into practice given the narrow institutional margins. If one takes into account the human factor, that is, the poor training of the indigenous teachers, it was evident that this proposal was doomed to failure. Although the attempt to implement the bicultural/bilingual proposal can be considered to be a victory of the indigenous movement and an emerging Discourse from the institutional sphere, bicultural/bilingual education itself was not able to overcome the previous proposals, mainly due to the lack of properly trained teachers.

Individuals that have conventionally taught in indigenous communities have had few training opportunities, even though they recognize themselves as part of the indigenous group and, in some cases, also speak the language in some cases. Moreover, many of them were subjects of the integrationist castellanización school. Hence, the proposal was not only hard to implement due to the conditions of participants (bilingual and non-bilingual teachers, with basic or high education), but results fell below expectations. It has been recognized, for instance, that the bilingual/bicultural approach was not fully taken to the classroom and that there was an exclusion of the indigenous cultural values as the monocultural mainstream Mexican culture prevailed (Moya, 1998). On the other hand, although theory referred to rescuing indigenous languages, such effort was hard to translate into practice given that most of the teachers no longer speak said languages or are not proficient in them (López & Viveros, 2003). Cases like that of San Quintín, Baja California where proficient teachers do not use the local language since their classes are attended by students from diverse ethnic backgrounds, have also been reported.

Intercultural/Bilingual Education: A Proposal for Diversity

Intercultural proposals have been discussed in social science for more than three decades (Abram, 2004; Comboni, 2003, López, 2001), although its adoption in some countries' official Discourse is rather recent (Aguilar Nery, 2004). For the Mexican case, two distinctive years can be identified: 1999 and 2000. During 1999, a new proposal called intercultural/bilingual indigenous education was distributed (SEP/Dirección General de Educación Indígena, 1999), whereas 2000 can be marked as the year when the concept was adopted by the political and educational discourses targeted at native populations (SEP, 2001).

Although this new education proposal officially came into effect in 1999, the General Office for Indigenous Education had adopted intercultural/ bilingual education some years earlier for curricular guidelines and teacher training programs (Gigante, 2004; Aguilar Nery, 2004). The incorporation of this concept to the indigenous Discourse relates to the forceful emergence of indigenous movements at the turn of the century (including the EZLN). Also, international organizations promoted a "greater sensitivity to the indigenous peoples" (Abram, 2004, p. iv). The Inter-American Development Bank included indigenous populations as one of its target groups in its 2001 Action Plan for Social Inclusion. National governments then became "sensitive" to the points of view portrayed in the documents produced by the said organizations, to the point that inclusion became a key element in current education public policies.

In 1999—and with renewed strength in 2001—the intercultural/bilingual political and pedagogical Discourse became official in Mexico. Opposed to the bicultural/bilingual Discourse, interculturality assumes diversity as a resource rather than an obstacle (Moya, 1998), recognizing cultural diversity and fully incorporating autochthonous populations in decision making at a national level. Mexican education authorities have insisted on the fact that "interculturality is part of the Nation project" (Schmelkes, 2005, p. 5).

As a concept and a nation project, interculturality emphasizes recognizing, valuing, and seizing the potential of the Mexican identity. In theory, it assumes a dialogue that takes place among actors on an equal basis. Conceptually, the term was defined as follows:

> Intercultural education will recognize and pay attention to linguistic and cultural identity, promote respect for difference and seek national unity based on the strengthening of local, regional and national identity and in the development of practices and attitudes in accordance with the ideals of liberty and justice for all. (SEP/Dirección General de Educación Indígena, 1999, p. 1)

Similar to what occurs in the political scene, the current education proposal highlights diversity, recognizing and working with it, while pointing out that homogenizing ways of teaching must be eradicated. This affirmation implicitly criticizes decades of integrationist indigenous policies and recognizes that ethnic groups have had uneven terms in their relationship with the rest of the Mexican society. Hence, it is impossible to separate educational policies from the context in which they emerge, so it becomes necessary to reestablish other kinds of social and political relations in which indigenous groups can find a response not only to their educational demands but also to their political, economic, and social needs.

The notion of interculturality has had its greater impact on the education field and the training process of indigenous teachers, although they attribute different meanings to it (Aguilar Nery, 2004). As a whole, the proposal promotes intercultural instruction in the totality of the basic education system; particularly, it promotes reproductive bilingualism in the indigenous education school system. However, this effort is highly questioned since its materialization depends on the degree of bilingualism among teachers, the community, the materials resources available, and the positions of teachers regarding the proposal itself.

Context of Study

In Baja California, attention to the children of indigenous migrant workers started in 1983. The greatest demand concentrated in San Quintín Valley, a place that has traditionally attracted immigrant workers, mostly of indigenous backgrounds. The last two decades of the twentieth century witnessed a shift in the mobility patterns of the immigrants (Velasco, 2007), as they passed from living temporarily in the region, dwelling in the landowners' camps, to settling down and founding colonies in the Valley. Oaxacan settlements close to the fields have been reported since the late 1970s (Velasco, 2003, quoted in Franzoni, 2006).

Two kinds of immigrant settlements can be distinguished in San Quintín Valley: camps, occupied by workers during their contract time, and colonies, founded by different ethnic groups at different times.

In 1991, a study conducted by the INI and funded by the National Solidarity Program (PRONASOL) surveyed a group of agricultural workers in order to know their ethnic composition. Mixtecs accounted for 60.28 percent of all workers in camps, whereas Zapotecs represented 22.32 percent, Triquis 10.44 percent, Purepechas 1.39 percent, and the remaining (5.57 percent) belonged to other ethnic groups. On the other hand, 82.62 percent of the colony settlers were Mixtecs. The study then concluded that the Mixtecs were the largest immigrant ethnic group in the region (INI/PRONASOL, 1991).

Velasco (2007) points out that, at present, the ethnic composition of camps and colonies has changed: in 2003 only 34 percent of the camps' population was indigenous—although most of them reported to be bilingual—and the age of inhabitants fluctuated between 15 and 35. On the other hand, 86 percent of the colonies' population was indigenous and had been born in another Mexican state.

In 1994, I interviewed 24 Mixtec teachers as part of an investigation that documented the pedagogical perspectives in the work of indigenous teachers, most of whom were founders of the first bicultural/bilingual schools in San Quintín Valley. The investigation was a case study, and sampling criteria included the teachers' year of arrival to the fields, their role as key actors in the schools' creation, and their adscription to elementary school. The sample was comprised of teachers that arrived between 1983 and 1986 and established the first 21 schools (Tinajero, 2007). The interviews conducted allowed for a documentation of the teachers' training background, as well as their opinion on the bicultural/bilingual model that then prevailed. In 2008, I conducted a new set of interviews with the teachers that were still in the region, this time related to the intercultural/bilingual proposal that had been implemented in the previous decade. The main objective of this exercise was to document their opinion on the newest approach and to assess their degree of appropriation of the new Discourse promoted by indigenous government agencies.

A Characterization of the Indigenous Teachers in San Quintín Valley

Three types of teachers can be identified in the indigenous education subsystem: (1) Bilingual promoters (a program that dates back to 1964), (2) Teachers graduated from a postsecondary teachers' college, and (3) Trained staff with middle school studies who are proficient in an indigenous language, hired under special circumstances, and trained by educational authorities.

Teachers interviewed in 1994 in San Quintín Valley belonged to the third category. Although some of them had been bilingual promoters in their native Oaxaca or had started undergraduate studies, most of them were hired *ex professo* to educate the children of agricultural workers of indigenous backgrounds. The indigenous education subsystem in San Quintín dates back to December 1983, when the first Oaxacan teacher arrived with her husband (who did not have a teaching position) to work in the one boarding school that existed in the region. A year later, five other teachers were assigned to the school—four of them stayed for only one year—the first teacher was promoted to be the school's principal and her husband was hired as a teacher. Eight more teachers from Oaxaca arrived on September 1984. Ten years later, only half of them remained in Baja California. After this initial hiring and in response to the demand of the workers' children, state authorities—through the INI—agreed to train some immigrant agricultural workers. Thus, 20 indigenous workers that met the criteria (basic education studies and language proficiency) were trained initially as cultural promoters in 1984. Five other teachers arrived from Mexico in school year 1986–1987, hired by the DGEI. Year after year, the number of teachers increased and in 1994, the San Quintín Valley sub-system had almost 100 teachers, 21 schools, and one supervision office.

The 24 teachers that were initially interviewed were pursuing undergraduate studies in Elementary and Pre-School Teaching for Active Indigenous Teachers (LEPPEPMI), a program that started in 1991 at National Pedagogical University (Universidad Pedagógica Nacional, UPN). By 1994, the teachers from the sample (24) had not finished their studies yet: 22 attended the fifth semester and two the third semester. 17 (71 percent) of them obtained their diplomas. Out of those who graduated, 11 pursued a Master's Degree in Intercultural Education at UPN and one graduated as a Master in Pedagogy from the state's teachers college school. As to their professional experience, most of them had worked as principals, due to the lack of staff and the need to manage the schools. One had been a supervisor; two had been union representatives and another one, a pedagogic technical advisor.

Of all teachers in this sample, one is outside the bilingual system, three are supervisors, seven are principals—officially designed as such—nine are still teaching, three are temporarily substituting for their principals, three are both principals and homeroom teachers, and one has a double position as a teacher (Table 1). In 2008, I was able to interview 17 teachers from the original sample of 24.

Table 1. Indigenous Teachers—Training and Main Activity

Name*	Year of arrival	Studies undertaken until 2008	Position held in 1994	Position held in 2008	Interviewed 1994	Interviewed 2008
1. L.M.	1983	Graduate student (internship)	Principal	Out of system	✓	
2. A.V.	1983	Graduate student	Classroom teacher	Classroom teacher	✓	✓
3. R. M.	1984	Graduate student Master of Intercultural Education (internship)	Principal	Supervisor	✓	
4. G.	1984	Graduate student	Classroom teacher	Supervisor	✓	✓
5. R.	1984	Graduate student Master of Intercultural Education (internship)	Classroom teacher	Supervisor	✓	✓
6. J. T.	1984	Graduate student (internship)	Classroom teacher	Principal	✓	✓
7. C.	1985	Graduate student (internship)	Classroom teacher		✓	
8. E. L.	1985	Graduate student Master of Intercultural Education (internship)	Classroom teacher	Principal	✓	✓
9. M. B.	1985	Graduate student Master of Intercultural Education (one year)	Classroom teacher	Principal	✓	✓
10. A.C.	1985	Graduate student	Classroom teacher	Principal	✓	✓

Continued on next page

Table 1 (*Continued*)

11. D.	1985	Graduate student Master of Intercultural Education (internship)	Classroom teacher	Principal	✓	✓
12. V.	1985	Graduate student Master of Intercultural Education (one semester)	Classroom teacher	Principal/ Classroom teacher	✓	✓
13. M.L.	1985	Graduate student Master of Intercultural Education (internship)	Classroom teacher	Principal	✓	✓
14. T. P	1985	Graduate student Master of Intercultural Education (internship)	Classroom teacher	Classroom teacher	✓	✓
15. S.	1985	Graduate student	Classroom teacher		✓	
16. L.	1985	Graduate student (internship)	Classroom teacher		✓	
17. F. S.	1985	Graduate student	Classroom teacher	Principal	✓	✓
18. F.	1985	Graduate student (internship)	Classroom teacher	Classroom teacher	✓	
19. L		Graduate student	Classroom teacher		✓	
20. A.	1985	Graduate student Master of Intercultural Education (internship)	Classroom teacher	Principal / Classroom teacher	✓	✓
21. R.	1986	Graduate student Master of Intercultural Education (internship)	Classroom teacher	Principal / Classroom teacher	✓	✓
22. M.S.	1986	Graduate student	Classroom teacher	Classroom teacher	✓	✓
23. M.	1986	Graduate student Master of Intercultural Education (internship)	Classroom teacher	Classroom teacher	✓	✓
24. F.	1986	Graduate student	Classroom teacher	Classroom teacher	✓	✓

*The number assigned to each teacher is the same during the 1994 and 2008 interviews.

Bicultural/Bilingual Education: An Inoperative Label

Analysis derived from the teachers' interpretations sought to identify the general dimensions of the indigenous Discourse as contained in the protocol material. Three categories, namely: (1) the school-community binomial, (2) language as trust, and (3) bilingual education as a label, give coherence to the teachers' Discourse.

The official Discourse imagines a bilingual teacher as one who works in an indigenous community and is therefore different from an urban teacher. Not only because he/she uses another language but also because he/she works with and in the community. It is believed that the bilingual teacher's work goes beyond the classroom and that influences community life.

According to the office in charge of DGEI, community work is one of the indigenous teacher's working objectives. Also, discursive texts produced during the 1980s stated that the school had to match the community's characteristics, capabilities, trends, possibilities, and ideals. Hence, the teacher should move beyond his/her immediate environment–that is, the classroom–in order to reach the school's lieu: the community (SEP, 1988). The teachers interviewed (Table 1) were convinced that their work should reach the community, independent of the official guidelines:

> That is why my activities target the community, they have a sense of solidarity, they respond to the problems of the community members. (Teacher # 20, 1994)

> Activities are done in the community, according to the most urgent needs that range from support in government paperwork to [community] problem-solving. (Teacher # 22, 1994)

Although the official Discourse defines the teacher's role in the community, indigenous teachers reinterpreted its meaning: community work was understood as reciprocity and solidarity (tequio),[3] giving the term a broader connotation since it implied helping their equals, individuals that teachers identified as similar to them, due to their background or affinity. The school-community relationship gains a greater meaning when teachers are clear on their life situation, a situation of externally imposed marginality:

> If we were all at the same level, no rescue campaign would be necessary. It is this situation of marginality that demands a change from us. (Teacher # 6, 1994)

San Quintín Valley schools are not characterized by their cultural or linguistic homogeneity. However, the term indigenous teacher (as an institutional identity) allowed for the expression of certain cultural elements shared

---

3 *Tequio* is a word from nahuatl that means work or tribute. Teachers referred to tequio as a tribute they pay to the community.

by members of different ethnic groups. On the other hand, communication between the school and the community was mainly established through the language's use and management. In the indigenous school, this has a specific meaning since teachers define their pedagogic stance vis-a-vis the bilingual model.

Indigenous teachers said they identified themselves with parents and students in the working community because of the indigenous language. Even when different languages were spoken, their bilingualism served as a vehicle for gaining acceptance between people with varying indigenous backgrounds. Hence, trust as a concept acquires an accurate meaning, being the key element for interpreting educational purposes. Bertely (1990) mentions that trust between students and teachers—and I would add between parents and teachers—"has been interpreted as the milestone of school legitimacy and is construed through what Erickson called 'existential phenomena' that emerge and are negotiated in everyday encounters at schools" (p. 56).

Trust (gained by speaking an indigenous language) was critical to the development of the first pedagogic tasks (school creation, school census on farms); it was the defining element of the indigenous school in San Quintín, and it was pointed out by teachers as part of their natural and institutional identities:

> There is more trust. The people, mainly the people, most of them see that we devote more time to education. (Teacher # 8, 1994)

> On the one hand, teachers that do speak their language, they can talk to them...if the teacher is equal to them, they see us with the same features and then there is more trust in a way, it seems like the kids come closer, one of the very particular conditions of indigenous education. (Teacher # 10, 1994)

Nevertheless, the fact that teachers used indigenous languages also implied marginalizing and belittling. To the nonindigenous community in San Quintín Valley, they were ordinary individuals, "oaxaquitas" that spoke a "dialect" regardless of their status as agricultural workers or teachers. Therefore, many teachers considered that the linguistic conflict was not within the indigenous school but rather in the context where the school was established: San Quintín Valley, a place where they did not belong, where people did not accept them as equals. Such context also gave place to opinions on the viability of education in an indigenous language. Some supported its use at the school: "I am one of those who disagree with an education that is merely in Spanish" (Teacher # 12, 1994), while others considered that, given the children's bilingualism and the parents' opposition to their children studying in their native language, teaching in Spanish was more advisable.

This situation was consistent with the practices promoted by the government decision-making spheres. A teacher pointed out that the bilingual or any other proposal would depend on the authorities' political will. Functioning of the subsystem is linked to the socioeconomic conditions and the scarce political participation of the indigenous population in Mexico:

> It will not be the language or the linguistic conflict among languages, be it indigenous or Spanish that will rescue these groups from their situation. I think it is rather that the poor government planning ability keeps us all from having a stable quality of life as Mexican citizens. (Teacher # 6, 1994)

In 1994, indigenous teachers in the Valley said that the bilingual model was just nominal–it was a "seal" or a "label." The main reasons why the bicultural/bilingual school did not work "as it was supposed to" in the Valley were that local authorities did not follow the guidelines that determined the system's characteristics (back in those years, state authorities were hiring non-indigenous teachers), nor did they supervise language utilization in the classroom. Also, there was a significant heterogeneity within the school groups (language variants and children with different ethnic backgrounds), some teachers and students spoke only Spanish, parents preferred Spanish, and finally, there were no didactic materials available for teaching any indigenous language in the classroom. Teachers accepted the model's failure by pointing out that:

> We say bilingual just from habit. (Teacher # 1, 1994)

> There is that contradiction regarding indigenous education; it is not used but it is just a...what can one say...hmm...hmm...it's like carrying a label... Now we know bilingual education does not exist, I repeat: kids are receiving some education but based on materials that have nothing to do with bicultural/bilingual. (Teacher # 2, 1994)

> Unfortunately, bilingual education has been managed by the government, controlled by the government and follows the government's interests; that is why it has not been possible to achieve bilingual education. (Teacher # 6, 1994)

> There is bilingual school, lot of people, right? I have heard about the bilingual school but really it...I mean, it cannot work. (Teacher # 11, 1994)

> I believe it has not been implemented at a national level, it has not been implemented as it should, perhaps it just has the name: bicultural/bilingual education. (Teacher # 12, 1994)

> The bicultural/bilingual education subsystem is alright, what I want for it is that all promises are delivered and that it does not become just a name. It is true that it does not work as it should. (Teacher #16, 1994)

When referring to the model, teachers formulated the conflict in which they were involved as professionals and members of a system (that did not work), as members of an ethnic group (to which they were more or less identified), and as representatives of a social institution, that is, the indigenous school (that did not respond to discursive texts). Although teachers did not agree with some of the guidelines defined by authorities—the reports they must prepare and the working pace, which was imposed—they followed them somehow, at least regarding the use of national textbooks and programs. Particular characteristics of the indigenous schools became blurry. A teacher pointed this out (Table 1):

> We are teachers and that means we are teaching how to read and write, we are working with the official programs that teachers from normal schools [teachers college] use countrywide, although we never attended normal school. (Teacher # 2, 1994)

Following Gee (2002), it can be said that the official Discourse's social positions and practices conflict with those of other Discourses, like the indigenous teachers'. This is demonstrated with a comment made by a teacher about school contents, specifically the Mexican Revolution. He wondered how he could explain the Revolution as a movement that changed the lives of Mexicans to a group of children who, like their parents, were agricultural workers at the large farms of San Quintín. This paradox indicates the conflict teachers must face when deciding whether to adopt an institutional identity that complies with discursive texts or to be identified with the rest of the indigenous community.

Members of diverse ethnic backgrounds have coexisted in the Valley (Mixtec, Triqui, Zapotec, Nahua, Totonaco, Purepecha, among others). There is language disparity even within the Mixtecs, the largest group, since they come from different regions and there are language variants. Under these circumstances, one may suppose that teachers had to alternate between Spanish for teaching how to read and write and an indigenous language for basic instructions and oral communication. Hence, as in the past, the school was playing an integrationist role by trying to level the children through the official language: Spanish. This must be related to the conditions under which the bicultural/bilingual school operated in San Quintín Valley, as well as to the kind of intercultural relations that were established with the non-indigenous population that manifestly despised other cultural forms.

Thanks to their natural identity and the trust they inspired by speaking an indigenous language, teachers were able to interact with parents, students, and the immigrant community at large. The working community recognized their proficiency in their native language and they were slowly identified institutionally as indigenous teachers. However, and given its operational conditions, the indigenous school once more became a Spanish-speaking site.

Intercultural Education: Positive but Not Effective

The official Discourse's intercultural approach is based on accurate considerations. For instance, it assumes diversity as a "source of possibilities" (SEP/Coordinación General para la Educación Intercultural Bilingüe, 2004: 10), "of wealth and...development" (Consejo Nacional de Población, 2001, p. 227). Based on this idea, authorities defined interculturality as one of "the milestones on which the identity of a sovereign, equitable, democratic and multicultural Nation-State [will] be based and built upon" (SEP/Coordinación General de Educación Intercultural Bilingüe, 2004, p. 27). For the first time, official Discourse targeted society at large, not only the indigenous peoples. Indigenous education continues to be the bilingual proposal—that is, teaching in indigenous languages. Adding the term "intercultural" allowed the state to define another level of intervention in education.

At the end of the 1990s, the new teaching model for indigenous schools was promoted. The then recently created General Office for Bilingual/Intercultural Education organized customized short courses and diplomas for indigenous teachers. Teachers in San Quintín Valley attended and participated:

> I've attended national meetings. I was in Hermosillo, in Chihuahua, in this state in various meetings, in Tijuana, in Ensenada, and what I've seen is that teachers that don't belong to the indigenous system are very willing to work with it [the intercultural approach], to implement that system. (Teacher # 5, 2008)

> We have been trained on interculturality, at the Intercultural Education Office still led by Silvia Schmelkes. She is the one that has helped us to learn more about intercuturality and yes, there has been great progress. (Teacher # 13, 2008)

Three categories summarize teachers' positions on the intercultural/ bilingual model/education [IBE] (1) positive but not effective, (2) it rescues language, and (3) it generates a commitment to the indigenous school. Analysis suggests that teachers tend to consider the model as "more of the same" and yet positive, but not effective. All in all, it is an imposed model:

> Intercultural education should flow through all levels, not only bilingual education. We used to talk about bicultural/bilingual education, then intercultural education. We are not talking about change, it is the same thing, it now just has a more global approach. (Teacher # 3, 2008)

> It is not very adequate for us, it's not only about indigenous languages interaction, what we need is real attention, a model to work within the indigenous education system...However, sometimes it is confusing and it is not clear even for us...Kids sort of walk away from schools or teachers because it does not make any sense to them, because the teacher does not belong to that culture. Therefore, I think that is what has really failed. We have been imposed a model that is not ours. (Teacher # 5, 2008)

> I consider it to be positive because at the national level, somehow, it can strengthen all the cultures, right? And somehow they are preserved, but considering it as a remedy for strengthening the indigenous question, to preserve the languages, above all to preserve the languages...I don't think it is an effective model for that. (Teacher # 6, 2008)

> Of course we are using that type of model...we talked about that before, it is just that the term has changed in time, interculturality, but we used to talk about bilingualism, biculturalism, we talked about two cultures: the ethnic or indigenous and Western culture, but that is what was said before, although internally we spoke about different cultures. That is what interculturality is about, various cultures. (Teacher # 17, 2008)

> It was like a public policy. The good thing was that, even now, as an Office [General Office for Indigenous Education], it has to be implemented and if it is not done, as I think it is, and it is in the program and does not follow it, then economic support is lost. (Teacher # 20, 2008)

Unlike 1994, when teachers considered bicultural/bilingual education [BBE] as a mere label, incapable of reaching its objectives, in 2008 they softened their position. In fact, 75 percent of the teachers interviewed in 2008 have a positive opinion of IBE. Although they consider it to be a bit "of the same," they recognize that the IBE model goes beyond the indigenous school and has spread throughout the education system. Nevertheless, some voices (Teacher # 5, 2008) insist on the fact that the model is "not adequate," since it should not only refer to reappraisal of indigenous languages, but teachers should also understand its educational purposes. This is why one teacher reports that school contents sometimes do not make sense to students. On the other hand, San Quintín Valley teachers were familiar with ethnic diversity, so they were able to reinterpret interculturality and consider it already a part of their work as teachers. However, the most significant element relates to the shift in intercultural relations among members of indigenous communities and the nonindigenous inhabitants of San Quintín Valley. Teachers are convinced of the fact that currently there is a greater acceptance of indigenous groups, which has in turn allowed for language reappraisal by the various ethnic populations. This new attitude has allowed them to reaffirm their ethnic identity.

It must be noted, however, that the perceived changes cannot be attributed to the implementation of IBE alone, since they also manifest one of the objectives set by BBE 20 years ago: an indigenous broadcasting station, that has highly contributed to language reappraisal. According to the teachers, the radio station implied a shift in intercultural relations and the possibility for them to express their own cultural forms. A teacher said that "radio was something that came to change the Valley" (Teacher # 6, 2008). It changed, above all, "people's mentality." Another teacher said that the radio station "has helped the teachers and the indigenous peoples not to be ashamed, to mainly speak their language" (Teacher # 22, 2008).

> Radio has given us great support because people listen, they hear from others, they listen to the children that go to the radio station and I think all that is good, not bad. Instead of feeling inhibited, they...I realize they get motivated, their self-esteem grows. (Teacher # 1, 2008)

> Another thing that has helped is the radio station, a communication channel in various, different languages, that has influenced the community a lot. If we speak an indigenous language we do not feel ashamed anymore. If we are at the shop or somewhere, we are no longer afraid to speak our language. It has become something natural, normal. (Teacher # 21, 2008)

Radio-mediated indigenous languages reappraisal has allowed teachers to incorporate and accept interculturality—a concept included in the official Discourse—into their work due to the fact that diversity is part of their day-to-day work:

> Yes, we have Zapotec, Triqui, Mixtec and Spanish; majority is Mixtec, followed by Spanish, Triqui and, finally, Zapotec. (Teacher #1, 2008)

> There are children that speak Purepecha. At least here, where I have to work, there are Nahua, Mazahua, Mixtec—both from the high and low regions—Triqui, Zapotec and many others. (Teacher # 5, 2008)

> In San Quintín Valley we have from 12 to 14 different languages. I say this because I work as school supervisor and I had to prepare a school database, so I knew there were many indigenous groups but I was also surprised because we found other indigenous groups that, although not numerous, deserve attention because they are spoken by one or two kids. (Teacher # 10, 2008)

That same diversity and the enrollment of Spanish monolingual children in the indigenous school legitimize one of the official postulates and is incorporated in to the teachers' Discourse: "We all respect each other, with our...language, our culture, because everything, everything is ours and sharing, co-existing...no culture is more or less than other" (Teacher #1, 2008). Co-existence and modified intercultural relations have also allowed them to recreate, as an ethnic group, their patron saint festivals:

> Lately in the San Quintín region, for about the past six to seven years, the cultural festivals of the groups that come from Oaxaca have been celebrated. Thus, with these festivals we are exhibiting and telling everyone we come from those roots, we have those origins and we preserve our customs, our religious beliefs. (Teacher # 6, 2008)

Most of the teachers interviewed have worked within the system for more than 20 years. They were central figures of the system's creation and they experienced discrimination when people scornfully called them "oaxaquitas," regardless of their ethnic background or region of origin. Their life experiences allow them to incorporate the concept of interculturality and assess it as positive because it facilitates their full incorporation into the community: "Even with the non-indigenous people we have... they have accepted us, respected us, now that interculturality works we have been accepted. They know our customs, our roots and finally accept us" (Teacher # 6, 2008). All of them worked with BBE, which they referred to as a "label proposal," and now they value the concept of interculturality because it allows them to work with the ethnic and linguistic diversity of San Quintín Valley. They also perceive they have a responsibility with the indigenous school:

> But we keep on with the work we have at school, we are not waiting for the government to tell us when to start. If it has to be taught, because it is indigenous, even if the government does not say it, we have to keep on working with that. (Teacher #13, 2008)

However, diversity in San Quintín's indigenous schools is an obstacle to reading and writing instruction in indigenous languages. Therefore, teachers consider the IBE model to be ineffective, arguing three main reasons: (1) the lack of adequate and sufficient didactic material, (2) the teachers' poor participation in linguistic matters, and (3) the persistence of monolingual, Spanish-speaking teachers.

Final Comments

One must bear in mind that the current indigenous groups are the product of previous intercultural practices that took place in contexts where they were treated and regarded as subordinate subjects (Comboni, 2003; López, 2001). Moya (1998) points out that the biculturality concept preceded that of interculturality and was used during the first stage of bilingual education, marked by a strong assimilationist approach. On the other hand, utilization of the concept of interculturality, although born in the same context, responds to different considerations. Although the Mexican official Discourse mentions the country's diversity, it has been limited to education services, without exploring a modification in power relations or giving greater political rights to indigenous populations.

Although ethnic cultures are recognized and valued in the indigenous Discourse and in the law, in practice there is not a correspondence with the theoretical implications of interculturality. It is doubtful that "the old problems [can disappear] just by using new education categories and models" (Muñoz Cruz, 2002, p. 14).

There is a clear contradiction between Discourse and the official actions that were promoted, as indicated by social development figures (88 percent of indigenous communities are considered to have high-marginalization rates) or those of educational achievements, according to which indigenous children's performance continues to fall below the national average. Further, these figures do not recognize the conditions and inequities that the indigenous school must face.

In 1994, teachers used a Discourse that differed from the official one. Their practice proved that the proposed model did not work, at least in the region under study. After all, the indigenous school is a socially and historically construed institution that groups the multiplicity of meanings it has received, depending on the public policies implemented and on the work of many teachers, indigenous or mestizo.

As mentioned before, various factors incited the teachers' incorporation into the system; once inside, they assumed their identity, although with many questions regarding school and pedagogy. At times, such questions entered into conflict with those of other members of the subsystem. It cannot be said that indigenous teachers are a monolithic group characterized by internal consensus. Rather, their previous experiences and training revealed a certain position on the model and the indigenous school. During the 1990s, some of them were in favor of the bilingual proposal as a whole whereas some considered that a few changes were necessary in order to reach efficacy. No one stood in favor of the subsystem's disappearance. Rather, discussion revolved around language use and management.

Hence, the study found teachers that: (1) were in favor of the bilingual proposal although they recommended a rearrangement of the ethnic contents according to regional characteristics. Their proposal takes into account the discursive identity and the need to use the indigenous language in the pedagogic work, or (2) believed the proposal was not viable because children were already bilingual, so there was no reason for linguistic conflict. They insisted on the fact that parents opposed to and resisted the indigenous school and its implications (marginalization and scorn). Nevertheless, the lack of resources for offering bilingual instruction did not imply its disappearance. The indigenous school was constituted as a space for ethnic legitimacy and encounters.

These conflicting positions are based on the teachers' experience and knowledge. It can be pointed out that they do not have a single pedagogic Discourse. Instead, it is a mix of shared and non-shared points of view that create a unique substance, something that differentiates it from the official Discourse. Incorporation of new concepts to the official Discourse—that is, interculturality—does not remove the conditions of inequality and social injustice in which the indigenous groups have been immersed. At the same time, thinking about intercultural education becomes difficult in these conditions, mainly due to the categories that are defined but are not explicit enough for teachers. As Muñoz (2002) points out, it cannot be considered feasible that the targeted population "appropriates the legal and institutional changes in favor of the construction and participation in a plural multicultural society" (pp. 12–13), because it is able to perceive the existing disparities between constitutional reforms and the practices that move toward a new state indigenism. To this extent, teachers interviewed in 2008 say that, although the model is positive, it is not effective in attaining an important aspect of the proposal's objective: reading and writing in indigenous languages.

Nevertheless, the context in which the current proposal is being developed, which differs completely from that of other regions of the country, allows teachers to consider interculturality as a tool when interacting with children from various ethnic backgrounds. However, they attribute the change in "others" toward them to two factors: the radio station and the diffusion of their cultural activities, like patron saint festivities that have been re created in San Quintín for almost a decade.

Teachers' positions are related to the fact that the proposal of intercultural/bilingual education is feasible within the context in which it developed. It has allowed for classroom work where children have diverse ethnic backgrounds. Language has been reappraised within the indigenous school, which in turn allows for the incorporation of other cultural elements. Nevertheless, this proposal is not feasible for teaching their mother tongue to children. The school—and the system—does not have the capacity needed for supporting all the children's languages, mainly due to linguistic diversity and the different understanding of teachers regarding the educational proposal.

References

Abram, M. (2004). *Estado del arte de la educación bilingüe intercultural en América Latina.* Borrador preliminar. Retrieved February 13, 2008, from http://www.iadb.org/sds/doc/IND-MAbramS.pdf.

Aguilar Nery, J. (2004) Hacia una memoria argumental sobre la educación bilingüe intercultural en México. Una narrativa desde la frontera norte. *Revista Mexicana de Investigación Educativa,* 9(20), 35–59.

Bertely, M. (1990). *Procesos de adaptación escolar y docente en una comunidad mazahua del Estado de México.* México: DIE /CINVESTAV.

Bonfil, B. G. (1987). *México profundo. Una civilización negada.* México: CIESAS/SEP.

Comboni, S. (2003) La cuestión de la interculturalidad y la educación latinoamericana. Retrieved August 12, 2007, from http://interbilingue.ajusco.upn.mx/modules.php?name=News&file=article&sid=140.

Comisión Nacional de los Pueblos Indígenas (2001). *Programa nacional para el desarrollo de los pueblos indígenas, 2001–2006.* México: Author.

Consejo Nacional de Población (2001). *Programa nacional de población, 2001–2006.* México: Author.

Constitución Política de los Estados Unidos Mexicanos. (2001). Artículo 2. Constitucional. Retrieved October 10, 2008 from http://info4.jurdicicas.unam.mx/ijure/fed/9/3.htm.

Díaz Polanco, H. (1992). *Autonomía regional. La autodeterminación de los pueblos indios.* México:

Siglo XXI Editores/UNAM.

Dietz, G. (2000). Entre Estado-Nación y comunidad indígena. La identidad del magisterio bilingüe purépecha en México. *Estudios Interdisciplinarios de América Latina y el Caribe, 11*(2). Retrieved November 13, 2008, from http://www.tau.ac.il/eial/XI_2/dietz.html.

Franzoni, J. (2006). Migración y organización indígena transnacional. En *Anuario de Espacios Urbanos, 2*, 297–329.

García, S. S. (2004). De la educación indígena a la educación bilingüe intercultural. *Revista Mexicana de Investigación Educativa, 9*(20), 61–81.

Gee, J. P. (2002). *La ideología de los Discursos*. Madrid: Morata.

Gigante, E. (2004) La construcción de una práctica pedagógica sensible a la problemática etnocultural y de género. In I. Sichra, (Ed.), *Género, etnicidad en América Latina* (pp. 139–156). España: Ediciones Morata.

Gómez Mont, C. (2005). Tejiendo hilos de comunicación. Los usos sociales de internet en los pueblos indígenas de México. Tesis para obtener el grado de doctora en ciencias políticas y sociales. México: UNAM.

González Casanova, P. (1971). *La democracia en México*. México: Era.

Greaves, C. (1999). Entre la teoría educativa y la práctica indigenista. La experiencia en Chiapas y la Tarahumara. In P. Gonzalbo, (Ed.), *Educación rural e indígena en Iberoamérica* (pp. 161–178). México: El Colegio de México / Universidad Nacional de Educación a Distancia.

Instituto Nacional de Evaluación Educativa (2006). *Panorama educativo de México. 2006. Indicadores del sistema educativo nacional.* México: Author.

Instituto Nacional Indigenista. (1992). *Perspectivas para el desarrollo de los pueblos indígenas de México*. México: Author.

Instituto Nacional Indigenista /Pronasol (1992). *Diagnóstico de las condiciones de vida y trabajo de los jornaleros agrícolas del Valle de San Quintín, B. C.* México: Author.

López, L. E. (2001). *La cuestión de la interculturalidad y la educación latinoamericana*. Séptima reunión del Comité Regional Intergubernamental del Proyecto Principal de Educación en América Latina y el Caribe. Retrieved, May 2, 2008, from http://www.aulaintercultural.org/IMG/pdf/lopez-unesco.pdf.

López, D., & Viveros, R. (2003). *Educación intercultural y pueblos indígenas en México: Elementos para analizar nuevas metáforas del siglo XXI*. Retrieved October 18, 2008, from http://www.uhu.es/agora/version01/digital/numeros/04/04articulos/monografico/pdf_4/02.PDF.

Loyo, E. (1999). Los centros de educación indígena y el papel en el medio rural. In P. Gonzalbo, (Ed.), *Educación rural e indígena en Iberoamérica* (pp. 139–160). México: El Colegio de México / Universidad Nacional de Educación a Distancia.

Martínez M., M. (1994). *La investigación etnográfica en educación. Manual teórico práctico*. México: Trillas.

Martínez Rizo, F. (2008). *¿Avanza o retrocede la calidad educativa? Tendencias y perspectivas de la educación básica en México. Informe anual 2008*. México: INEE.

Moya, R. (1998). Reformas educativas e interculturalidad en América Latina. *Revista Iberoamericana de Educación, 17*. Retrieved October 18, 2008, from http://www.oei.es/oeivirt/rie17a05.htm .

Muñoz Cruz, H. (2002). La diversidad en las reformas educativas interculturales. *Revista Electrónica de Investigación Educativa, 4*(2). Retrieved November 13, 2007, from http://redie.ens.uabc.mx/vol4no2/contenido-cruz.html.

Pérez Ruiz, M. (1990). Reflexiones sobre el estudio de la identidad étnica y la identidad nacional. In A. Warman & A. Argueta (Eds.), *Nuevos enfoques para el estudio de las etnias en*

México (pp.317-367). México: CIIH/UNAM.

Rebolledo, N. (2001). Educación indígena y neozapatismo. In T. Bertussi, (Ed.), *Anuario estadístico. Visión retrospectiva* (pp. 55-69). México: UPN /La Jornada.

Schmelkes, S. (2005). La interculturalidad en la educación básica. Retrieved June, 12 2008, from http://eib.sep.gob.mx/files/interculturalidad_educacion_basica.pdf.

Schmelkes, S. (2006). *México: Educación intercultural bilingüe destinada a los pueblos indígenas. Texto base. Foro Latinoamericano de Políticas Educativas–FLAPE V Foro Virtual*–Educación para la interculturalidad, migración-desplazamiento y derechos lingüísticos. Retrieved November 18, 2008, from http://www.lppuerj.net/olped/documentos/1225.pdf.

SEP (1988). *Programa nacional para la modernización de la educación indígena, 1990–1994*. México: Author.

SEP (1995). *Programa de desarrollo educativo, 1995–2000*. México: Author.

SEP (2001). *Programa nacional de educación, 2001–2006*. México: Author.

SEP (2007). *Programa sectorial de educación, 2007–2012*. México: Author.

SEP/Coordinación General para la Educación Intercultural Bilingüe (2004). *Marcos normativos para el trabajo intercultural bilingüe*. México: Author.

SEP/Dirección General de Educación Indígena. (1986). *Bases generales de la educación indígena*. México: Author.

SEP/Dirección General de Educación Indígena (1999). *Lineamientos generales para la educación intercultural bilingüe*. México: Author.

SEP/Dirección General de Educación Indígena (2008). *Estadísticas básicas del sistema de educación indígena*. México: Author.

Tinajero, G. (2007) *Las perspectivas pedagógicas de los docentes indígenas*. Baja California: UABC.

Tinajero, G. & Englander, K. (in press). Bilingual-intercultural education for indigenous children: The case of Mexico in an era of globalization and uprisings. *Intercultural Education*.

Torres, C. A. (2008). Democracia, educación y multiculturalismo: dilemas de la ciudadanía en el mundo global. In C. Mora-Ninci & G. Ruiz, (Eds.), *Sociología política de la educación en pers-pectiva internacional y comparada. Las contribuciones de Carlos Alberto Torres* (pp. 181-225). España: Niño y Dávila.

Varese, S. (1987). *Indígenas y educación en México*. México: CEE.

Velasco O., L. (2007). Diferenciación étnica en el Valle de San Quintín: Cambios recientes en el proceso de asentamiento y trabajo agrícola (un primer acercamiento a los resultados de investigación). En M. I. Ortega, P. Castañeda, & L. Sariego, (Eds.), *Los jornaleros agrícolas, invisibles productores de riqueza. Nuevos procesos de riqueza en el noroeste de México* (pp. 57-78). México: Plaza y Valdés / Fundación Ford.

Author Index

A

B

C

D

E

F

G

H

I

J

K

L

M

N

O

P

Q

R

S

T

U

V

W

Y

Subject Index

A

B

C

D

E

F

G

H

I

K

L

COUNTERPOINTS

Studies in the Postmodern Theory of Education

General Editor
Shirley R. Steinberg

Counterpoints publishes the most compelling and imaginative books being written in education today. Grounded on the theoretical advances in criticalism, feminism, and postmodernism in the last two decades of the twentieth century, Counterpoints engages the meaning of these innovations in various forms of educational expression. Committed to the proposition that theoretical literature should be accessible to a variety of audiences, the series insists that its authors avoid esoteric and jargonistic languages that transform educational scholarship into an elite discourse for the initiated. Scholarly work matters only to the degree it affects consciousness and practice at multiple sites. Counterpoints' editorial policy is based on these principles and the ability of scholars to break new ground, to open new conversations, to go where educators have never gone before.

For additional information about this series or for the submission of manuscripts, please contact:

Shirley R. Steinberg
c/o Peter Lang Publishing, Inc.
29 Broadway, 18th floor
New York, New York 10006